Whatever Happened to Tory Scotland?

Edited by David Torrance

EDINBURGH
University Press

For Douglas Pattullo and others in the 'coffee crew' who have
kept me informed and entertained over the past decade

© in this edition Edinburgh University Press, 2012
© in the individual contributions is retained by the authors

Edinburgh University Press Ltd
22 George Square, Edinburgh EH8 9LF
www.euppublishing.com

Typeset in Sabon by
Servis Filmsetting Ltd, Stockport, Cheshire and
printed and bound in Great Britain by
CPI Group (UK) Ltd, Croydon CR0 4YY

A CIP record for this book is available from the British Library

ISBN 978 0 7486 4687 6 (hardback)
ISBN 978 0 7486 4686 9 (paperback)
ISBN 978 0 7486 4688 3 (webready PDF)
ISBN 978 0 7486 7044 4 (epub)
ISBN 978 0 7486 7043 7 (Amazon ebook)

The right of the contributors to be identified as authors of this work has
been asserted in accordance with the Copyright, Designs and Patents Act
1988.

Contents

Notes on the Contributors

Margaret Arnott is Reader of Politics at Glasgow Caledonian University. Her main research interests include post-devolution territorial politics and governance in the UK, with a focus on education policy. She has written widely on post-Thatcherite public policy in Scotland and on the relationship between Nationalism and policy-making in Scotland. Her most recent research (with Professor Ozga) is on the SNP government and policy-making.

Antje Bednarek is a Research Assistant at Theological University Friedensau in Germany. She received her PhD, entitled 'Young Scottish Conservatives and Conservative values 2007–11' from the University of Aberdeen, and she has also published research articles in *Scottish Affairs* and Sociological Research Online. She is currently working on a qualitative research project exploring the mechanisms of upward social mobility through education among working-class students.

Alan Convery received his MA from the University of Glasgow in 2009 and his MSc from the University of Strathclyde in 2010. He is now a doctoral student at Strathclyde University where he is researching the Conservative Party.

John Curtice is Professor of Politics at the University of Strathclyde and Research Consultant with ScotCen Social Research, His publications include *Revolution or Evolution? The 2007 Scottish Elections* (2009), *Has Devolution Worked?* (2009), *Has Devolution*

Delivered? (2006) and *Devolution – Scottish Answers to Scottish Questions?* (2003), along with several studies of UK voting and social attitudes, including *The Rise of New Labour* (2001), *Labour's Last Chance?* (1994), *How Britain Votes* (1985) and the annual British Social Attitudes Report series.

Richard J. Finlay is Professor of Scottish History at the University of Strathclyde and the author of *Independent and Free: The Origins of the SNP, 1918–45* (1994) and *Modern Scotland, 1914–2000* (2004). He is currently working on a book which will examine Scotland, Africa and the New Imperialism.

Gerry Hassan is a writer, broadcaster and commentator on Scottish and UK politics and the author and editor of numerous books and publications. His recent books include *The Strange Death of Labour Scotland* (written with Eric Shaw; 2012), *Radical Scotland: Arguments for Self-Determination* (edited with Rosie Ilett; 2011), *The Modern SNP: From Protest to Power* (2009) and *After Blair: British Politics after the New Labour Decade* (2007). Gerry can be contacted at www.gerryhassan.com

Alvin Jackson is Sir Richard Lodge Professor of History and Head of the School of History, Classics and Archaeology at the University of Edinburgh. His most recent work is *The Two Unions: Ireland, Scotland and the Survival of the United Kingdom, 1707–2007* (2012). He has written extensively on modern Irish history, the British-Irish relationship and Irish Unionism: his books include *Ireland 1798–1998: War, Peace and Beyond* (second edition: 2010) and *Home Rule: An Irish History, 1800–2000* (2004).

Colin Kidd has recently taken up a Professorship of Modern History at the University of St Andrews. From 2010 to 2012 he was Professor of Intellectual History and Political Thought at Queen's University, Belfast, and before that he was Professor of Modern History at the University of Glasgow. He also holds a Fifty-Pound Fellowship of All Souls College, Oxford, and was elected a Fellow of the British Academy in 2010. His most recent book is *Union and Unionisms: Political Thought in Scotland 1500–2000* (2008). Previous publications include *Subverting Scotland's Past* (1993), *British Identities before Nationalism* (1999) and *The Forging of Races* (2006).

Catriona M. M. Macdonald is Reader in Late Modern Scottish History at the University of Glasgow. Her most recent book, *Whaur Extremes Meet: Scotland's Twentieth Century* (2009) won the Saltire Scottish History Book of the Year. Her interests lie mainly in the political and cultural history of modern Scotland, and publications in this field include *The Radical Thread* (2000), and the edited collections *Unionist Scotland* (1998) and *Scotland and the Great War* (1999). She currently co-edits the *Scottish Historical Review*.

Alex Massie is a freelance journalist based in the Scottish Borders. Educated at Glenalmond College and Trinity College, Dublin, he was *Scotland on Sunday*'s chief leader writer before moving to Washington, DC where he was a correspondent for *The Scotsman*, *Scotland on Sunday* and the *Daily Telegraph*. He writes a blog for the *Spectator* and is a regular contributor to *Foreign Policy*, the *New Republic* and The Daily Beast. He has written for the *New York Times*, the *Los Angeles Times*, Bloomberg Businessweek, the *Sunday Telegraph*, Slate, the *Observer* and numerous other publications.

David Melding is the Conservative Assembly Member (AM) for South Wales Central and the deputy Presiding Officer of the National Assembly for Wales. He was previously Shadow Minister for Economic Development and the Welsh Conservative Party's director of policy. As an AM he chaired the Health & Social Services and Standards of Conduct Committees. Born in Neath in 1962, Melding is the former manager of the Carers National Association in Wales and a former Deputy Director of the Welsh Centre for International Affairs. He is the author of a number of publications, most recently *Will Britain Survive Beyond 2020?* (2009).

James Mitchell is Professor of Politics at the University of Strathclyde. His most recent book, *The Scottish National Party: Transition to Power* (2012), is a study of the SNP membership co-authored with Rob Johns and Lynn Bennie. He is also author of *Conservatives and the Union* (1990), *Strategies for Self-Government: The Campaigns for a Scottish Parliament* (1996), *Governing Scotland: The Invention of Administrative Devolution* (2003) and *Devolution in the United Kingdom* (2009). He is currently completing a book on the 2011 Scottish elections with Chris Carman and Rob Johns.

David Torrance is a freelance writer, broadcaster and journalist. He is the author of five books on Scottish political history, *The Scottish Secretaries* (2006), *George Younger: A Life Well Lived* (2008), *'We in Scotland': Thatcherism in a Cold Climate* (2009), *Noel Skelton and the Property-Owning Democracy* (2010) and *Salmond: Against the Odds* (second edition: 2011). He is currently working on a biography of the former Liberal leader David Steel, and is a frequent commentator in the Scottish and UK media.

Tables

CHAPTER 1

Centenary Blues: 100 Years of Scottish Conservatism

David Torrance

> Lady Bracknell: What are your politics?
> Jack: Well, I am afraid I really have none. I am a Liberal Unionist.
> Lady Bracknell: Oh, they count as Tories.
> *The Importance of Being Earnest* by Oscar Wilde (1895)

Introduction

The centenary of any organisation ought to be time for celebration, an opportunity to look back with satisfaction on 100 years of achievement and, if nothing else, sheer longevity. Marking its half-century in 1962, that might have been true for what was then known as the 'Scottish Unionist Party'; but another fifty years later, and for what is now known, in full, as the 'Scottish Conservative and Unionist Party', there seems to be little worth celebrating.

Although the party has had its share of triumphs, not least the unique achievement in Scottish politics of securing not only a majority of the popular vote but also of MPs at the 1955 general election, its recent history has been a tale of managed decline. There is, however, a neat circularity in the condition of Scottish Conservatism circa 1912 and again in 2012. History might not repeat itself, as Mark Twain is supposed to have observed, but it does rhyme.

One impetus for the 'fusion' of Liberal Unionists (those who split from the Liberals in opposition to Irish Home Rule) and Conservatives a century ago was the then Liberal government's renewed push to tackle the Irish Question. Thus the 'Conservative' moniker was willingly dropped (it was considered a handicap) and the new party – the 'Scottish *Unionist* Party' – emphasised its opposition to Irish Home Rule in its very name. In 2012, meanwhile, a devolved Scottish Government's push to achieve 'Home Rule with Independence' informed almost everything the 'Scottish Conservative and *Unionist* Party' did, only the 'Unionist' portion of its name was now taken to refer to the Anglo-Scottish Union rather than that binding Great Britain and (Northern) Ireland.

There are other parallels. In 1912 Conservative representation in Scotland was relatively weak (nine Conservative and Liberal Unionist MPs were elected in December 1910);[1] in 2012 the party had just one MP and fifteen MSPs, derived from around 14 per cent of the popular vote. There is also a Liberal dimension. A hundred years ago one wing of the Liberals joined with the Conservatives to form a new party; in 2012 the Liberal Democrats are in coalition with the Conservatives at Westminster. Then, as now, Liberals make a virtue out of keeping their more instinctively right-wing bedfellows in check. On a memorable visit to Edinburgh in February 2012 the Prime Minister of that coalition government, David Cameron, had little choice but to acknowledge his party's weakness north of the border. 'I know that the Conservative Party is not currently – how can I put this – Scotland's most influential political movement,' he admitted. 'I am often reminded that I have been more successful in helping to get pandas into [Edinburgh] zoo than Conservative MPs elected in Scotland.'[2]

Acknowledging the same stark political reality a few months before, Murdo Fraser, a contender for the Scottish Conservative leadership, went even further, telling supporters that the party, 'in its current state, is not fit for purpose'. Not only was the Scottish Conservative and Unionist Party 'failing', he added, but it would 'never succeed in its current form'.[3] Ruth Davidson, who narrowly beat Fraser to lead the party, took a more optimistic view. The Scottish Tory mission, she told the 2012 Scottish Tory conference, 'was about more than simply restoring the electoral fortunes of the Scottish Conservatives ... more fundamentally it is to reclaim our place as the voice, and party of choice, for mainstream Scotland'.[4]

Fusion: the road to 1912

The dramatic political events of 1886 recalibrated UK politics. As soon as it became clear that William Gladstone, the Liberal leader and then Prime Minister, was serious in his conversion to Irish Home Rule, his party split along Home Rule and Unionist lines. At a national level, cooperation between the Conservatives and 'Liberal Unionists' was immediate, with the latter giving Lord Salisbury his majority (but not a formal coalition) after the 1886 general election, and going on to join his administration following the 1895 poll in what became known as the 'Unionist' government (thus Lady Bracknell's quip at the beginning of this chapter). The two parties, however, maintained separate organisations, not just in England and Wales, but also in Scotland, where Liberal Unionists easily outnumbered Conservatives, a context explored by Alvin Jackson in Chapter 2.

In 1911 the revived prospect of Home Rule for Ireland (the Parliament Act of that year having removed the House of Lords' power to veto it) encouraged a movement formally to merge the Conservatives and Liberal Unionists at a constituency and national organisation level. This had already happened to some extent in Ireland, and in most of England and Wales. In Scotland, however, pressure to form joint constituency parties had largely been resisted.

By May 1912 a formal merger of the two parties had created the 'Conservative and Unionist Party', although this applied only in England and Wales. 'We agreed that we could not bind the Scottish organisation in any way,' recalled Austen Chamberlain (a Liberal Unionist) in his memoirs, 'that the cause of Scotland must be separately treated, and that the Scotsmen must settle it for themselves.'[5] Unification had, however, already been discussed in Scotland, the Western Divisional Council of the Conservative Party having investigated the possibility in 1911. The following year a joint committee representing the National Union of Conservative Associations for Scotland (NUCAS), the East and North of Scotland Liberal Unionist Association (ENSLUA) and the West of Scotland Liberal Unionist Association (WSLUA) had been convened under the presidency of Sir George Younger. It recommended unification.[6]

This proposal was adopted by special conferences in Glasgow and Edinburgh on 5 December 1912, seven months after the merger south of the border. Both Liberal Unionists and Conservatives adopted the resolution 'that it is desirable that the present Central

Conservative and Liberal Unionist organisations in Scotland should be united to form one consolidated Scottish Unionist organisation'. This was to be known as the 'Scottish Unionist Association'.

Following luncheon at the Scottish Conservative Club (now Debenhams) on Edinburgh's Princes Street, Sir George explained the twin rationale behind the fusion: 'It would tend to greater economy of administration', and he hoped 'it would result in what they all earnestly desired, in sending into the wilderness at the earliest moment a party and a Government of which most people were heartily sick'. Similarly, at the final meeting of the ENSLUA, also in Edinburgh, the chairman argued that the merger enabled the two parties to present 'an unbroken front to the common enemy' which was, of course, H. H. Asquith's Liberal government.

The WSLUA, meanwhile, met at the Christian Institute in Glasgow, where one speaker, Mr J. Cumming, argued that not only had the Liberal Unionists 'carried on the principles of the true Liberal party, but they had brought their Conservative friends a good deal in their direction'. He continued:

> The word 'Tory' was all that remained of the old Tory, who revered things that existed simply because they existed, was as dead as the dodo. Personally, he was a Unionist because he was a Liberal. Unionism meant not only the union of Scotland, England and Ireland, but the union of all classes of the Empire, and also the union of all classes of the community in a homogenous whole.[7]

That 'homogenous whole', at least as applied to Scotland, soon became remarkably successful. Within a few years of the 1912 merger and name change the Unionists had been transformed from a pre-First World War rump into Scotland's pre-eminent political party.

Unionist Nationalism

As Richard Finlay, Margaret Arnott and Catriona M. M. Macdonald chart in Chapters 3 and 4, the Scottish Unionist Party did surprisingly well in the general election of 1918 (winning thirty seats), held its own in the 1920s, then dominated Scottish politics between 1931 and 1945, and to a lesser extent from 1951 to 1964. Yet as Finlay points out in Chapter 3, a bias in Scottish historical writing has predominantly excluded the Conservatives.

Compared with voluminous accounts of Labour and, more recently, SNP politics, academic studies are few and popular accounts almost non-existent. James Mitchell's *Conservatives and the Union: A Study of Conservative Party Attitudes to Scotland* (Edinburgh, 1990) appeared just as Margaret Thatcher's premiership was drawing to a close, while David Seawright's *An Important Matter of Principle: The Decline of the Scottish Conservative and Unionist Party* (Aldershot, 1999) was published as it experienced a modest rebirth courtesy of the devolved Scottish Parliament. Only Gerald Warner's *The Scottish Tory Party: A History* (London, 1988) looked at Conservatism in Scotland from a popular perspective, albeit from a generalised and party political viewpoint. This volume aims to revisit some past assumptions while bringing the story up to date, particularly the neglected post-1997 period.

Catriona M. M. Macdonald's edited volume, *Unionist Scotland 1800–1997* (Edinburgh, 1998), also contained useful contributions from a range of historians interested in Scottish Conservatism. As Macdonald charts in Chapter 4, the party was usually far from dogmatic, and saw no inconsistency in promoting a combination of patriotic Unionism, decentralisation and the Scottish dimension, be it rhetorically or via administrative devolution, most notably with the transfer of most Scottish Office functions to Edinburgh in 1939. Surely a good example of what Graeme Morton identified as 'Unionist Nationalism'.[8]

Indeed, the old Scottish Unionist Party, between 1912 and its rebranding in 1965, could be viewed as the SNP of its day: formidably organised, deploying a clear political message, enjoying prominent business support and, of course, electorally successful. All it lacked was a 1950s version of Alex Salmond, a populist and high-profile leader who personified the party, although it had no shortage of creative thinkers.[9] But party leaders were different creatures in those days, with the patrician James Stuart presiding over what was in many ways a coalition of different groups: Progressives in local government and, even at the electoral high point of 1955, National Liberal MPs who took the Unionist Whip.

Mass support for Scottish Conservatism began to ebb away at the general election of 1964, when even a popular Scottish Unionist Prime Minister, Sir Alec Douglas-Home, only managed to return twenty-four MPs in Scotland, a net loss of six since 1959 and a dozen since the triumph of 1955. Naturally, the party looked inward, prompting the first of many reorganisations designed to halt electoral decline. Aptly, presiding over this particular rejig – which added the word 'Conservative' to the party's name for the first time in half a century – was George Younger, the affable young MP for Ayr and great-grandson of the eponymous grandee behind the 1912 merger.[10]

Decline and fall

Later, many pinpointed the beginning of the party's decline to that removal of organisational and branding distinctiveness in 1965 and, although simplistic, it appeared to be confirmed by the loss of another four seats at a general election the following year. The UK party's new leader, Edward Heath, naturally was not impressed and, casting around for something to revive the Scottish party's fortunes and cement his modernising credentials, made his famous 'Declaration of Perth' at the 1968 Scottish Tory conference. Although this, as Macdonald argues, could be seen as the logical extension of a long-held commitment to administrative devolution (see p. 000), Heath failed to consult widely enough and ended up with a dangerously divided party.

Some younger Conservatives, who styled themselves as the 'Thistle Group', developed Heath's decentralism further, writing in 1969 that 'Fiscal independence is vital . . . The Scottish Parliament would raise her own revenue and remit a proportion to the Federal Treasury.'[11] This was, however, far from a mainstream view, and the Conservatives' forward-looking commitment to devolution suffered death by a thousand cuts at the hands of Margaret Thatcher, who ousted Heath as leader in early 1975. In retrospect, neither the party nor its new leader responded imaginatively enough to the electoral breakthrough of the SNP in the two elections of 1974 (at the latter, the Scottish Conservatives lost four seats to the Nationalists), becoming, if anything, more centralist as Scottish public opinion moved in the opposite direction.

As Colin Kidd explores in Chapter 5, the Scottish relationship with Mrs Thatcher and what became known as 'Thatcherism' was neither straightforward nor as caricature subsequently dictated.[12] Although initially popular, beyond a temporary boost to the Scottish Tory vote at the 1979 general election, Thatcher's impact on her party's northern fortunes was in the short term mixed, and in the longer term problematic. As Gerry Hassan sets out in Chapter

6, a deeply negative, yet effective, campaign by Opposition politicians eventually succeeded in making Scotland a 'Tory-free' zone.

By the time of the 1997 Labour landslide, Scottish Conservatism had become defensive and inflexible. Just as Mrs Thatcher had taken the 1979 devolution referendum to mean Scots were not serious about having a Scottish Assembly, the party had also misinterpreted the 1992 election result – in which its number of MPs and share of the vote enjoyed a modest recovery – viewing it as a vindication of John Major's muscular Unionism rather than the temporary reprieve it turned out to be. Even a final Unionist-Nationalist flourish from the Scottish Secretary, Michael Forsyth, did not work, for the show had already moved on. 'I tried, I tried,' Forsyth later lamented of schemes such as the repatriation of the Stone of Destiny. 'It was perhaps too late.'[13]

As set out in this author's own Chapter 7, having consistently – indeed vehemently – opposed a devolved Scottish Parliament, the Conservative Party in Scotland struggled to adapt to radically altered political terrain. Although it returned a respectable number of MSPs (eighteen with 15.6/15.4 per cent of the vote) to the new Parliament, as John Curtice concludes in Chapter 8, this did not indicate any electoral recovery beyond what had been delivered by a proportional system of voting.

Yet as David Melding argues in Chapter 9, political revival was possible given the right strategy. In the Principality – where, as in Scotland, 1997 took the party back to year zero – a genuine commitment to the National Assembly for Wales, creative policy-making and talented personnel took the Welsh Conservatives from a demoralised rump to second-largest party in 2011. In both Wales and Scotland the shifting sands of national identity was an important factor, as was the media. As Alex Massie writes in Chapter 10, the party in Scotland had few friends in print, and even those were often more of a hindrance than a help. Demographic changes also continued to rob Scottish Conservatism of support. As one broadcaster put it, 'This once great force is the political equivalent of the old *Scottish Daily Express*. Its readers didn't desert it, they simply died.'[14]

As the party weakened in Scotland, the view from London was – as it had been to varying degrees since the mid-1960s – one of polite frustration combined, increasingly, with Tory realpolitik. As former Cabinet minister Michael Portillo told Andrew Neil in 2006: 'From the point of political advantage, the Conservatives have a better chance of being in government if Scotland is not part of the affair . . . You are continuing to assume the Union is sacrosanct. That is not an assumption I make any more.'[15] The prospect of Scotland ceasing to be part of the UK 'affair' increased the following year when the SNP (increasingly pushing a form of Nationalist-Unionism) took office for the first time. In perhaps a last-ditch attempt to detoxify, the Scottish Conservatives negotiated an informal arrangement with Alex Salmond's minority government.

It was a bold move that bore little, if any, electoral fruit when Scotland next went to the polls in 2011. The Scottish Tory leader for the last six years had been Annabel Goldie who, although popular with the media and, according to polling, many voters, had struggled to increase Conservative support. As Antje Bednarek explores in Chapter 11, Goldie had represented a rich tradition of strong female characters in the party, from the Duchess of Atholl and Florence Horsbrugh in the 1930s, Betty Harvie Anderson in the 1970s, to Goldie and Ruth Davidson in the early twenty-first century.

Lines in the sand

'The tradition of all dead generations weighs like a nightmare on the brains of the living,' wrote Karl Marx in his critique of Napoleon III. He continued:

> And just as they seem to be occupied with revolutionizing themselves and things, creating something that did not exist before, precisely in such epochs of revolutionary crisis they anxiously conjure up the spirits of the past to their service, borrowing from them names, battle slogans, and costumes in order to present this new scene in world history in time-honoured disguise and borrowed language.[16]

Thus it proved when the Scottish Conservative Party chose a new leader – indeed its first leader chosen by party members[17] – in the autumn of 2011. Endorsing Ruth Davidson, the eventual victor, Michael Forsyth compared her with his political heroine and former patron, claiming Davidson had, like Margaret Thatcher, 'the balls to take on one of the hardest tasks in public life'.[18] Jackson Carlaw, meanwhile, paraphrased one of the Iron Lady's most famous speeches in order to attack Murdo Fraser's plan to form a new Centre-Right party: 'You disband if you want to, the party's not for disbanding.'[19]

But it was Fraser who alluded most to the past, emphasising the historical provenance of his 'revolutionary' plan to disband the Scottish Conservative Party and begin anew. 'For those people who think this is a leap in the dark,' he said at his campaign launch:

> let us remember that our most successful electoral period as a party came before 1965. We were not the Conservative Party then. We were a party which had a distinct Scottish identity. And in 1955, we gained the only absolute majority of votes in Scotland in the period of modern democracy. So this new party will take us back to our roots.[20]

The contest presented the party with two radically different visions for the future: Davidson offered continuity and a fresh face while Fraser embodied a break with the past (while drawing from it) and an experienced old hand. Both mentioned metaphorical lines in the sand. For Fraser, the election of May 2011 had to be a 'line in the sand' in terms of how the party conducted itself, while for Davidson the 'line in the sand' was constitutional. The partial fiscal autonomy offered by the Westminster-initiated Scotland Bill, she argued, ought to go no further. Margaret Mitchell, a late entrant in the leadership race, considered even the Calman Commission's recommendations a step too far, while Jackson Carlaw – who eventually became deputy leader – presented himself as 'experienced, assured and unionist' and promised to fight against 'separatists' in all parties.[21]

Ultimately, the debate came down to personality and the constitution. Little divided the candidates in policy terms, thus personalities came to the fore, Davidson's – young, female and openly gay – was 'counter-intuitive', while Fraser's, although he had been on a Michael Portillo-like journey from the Right to the Centre of the party, was perceived by many to carry a little too much Thatcherite baggage. The outcome was a close win for Davidson.

The new Scottish Conservative leader faced similar challenges to her Unionist predecessors in 1912: rebuilding support for a minority party while simultaneously defending the Union. The former had eluded the party since 1997, while the latter was made more difficult by pronouncements during the campaign. Davidson's assertion that 'when the referendum is done and Scotland in the Union has won the day, let that be an end to it'[22] was hardly consistent with David Cameron's subsequent offer to consider 'what further powers could be devolved' once Scotland had made its choice about 'the fundamental question of independence or the United Kingdom'.[23]

Drawing on the party's Unionist-Nationalist tradition might have produced a more creative solution. Both David Melding and Murdo Fraser spoke of 'New Unionism', the former proposing federalism (dismissed as 'risky' by Davidson),[24] and the latter a more decentralised, responsible Scottish Parliament through greater fiscal autonomy. The influential Tory commentator Tim Montgomerie reckoned the Prime Minister had the opportunity to 'score a triple crown of political victories' by offering Scots 'devo-plus' (another constitutional Third Way that emerged in late 2011), balancing it out with new arrangements for the government of England and thus replacing 'one of Europe's most centralised states with a political architecture fit for the 21st century'.[25] One veteran Scottish Tory fundraiser was even deselected as a council candidate when he concluded that independence was a 'very attractive option for Scotland'. 'Here's the party that stands up for independence of views, freedom of speech, freedom of action,' reasoned financier Peter de Vink, 'and yet we are so intolerant when it comes to this'[26] (de Vink was elected to Midlothian Council as an independent in May 2012).

But Cameron, whose style combined the consensual language of Harold Macmillan and the governing style of Margaret Thatcher, showed no signs of being so bold. Instead, he drew inspiration from his old boss John Major, echoing the former Prime Minister's 1992 'Taking Stock' exercise by simultaneously standing up for the Union while hinting at a compromise.[27] 'I am open-minded about the transfer of more powers,' Cameron repeated in March 2012, 'as long as those powers are truly about improving the lives of Scottish people – not just bargaining chips in a game of constitutional poker.'[28] Another Tory ghost, that of Lord Home, hovered over Cameron in this respect. His 1979 promise that if Scots voted 'no' to a Scottish Assembly then a Conservative government would bring forward better proposals had fuelled suspicions that Tories were not to be trusted when it came to the governance of Scotland. In early 2012 Alex Salmond suggested that Cameron was making the same mistake.

Private polling released by Murdo Fraser during the leadership election rather illustrated the point. Conducted in January 2011, it revealed that only 6 per cent of Scots considered the Conservatives put 'Scottish issues' first. South of the border, meanwhile, discontent on the Conservative backbenches appeared to be growing. 'Let them cut themselves loose, see if we care,' said one senior backbencher, another adding that the number of MPs who wanted Scottish independence for the sake of party advantage was 'definitely increasing. People are fed up.'[29] Central Office planning for the 2015 general election did not include Scotland, with many expecting to lose even the single seat held by David Mundell. 'Ruth Davidson has made a good start,' commented one Downing Street insider, 'but to rely on the Scottish Conservatives contributing anything substantial to the Westminster party after the next election would be a triumph of hope over experience.'[30]

'Enough of the hand-wringing and trying to be all things to all people,' Cameron told the 2012 Scottish Tory conference. 'Let's be clear about what we stand for – and what we won't put up with.'[31] Again, there was an apparent disconnect between the rhetoric and the ideological reality of the modern Scottish Conservative Party. Since 1999 the party had gravitated towards the social democratic centre ground of Scottish politics already occupied by most other parties. Often, it ended up attacking the Scottish Government from the Left, neatly illustrated by a U-turn on minimum alcohol pricing (from anti to pro) in early 2012. As a result, the former MSP Brian Monteith argued that the party was 'neither Scottish, Conservative, nor even Unionist'.[32] Ruth Davidson, meanwhile, initiated another policy review, ditched the party's existing 'tree' branding and promised a 'dynamic new logo and image'.[33]

Would it work? 'That is doubtful, even with a name change,' concluded Lord Fraser of Carmyllie in a pamphlet for the think tank Politeia. 'In my view the Scottish question will not be settled on the basis of existing unionism.'[34] The Prime Minister suggested the fight for the Union would imbue the Scottish Conservative Party with renewed vigour, as indeed it had when the Scottish Unionist Party was formed a century before. Or could it be that, as James Mitchell and Alan Convery posit in Chapter 12, that 'Conservative Unionism' is 'Prisoned in Marble'? A hundred years of Scottish Conservatism offered mixed messages for a party that had known better times and indeed better prospects. As Einstein, quoted by Murdo Fraser, once said, the definition of insanity was 'doing the same thing over and over again and expecting different results'.[35]

Notes

1. The Scottish Conservatives gained two more seats from Liberals in by-elections in December 1911 and September 1912, taking the tally to eleven by the time of the merger.
2. http://www.number10.gov.uk/news/transcript-pm-scotland-speech/
3. Murdo Fraser Leadership Campaign press release, 5 September 2011.
4. Scottish Conservative and Unionist Party press release, 24 March 2012.
5. Sir Austen Chamberlain, *Politics from the Inside: An Epistolary Chronicle 1906–1914* (London, 1936), p. 156.
6. Derek W. Urwin, 'Conservative Party organisation in Scotland', *Scottish Historical Review* 44:138 (October 1965), pp. 89–111.
7. *Scotsman*, 6 December 1912.
8. Graeme Morton, 'Scotland is Britain: the Union and Unionist-Nationalism, 1807–1907', *Journal of Irish Scottish Studies* 1:2 (March 2008), pp. 127–41.
9. See David Torrance, *Noel Skelton and the Property-Owning Democracy* (London, 2010).
10. See David Torrance, *George Younger: A Life Well Lived* (Edinburgh, 2008), pp. 66–7.
11. *Thistle 2: Devolution – A New Appraisal/Scottish Education* (Edinburgh, 1969).
12. See David Torrance, *'We in Scotland': Thatcherism in a Cold Climate* (Edinburgh, 2009).
13. *Scotland on Sunday*, 31 January 1999.
14. http://news.stv.tv/politics/259806-preventing-the-slow-death-of-scottish-labour/
15. *Prospfect* 191 (February 2012).
16. Karl Marx, *The Eighteenth Brumaire of Louis Bonaparte* (London, 1852).
17. The Scottish Conservatives' first leader, David McLetchie, had been elected by candidates and constituency chairmen, rather than party members, in 1998. When McLetchie resigned in 2005, Annabel Goldie was elected his successor unopposed.
18. *Mail on Sunday*, 11 September 2011.
19. Jackson 2011 press release, 5 September 2011.
20. Murdo Fraser Leadership Campaign press release, 5 September 2011. A subsequent leak revealed names under consideration

included the 'Scottish Unionists' as it was 'consistent' with the party's history, and also the 'Progressive Conservatives', which also drew on the party's local government heritage (*Scotland on Sunday*, 2 October 2011).

21. http://www.toryhoose.com/2011/09/jackson-carlaw-experienced-assured-unionist/

22. *Daily Telegraph*, 9 September 2011.

23. http://www.number10.gov.uk/news/transcript-pm-scotland-speech/

24. *Scotland on Sunday*, 4 September 2011.

25. *Guardian*, 20 February 2012.

26. *Sunday Herald*, 25 March 2012.

27. Curiously, by July 2011 Sir John Major's views had changed. 'Why not devolve all responsibilities except foreign policy, defence and management of the economy?' he said in a speech to the Ditchley Foundation. 'Why not let Scotland have wider tax-raising powers to pay for their policies and, in return, abolish the present block grant settlement, reduce Scottish representation in the Commons, and cut the legislative burden at Westminster?' (http://www.bbc.co.uk/news/uk-14093640).

28. Scottish Conservative Party press release, 23 March 2012.

29. *Prospect* 191 (February 2012).

30. http://conservativehome.blogs.com/majority_conservatism/2012/03/the-conservative-hq-plan-to-win-36-seats-from-labour-and-14-from-the-liberal-democrats.html

31. Scottish Conservative Party press release, 23 March 2012.

32. *Scotsman*, 12 March 2012.

33. Scottish Conservative Party press release, 24 March 2012.

34. Peter Fraser, *Divided We Stand: Scotland a Nation Once Again?* (London, 2012), p. 2.

35. Murdo Fraser Leadership Campaign press release, 5 September 2011.

CHAPTER 2

Sociability, Status and Solidarity: Scottish Unionism in the era of Irish Home Rule, 1886–1920

Alvin Jackson

Introduction

In 1912, in the context of the crisis over Ulster and the Union with Ireland, the Scottish Unionist Party was created as an amalgam of the Scottish Conservative and Liberal Unionist parties, and through this was forged an electoral machine with astonishingly sturdy and complex cultural roots and reach. This was a party that emerged with the largest number of Scottish seats in 1918, 1924, 1931 and 1935, and (famously) won a plurality of the Scottish vote as late as 1955. This was also a party that incorporated influential elements of the great Scottish Whig tradition of Unionism, dating back to the Treaty of 1707 and beyond; but, no less remarkably, it laid claim to a tradition of romantic, patriotic Toryism, which (now that the Stuarts were no longer an active challenge) was proud of its roots in Jacobite legitimism. The great appeal of Scottish Unionism was anchored partly in the fact that it simultaneously embraced the Union and the patriotic forces which, for a time, had sought to undermine it.

By the end of the nineteenth century Scottish Conservatism had attained some patriotic credibility and was beginning to combine urban working-class support in the West with its traditional landed base: it was identified with Protestantism (and to some extent Orangeism) in the West, and was loosely associated with the

Church of Scotland at a time when the Free Church was looking to the Liberals to deliver disestablishment. Scottish Conservatism had eventually adapted to the organisational needs of the reformed electorates of the nineteenth century, and continued to do so after the reforms of 1884–5.

What the party lacked, however, was a single accessible cause which had meaning and clarity throughout Scotland. This came when the Liberal Party renounced its historic association with the causes of both Irish and Scots Union, adopting Home Rule for Ireland in 1886 and for Scotland in 1888. As Catriona Burness has remarked, 'defence of the Union with Ireland was the political cry that cracked Liberal hegemony in Scotland'.[1] The cause of Union, together with an influential minority of Liberals who were unpersuaded by the new policy directions, were now effectively annexed by the Conservatives, who had already (under Disraeli) made a bid for the Palmerstonian legacy of aggressive foreign and imperial policies. The accession of the Liberal dissidents, or Liberal Unionists, brought great long-term possibilities, but in the short term came pressure for new policy stands on a range of social and economic questions, as well as challenges to some traditional vested interests within Toryism.

The 'Unionism' of the new Unionist Party of 1912 reflected concerns over Home Rule and Irish Nationalism, as well as the historic interconnections between the politics of the West of Scotland and those of the North of Ireland. But while Scottish Unionism, as formulated in 1912, was partly a response to Irish Home Rule, it was not just about the Irish. Given that Scottish Liberalism was now (after 1888) committed to Home Rule for Scotland, and given that the *jeunesse dorée* of the party was enrolled in the Nationalist youth movement, Young Scotland, and given, too, the (admittedly increasingly nominal) Home Rule commitments of Labour, the political space now existed for a party that offered a clear commitment, not just on the Irish Union, but on the Scots Union too. Of course, within a decade of its creation, the Scottish Unionist Party was wavering in its absolute commitment to both these unions, but this should not distract from the fact that its Unionism was intricately constructed, and that both 1707 and 1801 were closely interwoven in its fabric.

The Unionist alliance

The two main streams that coalesced in 1912 should, perhaps, be individually identified and analysed. Scottish Unionism derived its strength not merely from its Tory roots, but also from the accession of strength delivered in 1886 by Liberal Unionism.

Gladstone's great conversion to Home Rule, announced in December 1885, certainly (in its original formulation) looked set to sub-contract Irish business to a Dublin assembly, as well as substantially exclude the infinitely loquacious representatives of Ireland from Westminster; but of course in freeing up the timetable for the consideration of Scottish and other business, Gladstone was apparently favouring one Celtic Nationalism over another, and rewarding political dissent rather than political acquiescence. The launch of Gladstone's Irish Home Rule Bill in April 1886 drove Scottish Liberals in several directions. Some, Whig landowners like Rosebery, Right-of-Centre luminaries like Haldane and a few radicals, remained within the Gladstonian fold, masking their antipathies and (in the case of Rosebery and Haldane) waiting for the moment to advertise a more imperialist Liberalism.[2] Others turned to the advocacy of a separate settlement for Scotland, participating in the creation of the Scottish Home Rule Association (1886) and in the conversion of the Scottish Liberal Association to the idea of Scots Home Rule (1888). But still others dealt with the paradoxes of Gladstonian Liberalism through inching along the route that a handful of moderate Whigs had traversed since the 1830s – towards Conservatism.

At the general election of July 1886, following the defeat of the Home Rule Bill at its second reading in the House of Commons, seventeen former Gladstonians were elected as Liberal Unionists in Scotland.[3] This number dipped to eleven in 1892, but broadly remained static until tariff reform temporarily broke Unionism in Scotland at the general elections of 1906 and 1910. The notion that the Liberal split in Scotland (as in the House of Commons) was essentially a parting of 'Left' and 'Right' has been closely scrutinised and challenged.[4] Scottish Liberal Unionism was a socially and regionally complex phenomenon, embracing landed Whiggery throughout Scotland, as well as urban Whigs in the West of the country: there was an admixture of radicals, influenced by a variety of motives, including (perhaps) Joseph Chamberlain's lead, disillusion with Gladstone's linking of Home Rule with an apparent bail-out for Irish landlordism (in the form of land purchase) and disillusion, too, with his hesitant stand on disestablishment. Rejection of Gladstone did not, of course, mean at this stage any automatic or immediate marriage with Conservatism.

More generally, Liberal Unionism was fired by the close interconnections between, in particular, the West of Scotland and the North of Ireland: ties of trade, capital and technological exchange bound Glasgow and Belfast, while the movement of people was facilitated by speedy and cheap ferry boats across the North Channel and the Firth of Clyde (a snapshot study of the regional origins of Irish immigrants into the West of Scotland for the years 1876–81 suggests that the four most Protestant counties of Ireland were supplying the majority).[5]

Presbyterianism was central to the political and commercial cultures of both the north-east of Ireland and Scotland.[6] There was also a shared Liberal Unionist political community bridging the North Channel. For example, Archibald Cameron Corbett, the radical Unionist MP for Glasgow Tradeston between 1886 and his reversion to Liberalism in 1908, was a brother of Thomas Lorimer Corbett, the temperance-minded and emphatically Presbyterian Liberal Unionist MP for North Down (1900–10). Thomas Wallace Russell, MP for South Tyrone (1885–1910) and the leading Irish radical Unionist of the era, was the son of a Fife crofter. The Belfast-born mathematician and physicist William Thomson, Lord Kelvin, was President of the West of Scotland Liberal Unionist Association between 1886 and 1892.

The relationship between Scottish Conservatives and Liberal Unionists, like their counterparts in the North of Ireland, was never easy, and indeed was fraught from the beginning with jealousies and resentments concerning the representation of seats or the allocation of resource, to say nothing of larger policy issues.[7] In both Scotland and the North of Ireland, Liberal Unionism acted as a defensive junior partner in the alliance, sometimes (in the short term) diverting political energies into infighting within the Unionist family. But in the long term the accession of these Gladstonian dissidents brought critical strengths to Scottish, and wider, Unionism: in particular, the reforming pressure of Liberal Unionists on issues such as land helped to create a more socially responsive and progressive Unionism – a more viable Unionism – than would have been the case had Conservatism had sole proprietorial rights over the cause of Union.[8]

While it would be wrong to discount the longer tradition of progressive Toryism, and to overestimate the influence of Liberal Unionism, particularly after 1895, it is unquestionably the case that concern for the integrity of the Unionist alliance was a powerful motivating force in the evolution of Conservative reformism in the decade after 1886.[9] In Glasgow, Unionism emerged as a powerful collectivist and interventionist force, 'a reconstructed form of ethical Liberalism'. Détente between Conservatives and Liberals in the city was facilitated by, for example, Lord Kelvin's Imperial Union Club ('an outstanding example of the kind of harmony that ought to prevail amongst all good Unionists and . . . one of the most important political forces in the West of Scotland').[10] More widely, the success of Unionism, even allowing for the setbacks induced by tariff reform, represented in effect the end of Scotland's long decades of one-party politics, and the beginnings of a more competitive party environment.

Uniting with their Conservative allies in 1912, Liberal Unionists were unsure whether they were commemorating 'a birth, a marriage or a funeral'. But in a sense their relationship with Conservatism was educational rather than sacramental, for they taught Scottish Tories how to address an electorate beyond the Protestants of Glasgow or the landed proprietors of the New Club.[11]

Local organisation

After the mid-1880s Conservatives could appeal to Scotland on the basis of Protestantism, Union and Empire, tinctured (thanks to the Liberal Unionists) with a measure of social progressivism. In addition, or perhaps consequently, there is an array of evidence to suggest an intellectual and organisational vitality throughout the movement, stimulated in part by the debate over Irish Home Rule and its implications for the wider governance of the Empire.

The politics of the Home Rule era were closely associated with an organisationally vibrant Scottish Conservative Party – a party which possessed strong personal and structural ties with its Irish counterparts, and whose vibrancy was strongly stimulated by Irish politics. In general the records of Scottish Conservatism for the period between 1886 and the Great War suggest an active and well-organised enterprise, though there is certainly some evidence for periodic disarray (as in the years immediately after the election debacle of 1906). The key Eastern Division of the National Union of Conservative Associations (NUCA) coordinated meetings and finances across the East of Scotland in these years, employing a mixture of national leaders and Irish Unionists (MPs and others) as speakers ('failing Sir John Gorst, the Secretary was instructed to apply for Sir Edward Clarke KC MP, and failing him, Colonel [Edward] Saunderson MP').[12]

The Edinburgh Conservative Working Men's Association was relatively successful throughout the period in importing prominent orators. Speakers from the Irish Unionist Alliance were effectively deployed in the border counties of southern Scotland on the eve of the 1895 general election.[13] Smoking concerts and 'lantern lectures' were in demand (the Division's offering of lantern lectures included 'Egypt', 'the British Empire', 'the Navy', 'Parliament' and 'Fishermen', though there was a request in March 1903 for 'South Africa, to include Joseph Chamberlain's tour'); these provided some light relief from the formal political meetings although speakers such as Saunderson were in demand precisely because they offered an entertaining cocktail of pugnacity and humour.[14] Working men, including those from the North of Ireland, were frequently deployed as speakers in order to connect with the needs of the masses, although they were carefully monitored, and were not always deemed successful: 'the Secretary reported that a working man speaker had been sent by request to Berwickshire for a series of meetings, but that as his style and matter were unsatisfactory, the meetings had been cancelled'.[15] A Workers' League was created to give form and representation to the Unionist working classes: mimicking the masonic-style organisation of other aspirational artisan or working-class bodies, the League offered membership of 'lodges' and the possibilities of office and status; in 1909–10 it was judged to be developing 'with considerable success'.[16] Women and Liberal Unionists were cautiously brought into the fold of the formal Conservative organisation; a separate Scottish Women's Conservative Association was approved in March 1906, with local bodies being raised almost immediately.[17]

After the humiliation of 1906 there is some evidence of organisational, particularly financial, drift within both Irish and Scottish Unionism. Within each political movement, certainly in the county seats, there was a disproportionately great expectation that the landed classes would supply funds; but, with the political dissolution and reorientation of the late Edwardian period, this expectation was routinely disappointed in Scotland and Ireland.[18] For example, in the comparatively wealthy agricultural constituency of East Lothian it was reported in November 1909 (on the eve of the general election) that 'the many large landowners whose interests are bound with those of the Unionist party are conspicuous by their apathy'.[19] Financial irregularity and conspicuous consumption, rather than elite miserliness, lay at the root of the financial problems of the Leith Burghs in 1910; the Unionist Association accounts were confused with that of the related social club and 'the expenses of the club, so far as were ascertainable, were heavier than the circumstances justified'.[20] The balance of social benefits as against subscription cost alarmed the central managers of the Scottish party, with the installation of a telephone causing particular alarm.[21]

The experience of Leith Burghs underlines, however indirectly, that existing assessments of Scottish Conservatism fail to capture much of the spirit of middle-class and lower-middle-class Scots (or indeed Irish) Unionism in the Home Rule era. A valuable corrective and insight into this louche and rumbustious world is provided through the records of the Western Conservative Club of Edinburgh, which span the Edwardian era and indicate that (however important the stimulus of Ireland, or of Union) a complex of more visceral attractions permeated the popular culture of Edwardian Unionism.

The Club, located in central Edinburgh, served as a debating and networking forum and as a library for Edinburgh Unionists. It was a platform, too, for its long-standing vice chairman, the rising young lawyer Robert Horne, who would later serve (in quick succession) as Minister of Labour, President of the Board of Trade and Chancellor of the Exchequer in Lloyd George's post-war coalition government. Horne, however, was also (in Baldwin's characteristically censorious judgement) the 'Scots cad', and this (rather than his legal and ministerial grandeur) chimed more closely with the tenor of the Western Club. It was noisy, undisciplined and badly managed. Like other contemporary and later political clubs, there was a strong emphasis on recreation: billiards, whist (the lifeblood of twentieth-century Scottish Unionist society) and dominos were all taken seriously, and there were established prizes for the top performers.[22] Newspapers and periodicals were also taken in copious quantities, and old runs were auctioned off for club funds at the end of each year. Whisky was an unusually strong preoccupation (presumably on the principle, endorsed both by Burns and Mrs Thatcher, that 'freedom and whisky gang together'), and there was a recurrent concern over the quality, measure and price of the spirits provided in the club bar.[23]

Whisky, in true temperance narrative style, was in fact the undoing of the club. The club had a sustained history of drunken rowdiness; the police periodically complained about the noisiness of the merry-making.[24] An unexplained fire at the club in August 1906 was opaquely defined as 'evidence of carelessness'.[25] In May 1911 a member was censured for introducing 'visitors to the club whose conduct in the opinion of the committee was undesirable and preducial [sic] to the interests of the Club'.[26] The contents of the bar, or rather their elusiveness, were an ongoing problem ('the Secretary reported that he had taken stock, and found that all was not in order, there being a shortage which was accounted for by the Clubmaster [the paid manager] in a very unsatisfactory manner').[27] The club was peculiarly unfortunate in its (rapid) succession of managers, whose various falls from grace were solemnly recorded by the Secretary: in November 1906 the then manager was absent without leave on both days of Musselburgh races; in July 1907 there were accounting problems; in May 1908 there was renewed absence without leave; and in May 1914 there were suspicions concerning the measures of whisky dispensed. By December 1914, with the war raging on the Western Front, the club was deserted, more than £10 worth of stock was missing and the members could not pay the interest on the club's debt. Dissolution swiftly followed.

More predictably, there is also evidence of a somewhat more 'refined' and disciplined Conservative popular culture in Scotland, driven partly in urban areas by the Primrose League, and encompassing social events of somewhat more salubrious kinds than those organised by the 'Western Club'. The League arrived in Scotland in the autumn of 1885, and thus more or less simultaneously with the mounting political crisis over Irish Home Rule; and from then through to the First World War it flourished, garnering more than 100,000 members in its different grades. The minute book of the Grand Council of the Scottish Primrose League survives for the period between 1904 and 1920, and suggests a broadly thriving enterprise, with a trough in the mid-Edwardian period (when of the seventy-three local League associations or 'habitations' on the books, twenty-five were deemed to be either 'in abeyance', 'hopeless' or 'indifferent'), and a peak during the third Home Rule crisis, when much activity (including a 'Help the Ulster Women Scheme' and support for the Women's Covenant) focused on Unionist resistance in the North of Ireland.[28] As Martin Pugh's work underlines, the League placed great emphasis upon title and hierarchy, and the meetings of the Grand Scottish Council were preoccupied with the award of honours (the first and second grades of the League's 'Grand Star', clasps for 'Special Service', 'Banners of Merit' and the 'Champion Banner').[29] It is true that Pugh has warned against over-emphasising the popularity of the Primrose League outside of Glasgow and Edinburgh, but in fact in 1920 the last redoubts of the movement (those 'habitations' that most strenuously resisted dissolution) spanned not only Glasgow (the 'Arthur Balfour Habitation') and Edinburgh (the 'Walter Scott Habitation'), but also Fife, Dunbartonshire and the Solway coast.[30]

Ireland

Ireland was of course central to the work of the Primrose League, as it was to the work of Scottish Conservatism and Unionism more generally.[31] There were numerous individual Conservative linkages, illustrated most obviously and critically by the successive leaders, Arthur Balfour and Andrew Bonar Law – damned by H. J. Hanham as 'semi-Scots' – but also by Hugh Thom Barrie, a Scot who was Irish Unionist MP for North Londonderry (1906–22), and Sir William Mitchell-Thomson (Lord Selsdon), the son of a Lord Provost of Edinburgh, who was successively MP for North West Lanark (1906–10), North Down (1910–18) and Glasgow Maryhill (1918–22).[32] Ian Malcolm, of Poltalloch, Argyll (and after 1930 the seventeenth hereditary chief of the Clan MacCallum), sought, as secretary of the Union Defence League between 1907 and 1910, to reunite British Unionism around opposition to Irish Home Rule; his surviving letters to his friend and patron, Arthur Balfour, reveal a particular interest in the Irish Unionist mission effort within Scotland at this time.[33]

There was also, inevitably, a degree of denominational solidarity between the Church of Scotland and its sister communion, the Presbyterian Church in Ireland, which fed into the politics of Scottish Unionism. During the Plan of Campaign in Ireland, a Presbyterian minister, the Reverend J. W. Holms, was boycotted, and the Unionist editor of *The Scotsman*, Charles Cooper, was quick to seize upon Holms' plight, and to propose bringing him to Scotland to meet the ministers of the Church of Scotland and of the Free Church.[34] Similarly, during the sittings of the General Assembly of the Church of Scotland in 1913, the Eastern Division Council of the NUCA planned to organise a protest against Home Rule – 'to be run by one or more of the Protestant bodies in Ulster which it was hoped might be attended by many of the ministers and elders in Edinburgh at that time'.[35] The Eastern Division Council also decided to translate the Irish Presbyterian Church's appeal against Home Rule into Gaelic, for the consumption of sympathetic Highlanders and the Free Church.[36] But recent research on the Scottish Episcopal Church in the West of Scotland has also emphasised the (hitherto neglected) affinities between Scots Episcopalians and the Church of Ireland, and the extent to which that communion was largely recreated in the nineteenth century, after the assaults of the eighteenth century, through the immigration of Irish Protestant Episcopalians.[37]

Emotions ran high over Ulster in 1912–14, even in relatively imperturbable quarters of Scottish Unionism.[38] Edward Carson rousingly addressed the 'Grand Habitation' of the Scots Primrose League in September 1912, and Ulster Unionism was more generally central to the concerns of its Scottish brethren at this time.[39] The Ulster Women's Unionist Council, confident of success, planned to extend its organisation to Scotland in November 1912. Though this was a relatively tactless overture (and there were others like it), in general Irish Unionist organisations were regarded as an asset to the Scottish Unionist enterprise: for example, the intervention of the Unionist Associations of Ireland was thought to have been useful in securing the South Lanarkshire victory for the party in late 1913.[40] The otherwise insouciant members of the Western Conservative Club were roused to defiance in February 1914, when they resolved to 'pledge ourselves to assist the loyalists of Ulster in their determined stand against the Government of Ireland being handed over to the enemies of Great Britain without the opinion of the electors being taken at a general election'.[41]

Ireland and Scotland were being defined increasingly according to the preconceptions and needs of British tourists; and politics, education, recreation and leisure were combined and intersected with the development of a 'political' tourism at this time – trips of Scots (and others) to Ulster to see at first hand the 'achievements' of Unionism and the 'depredations' of Irish Nationalism. The

Council of the SUA's Eastern Division granted £250 to subsidise excursions to Ireland in June 1914, although the party chairman, Sir Arthur Steel Maitland, 'stipulated that these visits should be of an educative nature and not merely excursions' (and sensibly vetoed the potentially disastrous idea of a trip on 11 July, the eve of the Orangemen's annual festival).[42]

However, there was also some restraint or caution: the flamboyance of Irish Unionism was, generally, better attuned to a Scots audience than to an English one, but one Irish outdoor speaker in 1914 overstepped the boundaries of Edinburgh's (public) bourgeois decorum through speechifying in the uniform of the Ulster Volunteer Force ('such action in Scotland at any rate was calculated to bring the Ulster Army and the case against Home Rule into ridicule').[43] And (confirming the scholarly insights of W. S. Rodner) it should be stressed that not every Scottish Unionist gave unqualified support to Ulster Unionist militancy.[44] For example, the British Covenant in Support of Ulster was (it was calculated) signed by 102,000 people in the West of Scotland by the spring of 1914, but not all were swayed by the emotions of the moment: addressing the Committee of the Western Division of the NUCA

> the Hon. F. Elliott desired more information on the [British Covenant], with regard particularly to passive resistance, and he urged before coming to any decision in the matter they should know exactly how far they were committing themselves in signing, and in asking others to sign.[45]

There was also a lingering, if discreet, view among certain Scots Tories that devolution for Scotland was desirable; and, accordingly, men such as Alexander Bruce, Lord Balfour of Burleigh, were 'afraid of finding myself committed to opposing things for Ireland, when I would take them for my own country, and would [thus] be in an impossible situation so far as Scotland is concerned'.[46] Complementing this was the elite suspicion, as expressed by Balfour of Burleigh, that the Ulster Orangemen were not desirable political company: 'I am anxious not to be connected with what I hope I may describe without offence as the extreme "Orange" position', Balfour informed a doubtless apoplectic Walter Long in February 1907.[47]

What, indeed, of Scottish Home Rule at this time? As in the 1880s, so in 1914, the campaign for Irish Home Rule stimulated some interest in Scotland on the question of a devolved parliament. But there was in general little public passion, and the Scottish Unionist Party took a very leisurely approach to the question. The Committee of the Western Division of the SUA thought, for example, that 'the question did not interest the electors very much, but it was felt that as a parliament for Scotland was now part of the official Liberal programme, some information should be prepared for the use of candidates and others'.[48] The Eastern Division of the SUA held a discussion on 'objections to Home Rule All Round' in January 1914 and organised a sub-committee to report on the issue ('as a question of present political importance').[49] But, certainly for Scottish Unionists, Home Rule for Scotland was thoroughly overshadowed by the mounting crisis in Ireland.

It is true that this relatively vibrant platform did not overturn Liberal dominance in Scotland in the 1885–1918 era, and indeed it would be a profound mistake to ignore some of the more negative features of the movement at this time. Undermined by the divisions created through tariff reform, much of the progress sustained by Conservatives between 1886 and 1900 was undone at the general election of 1906, when the combined Unionist tally of seats was only ten out of the seventy available.[50] However, the defeat of Scottish Unionism in 1906 (as was the case with Ulster Unionism) produced an immediate and extensive reawakening and professionalisation of constituency organisation.[51] And if Liberalism's dominance remained, then its hegemony was certainly challenged in these years. In 1895 the Unionists secured thirty-one of Scotland's seats, and in 1900 they briefly emerged as the dominant force in Scottish politics, with thirty-six seats to the Liberals' thirty-four. Moreover, as has been outlined, Ulster provided a critical galvanising stimulus between 1910 and 1914, as the surviving Scottish Unionist records indicate. They also suggest that sociability, professional networking and status were significant concerns alongside defence of faith and Union.[52]

By December 1918, with tariff reform forgotten, and working on the basis of some constituency redistribution and universal male suffrage, Scottish Unionists gained twenty-eight of the seventy-one seats available. They were now poised both to exploit the wartime divisions within Liberalism by making a bid for the middle-class vote, and to challenge Labour for the support of the Protestant working classes.[53]

Notes

1. Catriona Burness, *Strange Associations: The Irish Question and the Making of Scottish Unionism, 1886–1918* (East Linton, 2003), p. 215.
2. I. G. C. Hutchison, *A Political History of Scotland, 1832–1924: Parties, Elections and Issues* (Edinburgh, 1984), p. 162.
3. Burness, *Strange Associations*, p. 68.
4. Burness, *Strange Associations*, p. 47; Michael Fry, *Patronage and Principle: A Political History of Modern Scotland* (Aberdeen, 1988), p. 103. See also W. C. Lubenow, *Parliamentary Politics and the Home Rule Crisis: The British House of Commons in 1886* (Oxford, 1986).
5. Quoted in Burness, *Strange Associations*, p. 10.
6. Hutchison, *Political History of Scotland*, pp. 154–5, 162ff.
7. Alvin Jackson, *The Ulster Party: Irish Unionists in the House of Commons, 1884–1911* (Oxford, 1989), pp. 214–15.
8. Burness, *Strange Associations*, pp. 70, 217.
9. Ibid. p. 70.
10. Bodleian Library, J. S. Sandars Papers, c761, ff111, 134: Secretary to Balfour, 23 September 1910; Scott Dickson to Balfour, 27 September 1910. See Fry, *Patronage and Principle*, p. 110.
11. Burness, *Strange Associations*, p. 213; Harry Cockburn, *A History of the New Club, Edinburgh, 1787–1837* (Edinburgh, 1938).
12. National Library of Scotland, Scottish Conservative and Unionist Association Papers [hereafter SCUA Papers], Acc 10424/39: 21 February 1894.
13. SCUA Papers, Acc 10424/39: 6 February 1895.
14. Alvin Jackson, *Colonel Edward Saunderson: Land and Loyalty in Victorian Ireland* (Oxford, 1995), pp. 102–4. See also SCUA Papers, Acc 10424/42: 25 March 1903.
15. SCUA Papers, Acc 10424/42: 24 June 1903.
16. SCUA Papers, Acc 10424/42: Report of the Eastern Divisional Council, NUCA Scotland, 1909–10.
17. SCUA Papers, Acc 10424/42: 25 March 1906.
18. Jackson, *The Ulster Party*, p. 205.
19. SCUA Papers, Acc 10424/42: 19 November 1909.
20. SCUA Papers, Acc 10424/42: 25 May 1910.
21. SCUA Papers, Acc 10424/42: 25 May 1910.

22. SCUA Papers, Acc 11368/34: 11 July 1906.
23. SCUA Papers, Acc 11368/34: 13 November 1907, 14 October 1908. See also David Torrance, 'We in Scotland': Thatcherism in a Cold Climate (Edinburgh, 2009), p. 140.
24. SCUA Papers, Acc 11368/34: 10 October 1906, 6–9 May 1907.
25. SCUA Papers, Acc 11368/34: 6 August 1906.
26. SCUA Papers, Acc 11368/34: 10 May 1911.
27. SCUA Papers, Acc 11368/34: 12 July 1907.
28. SCUA Papers, Acc 10424/2: 19 January 1905, 16 December 1913, 20 January 1914.
29. SCUA Papers, Acc 10424/2: 21 November 1905. See also Martin Pugh, The Tories and the People, 1880–1935 (Oxford, 1985).
30. Burness, Strange Associations, p. 82; Hutchison, Political History of Scotland, p. 198; Pugh, Tories and the People, pp. 128–33. See also SCUA Papers, Acc 10424/2: 2 February 1920.
31. See Daniel Jackson, Popular Opposition to Irish Home Rule in Edwardian Britain (Liverpool, 2009), pp. 113–19, 147–51, 184; cf. Ewen A. Cameron, Impaled Upon a Thistle: Scotland since 1880 (Edinburgh, 2010), p. 100.
32. Hanham, Scottish Nationalism (London, 1969), p. 103. See also R. J. Q. Adams, Bonar Law (London, 1999), and Catherine Shannon, Arthur J. Balfour and Ireland, 1874–1922 (Washington, DC, 1988).
33. Arthur Balfour Papers, Add MS 49859, ff205, 207: Malcolm to Balfour, 2 December 1907, 15 December 1907.
34. Bodleian Library Oxford, Selborne Papers, v26, f57: Cooper to Wolmer, 7 October 1890.
35. SCUA Papers, Acc 10424/42: 24 November 1912.
36. SCUA Papers, Acc 10424/45: 30 April 1914.
37. See Ian Meredith, 'Irish migrants in the Scottish Episcopal Church in the nineteenth century', in Martin Mitchell (ed.), New Perspectives on the Irish in Scotland (Edinburgh, 2008).
38. Cf. Cameron, Impaled Upon a Thistle, p. 100. See also the discussion of Ulster Unionist campaigning in Jackson, Popular Opposition to Irish Home Rule.
39. Burness, Strange Associations; SCUA Papers, Acc 10424/2: 1 October 1912.
40. SCUA Papers, Acc 10424/28: 17 December 1913.
41. SCUA Papers, Acc 11368/34: 6 February 1914.

42. SCUA Papers, Acc 10424/43: 24 June 1914; Acc 10424/45: 27 May 1914.
43. SCUA Papers, Acc 10424/45: 24 June 1914.
44. See W. S. Rodner, 'Covenanters, Leaguers, Moderates: British support for Ulster, 1913–14', *Eire-Ireland* 17:3 (1982), pp. 68–85.
45. SCUA Papers, Acc 10424/28: 18 March 1914.
46. British Library, Walter Long Papers, Add MS 62411, f70: Balfour of Burleigh to Long, 2 February 1907.
47. Walter Long Papers, Add MS 62411, f67: Balfour of Burleigh to Long, 23 January 1907. On the other hand, intimate contact existed between leading Orange and Unionist figures in the North of Ireland and West of Scotland; see, for example, Public Records Office, Northern Ireland, Wallace Papers, D1889/1/2/3: Wallace to J. Rice, 17 March 1911.
48. SCUA Papers, Acc 10424/28: 18 March 1914.
49. SCUA Papers, Acc 10424/43: 28 January 1914.
50. Alan Sykes, *Tariff Reform in British Politics, 1903–13* (Oxford, 1979).
51. See Jackson, *Ulster Party*, and Hutchison, *Political History of Scotland*, p. 222.
52. Cameron, *Impaled Upon a Thistle*, p. 100.
53. For an expansion of the evidence, ideas and themes of this essay see Alvin Jackson, *The Two Unions: Ireland, Scotland and the Survival of the United Kingdom, 1707–2007* (Oxford, 2011), pp. 219–80.

CHAPTER 3

Patriotism, Paternalism and Pragmatism: Scottish Toryism, Union and Empire, 1912–65

Richard J. Finlay

Introduction

In a volume such as this there is little need to reiterate the point that the Scottish Unionist Party was the most successful organisation in Scottish politics in the period from after the Great War to the mid-1960s. Rather than offer a conventional blow-by-blow account of political and electoral history, which can be found elsewhere, this chapter will instead focus on the three key themes of patriotism, paternalism and pragmatism that formed the basis of a Scottish Tory outlook that served them so well in this period.[1] Given that the current travails of the party largely centre around issues of identity, a 'back to basics' approach to the fundamental importance of political philosophy might be helpful, but that is not to deny the importance of other issues such as party organisation and class appeal in explaining Conservative success. While these themes, especially paternalism and patriotism, have an old-fashioned ring to them, what this chapter will hope to demonstrate is the way in which they were suited to the socio-economic environment in the period from 1918 to 1964.

Patriotism

Patriotism, but not Nationalism, has always been a central component of Conservative philosophy. Without taking a detour into the by-ways of semantics, the distinction between a 'healthy' interest in the nation's international standing and a commitment to an all-embracing ideology that stressed the nation before the individual was an important one for Tories, especially in the 1930s when militant Nationalism was associated with foreign, goose-stepping, uniform-wearing Europeans. In other words, it was most un-British. Scottish Tory patriotism was made up of three interlocking and mutually reinforcing elements: Scottish, British and Imperial. Locality might also be added to that list. Conventional historical accounts of Scottish politics tend to abrogate the role of foreign policy to British history, largely because it is easier to chart the electoral impact of domestic socio-economic policy. Yet this has arguably left the story lopsided. There is no reason to assume that foreign affairs were any less important to the Scottish voter and that they did not influence their political loyalties.[2] Indeed, there is a historical consensus that the Scots were more imperially minded than other parts of the United Kingdom. Furthermore, the period under review was one in which foreign affairs were of paramount political importance.

The Great War, the economic crisis of the 1930s, appeasement, the Second World War, decolonisation and the Cold War were all major facets of British and therefore Scottish politics during this time. Indeed, for the period under review, it is probably more accurate to talk about British politics in Scotland. Furthermore, in foreign affairs a distinctive Scottish dimension can be traced and it therefore goes without saying that the reaction of the political parties in Scotland to these issues was of fundamental importance in determining electoral fortunes.[3] Admittedly, because of the tendency to insulate historical accounts of Scottish politics from the wider British dimension, this is an area that has not been studied or researched in any significant depth, but a number of pointers will hopefully illustrate the point.

While the First and Second World Wars have conventionally been seen to mark important landmarks in the disintegration of the British Empire, it should be remembered that this was not how it was seen by contemporary public opinion. After all, on both occasions Britain emerged triumphant and the Empire rallied round and made a significant contribution to victory.[4] At the end of the Great War, the Empire increased its size and although the period after the Second World War marked the beginning of decolonisation, it was to some extent camouflaged by the Commonwealth ideal and the exigencies of Cold War strategic imperatives. Like nothing else could, both world wars demonstrated the critical importance of the Empire and as the party most associated with the British Imperial project, the Conservatives were the natural heirs to what has been described as 'Britannic' national identity, that is one that was made up of all the 'British' peoples across the world.[5] Labour, especially in Scotland, was always decidedly ambivalent on Imperial issues. The economic crisis of the 1930s, likewise, increased attention towards the Empire as a potential market to compensate those lost in the global downturn. Indeed, Sir James Lithgow, who was in charge of the project to promote Imperial Preference and, if somewhat naively, believed that all future shipbuilding contracts in the Empire would come to Britain.[6] It is also worth pointing out that the Empire increased its proportionate share of global British trade in this period. The 1938 Empire Exhibition in Glasgow showed how much the Imperial project was linked to the future welfare of Scotland in the popular imagination. Although the mooted closer connections with the Empire never really solved the fundamental problems of the Scottish economy in the inter-war period, it certainly did not do the Scottish Tories any harm.

When the economy picked up as a result of rearmament in the late 1930s and carried on through the war, this again was determined by foreign and global policy. In the post-war era, the sterling area was recognised by the Scottish press as being of fundamental importance to the economy and a boost was given to Scottish industry by rearmament during the Korean War.[7] In the 1950s, a high point of Tory success in Scotland, the Conservative government pursued a robust foreign policy that dealt with the thorny issue of decolonisation that increasingly was determined by strategic considerations relating to the Cold War. The communist insurrection in Malaya and the Mau Mau rebellion in Kenya, not to mention the Korean War, all witnessed the deployment of Scottish troops in both holding up the Empire and staving off the threat of Soviet domination.[8] Even though it ended in the debacle of Suez, there were few Scottish protests against an adventurous foreign policy. Interestingly, but erroneously, the American magazine *Life* claimed that Macmillan was 'a Scotsman to the rescue' when he replaced

Eden.[9] Labour's dalliance with nuclear disarmament in the 1950s, as it likewise was in the 1980s, is another factor that ought to be borne in mind when assessing the significance of foreign affairs on Scottish politics. Although the Church of Scotland welcomed African decolonisation mediated through the auspices of the Commonwealth, it did not have any truck with the Soviet Union.[10] Extensive Scottish emigration to Canada and Australia in the 1950s and 1960s, likewise, may be said to have contributed to the continence of the 'Britannic' sense of identity. Finally, it is also worth mentioning the public support given to the Commonwealth Games held in Edinburgh in 1970, the first to have the presence of the Queen in person.

British patriotism and a strong sense of British identity remained powerful in Scotland throughout this period. It was not, however, an assimilationist or homogeneous notion of Britain, but one that stressed the importance of a distinctive sense of Scottish identity as a key element in making up that wider sense of Britishness. When Scottish Nationalism appeared on the political scene in the early 1930s, it alarmed the Tories more than Labour because the groundswell of discontent seemed to emanate from traditional Conservative voters.[11] As John Buchan noted, Scottish Nationalism appealed to the professional and middle classes, but they were hardly the stuff of revolution.[12]

A key component of the Gilmour Report and increased administrative devolution in the 1930s was the perceived need to acknowledge the significance of a distinctive sense of Scottish identity.[13] Although Unionism between the wars took on a negative sheen in that the nineteenth-century celebration of Scottish over-achievement within the Union was replaced by an emphasis on dependence on the richer neighbour, the policy of universalising unemployment benefit – thus taking it out of the hands of cash-strapped local authorities – meant that Scotland had a comparatively generous system of social security.[14] Also, in terms of public expenditure, there was a net inflow into Scotland that was used as a means of supporting the efficacy of the Union.

The Second World War gave rise to a redefined sense of Britishness, much of it perpetuated by the Ministry of Information, that emphasised fairness and social justice.[15] It was a vision that many Scots bought into largely because of the legacy of socio-economic problems experienced during the Great Depression. More than anything the Second World War was a shared British experience, although the tendency to use 'England' and 'English' did manage to get up many Scottish noses, which, if nothing else, demonstrated that the Scots were aware of their own distinctive national identity and, more significantly, their own contribution to the war effort.[16] Whether or not this renewed sense of Britishness worked to the Labour or Conservative Party's benefit in Scotland is a matter of contention. In 1945 the Tory share of the popular vote in Scotland was the same as in England, while Labour's was marginally less. In other words, the Labour surge was not as pronounced in Scotland, as London party managers sharply pointed out to their Scottish colleagues.[17] Furthermore, given the social structure of Scotland, with its bastions of heavy industrial workers in the 1940s and 1950s, it might have been expected to see Labour romp ahead, as was the case in Wales where the party won more than half the vote, while the Tories struggled to reach the 30 per cent mark. In the late 1940s and early 1950s Scottish national sentiment made a number of forays into political and public life. There was the agitation surrounding the National Covenant for Home Rule, the controversy over the numeral 'II' in the coronation, the stealing of the Stone of Destiny and the alarm over 'bishops in the pews'. While such issues, either collectively or on their own, did not have the potential to crystallise into a significant political movement or moment, what they do illustrate is that there was a fairly extensive reservoir of Scottish small 'n' nationalist sentiment in the air. Arguably, Scottish Tories were best able to capitalise on this. As Churchill himself put it in a speech in Edinburgh in 1950, he too would be a Scottish Nationalist if the Labour government through its policy of nationalisation sought to impose greater control from London.[18] This theme of increasing London centralisation formed a central plank of the Tory campaign in the 1950 election.[19]

The publication of the 1954 Balfour Report on Scottish administration brought howls of Scottish Tory indignation as Scotland was referred to as a 'region'. Even the furore over the numeral of the Queen illustrated a widespread Scottish royalism that was affronted by the indignity done to the Scottish crown. Her Majesty's arrival in Edinburgh to receive the Scottish regalia in St Giles' wearing a twin set did little to calm things, nor did her reference to herself as Queen of England in the Christmas broadcast to New Zealand. Needless to say, the monarchy soon recovered from these early gaffes and successfully tartanised itself to an extent not seen since the days of Queen Victoria.[20] One final incident can be cited to demonstrate the resilience of Scottish/British identity in the post-war era: the campaign to save the Argyll and Sutherland Highland regiment. It ought to be remembered that more public support was forthcoming on this issue than there was against the decision to base Polaris on the Clyde.

Paternalism

It might be argued that by the mid-1960s, the high point of Imperial identity in Scotland had passed as Britain came to terms with the loss of Empire and struggled to find a role. While the changed global realities affected both Labour and Conservatives, the Tories had made more of an investment in a robust defence of Britain's world position, but it was one that increasingly paid less of a dividend and arguably gave the Tories less of a distinctive dimension in its electoral appeal. Paternalism and its associated notions of deference to social superiors has not received the historical attention it is due largely because the dominant historiography of twentieth-century Scotland has been overwhelmingly concerned with the rise of the Labour Party. One consequence of the growing political strength of Labour in Scotland in the 1960s was to reflect this dominance back into the past. If one thinks of the fairly voluminous academic writings on Red Clydeside, for example, and then compares them to the fact that the Scottish Unionist Party did better in the general election of 1918, held its own in the 1920s and dominated from 1931 to 1945 and again from 1951 to 1964, it is fairly obvious that they at least ought to have parity in terms of objective historical inquiry compared to Labour.[21] In Scottish historical writing a bias has emerged towards the central belt, urban, industrial, working-class nature of Scottish society to the exclusion of its middle-class, rural/semi-rural, suburban and what for want of a better word might be described as its 'traditional' nature. The point is an important one because numerically most Scots have not worked in heavy industry nor did they live in large urban conurbations. The family-owned and run factory situated in a semi-rural environment, for example, survived well into the twentieth century where paternalistic and deferential traditions continued. Church attendance rates remained stable until the 1960s. As Iain Hutchison has pointed out, the Scottish Tory party in the period after the Second World War became more gentrified and tweedy than its counterpart in the south, but it did not do it any electoral harm in the 1950s.[22] It is an intriguing to speculate whether this was, rather than being out of touch, more in tune with a deferential and paternalistic Scottish society?

The beginning of the inter-war period, as many historians have noted, was marked by class conflict in which the rise of socialism led to a realignment on the Right with the Liberals and Conservatives vying to best display their anti-socialist credentials. The spectre of the 'red menace' was not just confined to the Clyde, but manifested itself throughout Scotland. The fear of socialism was enough to force the Liberal and Tory parties in Scotland into a form of official and unofficial collaboration until 1923 when Liberal support for a minority Labour government undermined the former's anti-socialist credentials.[23] For the Unionists, this left the field clear to build a political coalition around the anti-socialist banner. The young, women and the small town/rural hinterland were its principal areas of strength. This could best be described as a 'traditional' Scotland that was alarmed by the forces of change that had been unleashed during the Great War. A central theme that emerged during the Conservative election campaigns during the inter-war era was its emphasis on tradition and family values, sound fiscal policy and a return to 'normalcy'.[24]

Tory policy made great play towards winning the women's vote by an appeal to the family budget and the supposed threat from socialism to traditional family life. This tactic was also very much in evidence in the 1950s, especially capitalising on the hardships endured by mothers as a result of rationing. The threat to traditional family values and social norms was reinforced in the 1930s as a result of gang violence and widespread reporting of 'errant fathers' who were having children in order to increase their dole payments. By focusing on the rural vote and in particular the newly propertied farming class after the First World War and the young aspirant middle class, the Conservatives were able to build a strong electoral base. Also, the party had to stretch out to encompass what has been described as the 'Tory Liberal' vote with a number of 'National Liberals' who were virtually indistinguishable from their Conservative counterparts.[25]

That said, many skilled workers must have also been attracted to the Tories, who may have belonged to the tradition of independent, craft-based workers who were employed by small business owners who proliferated within the sub-contracting culture of the Scottish economy in the period between the end of the First World War and the 1960s. Although the Tory working-class voter is an area that requires more extensive research, a number of points can be made. First, the middle class, which was disproportionately small in Scotland, could not account on its own for the success of the Conservative Party in Scotland between 1914 and 1964 as it only represented about a quarter of the electorate, whereas the Tory poll was usually in excess of 40 per cent. Arithmetically, it is clear that a significant section of the working class voted Conservative. The reasons why the Conservative Party was attractive to so many working-class Scots can only be speculated on at the moment. The structure of the Scottish economy changed little in its fundamentals from the late nineteenth century and while many historians have commented on the transition from a Liberal political culture to a Labour one, little has been said about the ways in which it could in many respects translate into a Tory one.[26]

First, the highly individualistic nature of many of the skilled working class may have felt equally at home in the Conservative fold as with Labour, whose collectivism went against this fundamental tenet. Second, maintaining the skills hierarchy, especially in heavy industries, may have encouraged some workers to adopt a traditional and therefore Conservative political outlook. Third, the small-scale unit of production may have helped notions of paternalism to survive. Fourth, the development of large-scale trade unions that predominantly represented the unskilled and semi-skilled workers may have been seen as a threat to traditional skill and craft differentials. Given that the structure of the Scottish economy remained virtually unchanged throughout the period of Conservative electoral success and that the economy was more dependent on traditional heavy industry in the late 1950s, at the high point of Tory electoral success, as it was in the 1930s, perhaps some of the explanation can be found in this basic structural factor.

As many commentators have noted, Scottish institutions were notorious for their strong sense of authoritarianism and hierarchy. Education was profoundly elitist with learning imparted by teachers who 'were paid to know'.[27] Potential council tenants were assessed on their suitability, junior lecturers opened windows for the professor and a thousand petty tyrants presided over planning applications and the like. Even the Labour Party had an authoritarian tone as the absence of social amenities on council estates demonstrated. The traditionalist nature of both management and workers which was regularly bemoaned by economic commentators is further evidence that Scotland was, if nothing else, a nation of small 'c' conservatives.[28] While the expansion of government agencies and the welfare state is commonly seen as a movement of the Left, it should not be forgotten that it created a host of new opportunities for the professions and middle management whose traditional social bias would arguably lead them towards the Tory Party.[29] In an age before the public/private dichotomy, social class was the key political divider and the expansion of the state sector provided both opportunities and positions for the aspirant middle class.

Traditional accounts of the decline of Scottish Conservatism usually begin in the mid-1960s and a number of factors are cited in support of this explanation. The growth of Labour-led state intervention, the collapse of the Orange vote, ditching the Unionist brand and organisational difficulties are most often discussed.[30] This chapter does not wish to detract from these issues but would rather posit a more nuanced explanation. First, the mid-1960s witnessed a fairly vigorous assault on the bastions of traditional Scottish society. It was in this era that 'new towns' and the baby boomers came into their own. Also, there was the growth of the new sector of branch-plant manufacturing that was not tied to the traditional heavy industries. Secularisation began to kick in with the middle class first beginning the exodus away from the Kirk.[31] In many respects, it can be argued that there were two key aspects to this period in charting Tory decline. First, as tradition and deference began to collapse, this arguably worked more to the benefit of Labour as those were values more intrinsic to the Conservative political outlook. Second, Labour were more able to present themselves as more effective modernisers and economic managers. The extent to which this marked an inevitable decline for Tory Party fortunes in Scotland is, however, far from clear.

In the main, the primary explanation for the perception of Tory decline lies in two factors. First, Labour had greater vote efficiency in that it took fewer votes to deliver a MP than was the case for the Conservatives. A perfect illustration of this can be found in the general election of 1959 when the Conservative share of the vote at 47.2 per cent delivered thirty-one seats whereas Labour with slightly less of the share of the vote at 46.7 per cent secured thirty-eight MPs. Second, Labour's vote remained steady and increased by 2.2 per cent between 1959 and 1966 whereas the Tory vote began to fragment towards the SNP and Liberals. Although it was not a major haemorrhage, a decline of 10 per cent was enough to result in the significant loss of eleven seats. Labour's electoral surge in the 1960s was not a result of a surge in the popularity of the party, but was rather dependent on the peculiarities of the first-past-the-post electoral system that disproportionately punished the Conservatives.[32] Paradoxically, because the Conservative vote was more geographically scattered, it can be argued that it was more genuinely reflective of a broad cross-section of Scottish society than the Labour vote, which was concentrated in the party's industrial heartland.

Pragmatism

Pragmatism and the ability to adapt to changing circumstances was key to Scottish Tory success in the period from 1912 to 1964. Once the Irish issue effectively ceased to matter, the Tories were able to drop the 'die-hard' mentality that had dominated the Edwardian period when the party felt that it was about to be doomed to electoral impotence. Pragmatism was central to the anti-socialist alliance with the Liberals, even if it was unpopular with the rank and file.[33] Modernisation and reorganisation of the party machinery was a central aspect of the period after the First World War. The new electoral opportunities of female suffrage, young middle-class males and the rural/semi-rural constituency were seized. Also, during the Depression, the party did not allow the middle-class constituency and its own class warriors to dictate the terms of social policy that were comparatively generous when set in an international context. Nor did the party endorse the populism of religious sectarianism and set its face against any radicalisation of the Right that was experienced throughout mainland Europe. The proposals in the Gilmour Report on administrative devolution likewise demonstrated a pragmatic response to Scottish concerns about remote government. Finally, Secretaries of State for Scotland were always of a moderate hue.[34] While the corporatism of the post-war era has tended to be portrayed as a Left-of-Centre phenomenon, it is worth pointing out that its origins in the inter-war era were largely a Tory creation.[35]

While there was considerable grumbling among the backbenches that the welfare state was a charter for unwed mothers and other social evils, the party embraced state intervention on the one hand, while on the other it extolled the virtues of free enterprise.[36] For many ordinary Scots, the liberation of the economy from rationing and tightly controlled state regulation was a welcome relief that rebounded to the benefit of the Tories. In doing so, the Conservatives were able to present themselves as offering the best of both worlds and as such posited themselves as a compromise 'middle way'. It should be remembered that more council houses were built under Conservative administrations than Labour and Harold Macmillan rejoiced in his ability to complete new-build homes ahead of target. Part of the glue that held the consensus politics together was that both Labour and the Conservatives could advocate similar policies of state intervention but believed that it would create outcomes favourable to that particular party. After all, the 'affluent society' could be interpreted as a spur both to Conservative social mobility and to Labour socialist redistribution. Similarly, the expansion of higher education would demonstrate to a new generation the virtues of socialist state planning or increase the number of potential Tory graduate voters.

Arguably, it was the inability to adapt pragmatically to the changing socio-economic circumstances of the 1960s that undermined traditional Tory notions of patriotism and paternalism. With the decline of Britannic patriotism in the late 1960s, the Conservatives in Scotland fumbled around in reaction to the growth of Scottish Nationalism. The leadership's decision to make sympathetic noises towards devolution was unpopular with the rank and file. A clear policy on the importance of Scottish patriotism to the Union project did not emerge and it is worth pointing out that an accommodation with Scottish patriotism should have been theoretically more ideologically comfortable to the Tories than to Labour. Also, as domestic socio-economic issues were elevated up the list of Scottish political priorities as a result of the travails of the economy that required more and more state intervention to keep things going, the Tories seemed to always be playing catch up to Labour. Unlike the period after 1918, the party seemed unable to adapt to the new socio-economic realities, many of which were undermining traditional notions of paternalism and deference. The failure to create a new business class to the same extent as in England was a good case in point. Finally, as Iain Hutchison has noted, the party by the mid-1960s was having difficulty in mobilising supporters, which if nothing else reveals that the Conservative Party in Scotland was failing to renew itself.[37]

Notes

1. See in particular I. G. C. Hutchison, *A Political History of Scotland, 1832–1924: Elections, Parties, Issues* (Edinburgh, 1986), pp. 314–26, and *Scottish Politics in the Twentieth Century* (Basingstoke, 2001). For a more recent synopsis see Ewen A. Cameron, *Impaled Upon a Thistle: Scotland Since 1800* (Edinburgh, 2010), pp. 263–89.
2. For a good example of the issue of foreign politics in a Scottish political context see S. R. Ball, 'The politics of appeasement: the fall of the Duchess of Atholl and the Kinross and West Perthshire by-election, December 1938', *Scottish Historical Review* 69 (1990), pp. 49–83, and for the role of the British Empire in Nationalist politics see Richard J. Finlay, 'For or against? Scottish Nationalism and the Empire', *Scottish Historical Review* 191/2 (1992), pp. 184–206.
3. For some examples of Scottish Labour's trenchant criticism of rearmament see Thomas Burns, *A Plan For Scotland* (Perth, 1937) and *The Real Rulers of Scotland* (Glasgow, 1940), which were highly critical of the links between industry and rearmament.
4. See in particular John Darwin, *The Empire Project: The Rise and Fall of the British World System, 1830–1970* (Cambridge, 2009), and for the impact of the Second World War in Scotland see Trevor Royle, *A Time of Tyrants: Scotland and the Second World War* (Edinburgh, 2011).
5. See C. R. Blake, *Scotland of the Scots* (London, 1918), p. 61.
6. *National Review* 95 (1930), p. 874.
7. Till Geiger, *Britain and the Economic Problem of the Cold War: The Political Economy and the Impact of the British Defence Effort, 1945–55* (London, 2004), pp. 283–92.
8. See the coverage in *The Scotsman*, 7 February 1950, 'Resisting Communism in South East Asia', and 15 November and 2 December 1954 for 'Mau Mau Atrocities'.
9. *Life*, 21 January 1957.
10. E. W. McFarland and R. J. Johnstone, 'The Church of Scotland's Special Commission on Communism, 1949–1954: "Tackling Christianity's most serious competitor"', *Contemporary British History* 23:3 (2009), pp. 337–61.
11. Richard J. Finlay, 'National identity in crisis? Politicians, intel-

lectuals and the end of Scotland, 1920–39', *History* 79:256 (1994), pp. 242–59.

12. House of Commons Debates [hereafter HC Debs], second series, 272, 22 November 1932, col. 262.

13. Earl of Mansfield, House of Lords Debates, 107, 15 December 1937, col. 514.

14. Sir Robert Horne, HC Debs, 272, 24 November, col. 242–3.

15. Sonya O. Rose, *Which People's War? National Identity and Citizenship in Wartime Britain, 1939–45* (Oxford, 2004), pp. 197–285.

16. For example, the criticism in the *Glasgow Herald*, 3 April 1942.

17. Hutchison, *Scottish Politics*, p. 71.

18. *Scotsman*, 15 February 1950.

19. *Scottish Control of Scottish Affairs: Unionist Policy* (Glasgow, 1949).

20. Richard J. Finlay, 'Scottish monarchy in the twentieth century', in W. L. Miller (ed.), *Anglo-Scottish Relations From 1900 to Devolution* (Oxford, 2004), pp. 62–75.

21. See Iain Donnachie, Christopher Harvie and I. S. Wood (eds), *Forward! Labour Politics in Scotland, 1888–1988* (Edinburgh, 1989), pp. 7–49; Hutchison, *Political History of Scotland*, pp. 277–309; J. J. Smyth, *Labour in Glasgow 1896–1936: Socialism, Suffrage, Sectarianism* (East Linton, 2000), pp. 70–125; John Holford, *Reshaping Labour: Organisation, Work and Politics: Edinburgh in the Great War and After* (Beckenham, 1988); Alan McKinlay and R. J. Morris (eds), *The ILP on Clydeside 1893–1932: From Foundation to Disintegration* (Manchester, 1991), pp. 123–77; and William Kenefick, *Red Scotland: The Rise and Fall of the Radical Left, c1872–1932* (Edinburgh, 2007), pp. 159–84.

22. Hutchison, *Scottish Politics*, p. 113.

23. See Hutchison, *Political History*, pp. 322–6.

24. *The Campaign Guide* (London, 1924).

25. The number of 'National' Liberal MPs in Scotland was five in 1945 and six in 1955.

26. For the continuity of Liberal traditions into Labour ones see Richard J. Finlay, 'Continuity or change: Scottish politics 1900–1945', in T. M. Devine and Richard J. Finlay (eds), *Scotland in the Twentieth Century* (Edinburgh, 1996), pp. 64–85, and Catriona M. M. Macdonald, *The Radical Thread:*

Political Change in Scotland. Paisley Politics, 1895–1924 (Edinburgh, 2000).

27. T. C. Smout, *A Century of the Scottish People, 1830–1950* (London, 1997).
28. J. N. Toothill, *Inquiry into the Scottish Economy 1960–1961*, Scottish Council (Development and Industry), 1961.
29. Scottish Statistical Office, *Digest of Scottish Statistics*, 28 October 1966, p. 33, for the growth in employment in professional services which increased by about 50,000 between 1960 and 1965.
30. Hutchison, *Scottish Politics*, pp. 104–8 and James Mitchell, *Conservatives and the Union: A Study of Conservative Party Attitudes to Scotland* (Edinburgh, 1990).
31. Richard J. Finlay, *Modern Scotland, 1914–2000* (London, 2004), pp. 273–316.
32. http://www.parliament.uk/documents/commons/lib/research/rp 2004/rp04-061.pdf
33. S. R. Ball, 'Asquith's decline and the general election of 1918', *Scottish Historical Review* 61 (1982), pp. 49–83.
34. R. H. Campbell, 'The committee of ex-Secretaries of State for Scotland and industrial policy', *Scottish Industrial History* 2 (1979), pp. 1–10.
35. R. H. Campbell, 'The Scottish Office and the Special Areas in the 1930s', *Historical Journal* 22 (1979), pp. 167–83.
36. See, for example, the debate on Scottish industry, HC Debs 466, 7 July 1949, cols 2,350–470.
37. Hutchison, *Scottish Politics*, pp. 108–9.

CHAPTER 4

More than a Name: The Union and the Un-doing of Scottish Conservatism in the Twentieth Century

Margaret Arnott and Catriona M. M. Macdonald

The Unionist Party in Scotland should recognise that no London Government will ever solve any of our problems until we have a SCOTTISH PARLIAMENT FOR SCOTTISH AFFAIRS. Lest it be accused of fraud and failure to keep its election pledges, let the Unionist party remember that it is a <u>Scottish</u> Party and that COUNTRY BEFORE PARTY is not just another shallow platitude.

> The Scottish Covenant Association, 'The Unionist Party and Scotland' (Glasgow, 1953)

Introduction

Since 1912, if not long before, putting country before party has been no easy challenge for the Scottish Tories: the growth to maturity of administrative devolution and shifting political alliances at key points in the development of the British state meant that neither the country nor the party to which loyalty was owed was necessarily clear. In part, this might be explained by the fact that, with the possible exception of 1997, at no point in the twentieth century was the defence of the 1707 Treaty of Union a *defining* feature of Scottish Toryism in the eyes of the electorate – at least not in the same way or to the same extent that defence of the unity of the UK distinguished the Ulster Unionists. It also pays to be reminded that Unionists in Scotland regularly stood for election as political hybrids – 'Liberal Unionists', 'Coalition Unionists', 'National Unionists' – and that in times of national emergency they were, on occasion, happy to step aside and endorse avowed supporters of Home Rule as the surest way of defeating the greater menace of socialism. One might suggest that this flexibility is simply symptomatic of traditional Conservative suspicions of dogma and doctrine. Yet, the opaque quality of the rendering of nationhood in the history of Scottish Unionism took pragmatism to an extent that challenged core Conservative beliefs in the unitary state. Arguably, this was clearly revealed during the Thatcher governments when a more doctrinaire 'One Nation' approach infused with neo-liberalism threw into relief the ways in which the interface between nationhood and statehood had at times confounded the Unionist Party in Scotland, and the extent to which Burkean notions of traditionalism, for Scottish Tories, had always drawn on a distinctive rendering of *Scottish* values and interests as much as British mores and priorities.

Until the 1970s, '1707' was rarely mentioned in the campaign literature of Scottish Tories. While, on first appraisal, this might be surprising, it is readily explained when a more complex approach to what constituted 'the Union' is adopted. After all, the marriage of convenience between Liberal Unionists and Conservatives in Scotland which gave birth to the Scottish Unionist Association (SUA) in 1912 was intended to defend the Acts of Union between Great Britain and Ireland that came into effect in 1801, *not* the older Union of 1707 that had merged the parliaments of Scotland and England, which was not perceived to be under any serious threat until the 1960s when the SNP began to make electoral inroads. But the complexity goes beyond the origins of the party and constitutional particulars. Why, for example, politicians committed to one treaty, particularly after the emergence of the Irish Free State in 1922, moved effortlessly to the defence of another in the way they did is not as obvious as it might appear.[1] To say, as does James Mitchell, that 'Implicit in the notion of Unionism lay the belief in British Greatness – a notion challenged by Irish secession, later decolonization, and by Scottish nationalism still later', is to impose with hindsight a very even logic on a very uneven process, and to underplay the role of Unionists in the partition of Ireland and the influence of Scottish Home Rulers within the Scottish Unionist Party itself.[2]

Scottish Unionism throughout its history had at its centre a commitment to the Scottish nation as expressed in economic, civic and cultural terms that asserted loyalties to traditions below the level of the state and often in opposition to it. Similarly, it endorsed a transnational vision of the Scottish nation that was sustained by the Empire until 1945. In this way, the Union was seldom defended for its own sake. Until recently, Scottish Conservatives had (since at least the mid-nineteenth century) evidenced a keen awareness of Scottish sensitivities in the Union state and a commitment to administrative devolution. As Alex Tyrrell has recently shown, mid-Victorian Scottish Nationalism, as expressed in the rhetoric and activities of the National Association for the Vindication of Scottish Rights, owed much to Tory patronage and in turn influenced Scottish Conservative discourse on constitutional matters.[3] For Scottish governance, the consequences were profound. While pressure from Scottish Liberals like Lord Rosebery was certainly influential in the creation of the Scottish Office in 1885, it was ultimately a Conservative administration that delivered on Liberal promises, and in the years that followed, successive Unionist governments were instrumental in granting the Scottish Secretary first cabinet rank (1892), then elevation to Secretary of State (1926), before relocating the Scottish Office to Edinburgh in 1939.

By foregrounding the ways in which Scottish identity formed 'a key component of traditional Unionism', an alternative reading of 'the Conservative century' is possible in which historical and party-political contexts loom large.[4] By historicising Unionism, instead of reading from the singularity of a historic constitutional settlement a singularity of meaning over time, it will be shown how merger with the Liberal Unionists in 1912, far from an unalloyed advantage, acted as a brake on the organic development of Conservatism in Scotland, and how pacts and alliances between 1916 and 1945 then further compromised the evolution of Tory approaches to Home Rule in Scotland. Thereafter, the 1950s – far from being the 'high noon' of Unionism – showed in the coincidence of Conservative localism and administrative devolution, a winning utilitarian approach to the Union in which Scottish interests took precedence over the convenience of Whitehall.[5] Read in this way, Edward Heath's Declaration of Perth (1968) is less of an aberration than a missed opportunity to take a long-held commitment to administrative devolution all the way to a legislative end. It would not be until after the 1997 referendum on Scottish devolution that the party in Scotland was able to explicitly articulate a pro-devolutionist brand of Unionism again. Nevertheless, the legacy of the assimilationist brand of Unionism favoured by Thatcherites in the 1980s and 1990s remains with the party today.

1886–1916

Over the years, most historians have in a variety of ways agreed with John McCaffrey's 1971 statement that in 1886 the Liberal Unionists gave a 'boost' to the Conservative cause in Scotland.[6] Yet, beyond a short-term electoral upsurge, opinion is divided as to how long this advantage actually lasted. In some areas the Liberal Unionist–Conservative alliance was little more than confirmation of a 'class' divide premised on the defence of the established status of the Church of Scotland, and had little to do with broader constitutional principles. In addition, the Liberal Unionists' commitment to free trade led to 'deep fissures' opening up between them and their Tory allies over tariff reform in the early years of the twentieth century, and after merger in 1912 the energising influence of Liberalism that was imported into the Unionist ranks declined over time.[7] The adoption of the Unionist epithet (and the abandonment of the Conservative alternative) also prioritised a certain appreciation of the British constitution that distorted Tory identity in Scotland. After all, with its Jacobite roots, Unionism was hardly foundational for the Tories in Scotland, and a decade after the formation of the SUA the 'Union' to which their new appellation referred had been undone by an administration that boasted a significant Unionist presence.

The late Victorian rhetoric of Unionism also risked a breach with Scottish Tories' Nationalist traditions. As early as 1895 the annual report of the National Union of Conservative Associations in Scotland was drawing the political battle lines squarely between 'Unionists' and 'Separatists', thus eschewing the more nuanced appreciation of Unionism that earlier Scottish Tories appeared to have relished.[8] Perhaps it is time to look again at 1886 as a brake on Scottish Conservative devolutionary sympathies, and to identify in the merger of 1912 an alliance that even at the point of formalisation had, perhaps, outlived its usefulness. A year hence, the Ulster question would undercut the absolutes of Home Rule and Union with assertions of the rights of minorities, and in the years that followed, the resolution of the disestablishment question and the reunification of the Church of Scotland compromised the religious dynamic that had earlier facilitated Liberal Unionist–Conservative friendship to the extent that little remained of its original sentiments beyond sectarianism.

1916–45

Michael Dyer has described Scottish Unionism as 'decidedly mongrel', and has highlighted the extent to which the politics of the Centre Right in inter-war Scotland evidenced 'an acceptance of ideological heterodoxy and organisational flexibility in a culture of coalitionism'.[9] Commencing in 1915 with the short-lived coalition government of H. H. Asquith, and continuing into the Lloyd George coalition of 1916–22, Scottish Unionists worked in partnership with Liberals at both a national and a local level, and were more reluctant than their English counterparts to break this understanding at the famous Carlton Club meeting of 19 October 1922. Sir Robert Horne (the Chancellor of the Exchequer), standing as the sitting Unionist member for Glasgow Hillhead, noted in his general election address that November that:

> I regard co-operation with the National Liberals – with whom we share a common policy – as vital to the interests of the nation . . . I am glad to think that in Scotland the Unionist party takes the view which I hold.[10]

After contesting the 1923 and 1924 elections as Unionists, the pursuit of 'a common policy' reasserted itself; 1931 again saw the Scottish Unionists campaigning for the public vote as part of a coalition that would last – in various manifestations – until 1945.

Pacts with Liberals at a local level combined with formal coalitionism at a national level compromised the identity of the Scottish Unionist Party between 1916 and 1945, and this had clear implications for the Unionist approach to Home Rule for Scotland, which itself lacked definition. Unionist candidates at the 1918 general election embraced a wide spectrum of approaches to Scottish self-government. While most were silent on the issue, many Coalition Unionists such as Major William Murray (a former Liberal Unionist), a candidate in the Dumfriesshire constituency, declared their support for the government's reconstruction proposals, including 'Home Rule for Ireland excluding Ulster, and Home

Rule for Scotland'.[11] Some went further. In Glasgow Camlachie, Halford John Mackinder, the sitting Unionist MP, declared that 'we should be ready to contemplate a considerable measure of devolution to all the constituent parts of the United Kingdom'.[12] Gideon Murray, in Glasgow St Rollox, was even prepared to countenance 'a measure of Home Rule for Scotland, involving the devolution to a Scottish Parliament of much purely Scottish business now transacted in the House of Commons'. Federalism also appealed to others: D. H. MacDonald, the Coalition Unionist candidate for Bothwell, approved of 'the general principle of all-round Devolution or Federation, so as to relieve the Imperial Parliament of the consideration of many matters which could be better dealt with by Federal Legislatures'.[13]

The annual reports of the SUA would suggest that the politicisation of Scottish Nationalism in the 1920s caused nothing in the way of alarm.[14] Yet, as Richard Finlay rightly suggests, the formation of the National Party of Scotland (NPS) in 1928 and the Scottish National Party (SNP) in 1934 acted as a 'political catalyst' on the politics of the later inter-war period.[15] In the 1929 general election the Unionists were clearly playing the 'Scottish card' far more than they had done in the past. What this meant varied according to the candidate. In the Ayr Burghs, Lt Gen. Sir Aylmer Hunter-Weston considered it enough merely to emphasise that his family connection to the constituency went back to 'a very early period of Scottish history', and that his regard for the place was 'bred in my bones'.[16] Yet in Glasgow Kelvingrove, Andrew Dewar Gibb – later a founder member of the SNP – standing (ultimately unsuccessfully) in the Unionist interest offered more detailed proposals:

> So far as Scottish affairs are concerned, I desire earnestly to see far more Parliamentary time available for the discussion and solution of our peculiar problems. I would also support a measure to ensure that all Private bill legislation . . . is effected in Scotland and not in London. I regard the modern process of rationalisation in industry as one which must be carefully watched in the interests of Scotland, because in so many cases this process involves the closing down of Scottish factories and workshops, and the consequent throwing out of employment of Scottish workers . . .[17]

Gibb was not exceptional among Unionists in his desire for greater Scottish control of Scottish affairs. As discussed, this was evident in the acceleration of administrative devolution under the National Government from 1931, and is further confirmed by the explicit Nationalist sympathies of leading Unionists in the 1930s, the preparedness of the Baldwin regime to embrace the rhetoric of Scottish identity and ultimately the presence of Tories in the Nationalist parties in the inter-war years.[18] John Buchan, a Combined Scottish Universities MP between 1927 and 1935, was adamant about the defence of a distinct Scottish voice at Westminster, and as Gabrielle Ward-Smith has noted, such sentiments were echoed in Stanley Baldwin's regular populist speeches to Scottish audiences that were infused with references to Scottish values and Scottish history.[19] Yet for many Unionists, expectations raised by such sentimental effusions proved incapable of realisation within the party. Economic depression on a global scale was encouraging a cautious approach in the party hierarchy, even in Scotland. In 1932 the Annual Conference of the SUA passed a resolution declaring its belief that 'the setting up of a separate Parliament would be gravely injurious both to the economic and to the cultural life of Scotland and of Great Britain as a whole'.[20] For Unionists such as Dewar Gibb and the Duke of Montrose the solution was membership of the Scottish Party, then the SNP.[21]

While in the 1890s the 'Separatists' against which Scottish Tories defined their Unionism were the Liberals, by the 1930s this epithet was awarded to the Nationalists. It is hardly surprising, therefore, that there was no easy transfusion of loyalties and little in the way of doctrinal consistency in the Unionist approach to the constitution. Ulster would resurface now and again as a stumbling block for both pro- and anti-devolutionists in the Scottish arena. The Stormont Parliament could be used as a precedent for greater Scottish liberty within the Union state, but it also served to convince other Unionists that devolution harboured grave prospects for the Scottish minority in the UK. Arguably the Irish question continued to act as a brake on Scottish Unionists' devolutionary sympathies: while supporting practical measures of administrative devolution, the Unionist Party refused to support legislative devolution. Standing against the Nationalist leader, John MacCormick, in Glasgow Hillhead in 1937, the National Unionist candidate J. S. C. Reid (Solicitor General for Scotland), reminded constituents:

The National Government has not been unmindful of Scotland. Our problems are in many respects more difficult than those of England.

In many cases they have received special treatment. We have a housing subsidy while England has none. Government grants to Local Authorities have been largely increased. The new provision for Maternity and Child Welfare are [sic] more extensive in Scotland. In future the Government will be in more direct touch with Scotland as a result of the Scottish administrative department being concentrated in Edinburgh.[22]

For the time being, this was enough: National Government candidates secured just short of 54 per cent of the Scottish vote in 1931 and almost 50 per cent in 1935, and the cessation of party campaigning during the war years sustained the National Government into 1945. Yet on the eve of war the emergence of political Nationalism was throwing into relief the intrinsic vulnerability of Scottish Toryism when shorn of its associates. In the 1935 general election W. Oliver Brown, standing for the SNP in Renfrewshire East, was scathing:

Just as in the Khaki Election, the Coupon Election, the Zinoviev Letter Election, the Crisis Election, the Press and the Government have combined in an effort to stampede the electorate so that the Conservative party disguised as a 'National' Government may secure a majority which it could never obtain if it appealed to calm reason and cool judgement.[23]

1945–68

While the Labour landslide in 1945 may have appeared to prove Brown's thesis, Unionist success in the 1950s – when Scottish Unionists stood under their own banner – suggests a rather different story. In 1945, 1951 and 1955 the Scottish Unionists' share of the poll either equalled or exceeded the proportionate share given to the Conservative Party in England, and remained above 40 per cent of the Scottish electorate in the 1959 and 1964 general elections.[24] Yet such success ought not to be attributed to an unwavering and conservative 'take' on the Union. Rather, Unionist success in these years owed much to an anti-centralising agenda in British Conservatism at large and parallel localising tendencies in party policy. This suggests that devolutionary tendencies in Scottish Unionism in these years – far from the aberration some have styled them – *complemented* tendencies in English Conservatism while, as we have seen, drawing on a long heritage of Tory Nationalism. Further, the manner in which the Scottish Unionists embraced the modernising and progressive agenda of the Macmillan years also strongly suggests that the party's change of name in 1965 to the Scottish Conservative and Unionist Party was the logical expression of long-held suspicions in the party that Unionism's time had passed, or at least that the Union had to change.[25]

It is hardly surprising that after six years during which both citizenry and soldiery had been mobilised in pursuit of 'total war' and a further five years of a nationalising Labour government, Scottish Unionists – alongside their English Conservative colleagues – would appeal to the electorate in 1950 as the party that would halt the advance of the centralising state.[26] T. G. D. Galbraith, Unionist candidate for Glasgow Hillhead in 1950, was near typical in this regard when he complained that 'The independence of industry and of local government have been curtailed everywhere by Socialist planning. Unionists believe that the concentration of so much power at the centre is inefficient and undemocratic.'[27] But while in England such a strategy would halt at a local or regional emphasis in policy, in Scotland Unionist Nationalism was re-energised. Walter Elliot – the sitting Unionist MP for Glasgow (Kelvingrove) – would claim in 1950 that 'Scotland has been shackled by remote control', and proposed that the Unionists would 'bring the control of nationalised industries to Scotland and . . . have a resident minister in Scotland so that there shall always be responsibility here and not merely officialdom'.[28] A year later the Unionist Charles McFarlane in Glasgow Camlachie would insist that 'The United Kingdom cannot be kept in a Whitehall strait-jacket. The Unionist Policy for Scotland will be vigorously pressed forward.'[29] Yet W. Ross McLean, the Unionist candidate for Greenock that year, would go further. He announced his belief that 'Scotland should have legislative and administrative control of her purely domestic affairs.'[30] Read against the backdrop of the popularity of the Scottish Covenant movement that by 1950 had secured two million signatures in favour of legislative devolution for Scotland within the UK, such rhetoric might be styled as simple electoral opportunism. However, there are sufficient echoes in such sentiments with earlier Unionist claims for Scottish distinctiveness to confirm that this was more than simple political cunning and classical Tory pragmatism. After all, in 1951 the newly elected Conservative government established a Royal Commission on Scottish Affairs under Lord Balfour.[31]

Conservative strategy was to encourage a 'de-centred but still united Britain', and administrative devolution in Scotland in these years should, in part, be seen as symptomatic of this initiative and as an expression of Scotland's embrace of progressive conservatism.[32] The interventionism of the Macmillan years, marrying economic planning, regulated capitalism and a strong social welfare agenda, was popular among Scottish Unionists who made much of what it was doing for Scotland. In 1955 the party manifesto in Scotland would boast that 'Never before in Scottish history has the rate of house-building been so high as in these years of Unionist Government'[33], and in 1964 Kenneth Bruce Miller, the Unionist candidate in Glasgow Provan, would assert that 'For every £10 per head spent in England, Scotland received £12 for education, £12 10/- for hospitals, £13 for roads and £17 for housing.'[34] Even more significantly, in Glasgow Scotstoun, Ronald Anderson, the Unionist candidate that year, would attack the 'Socialists' for having 'no separate plan for Scotland'.[35]

The Scottish Unionist Association changed its name in 1965 to re-introduce a reference to its Conservative roots, and thereafter increasingly referred to itself as the Conservative Party. In light of its experience in the 1950s and early 1960s, this was surely hardly surprising. Conservative governments had delivered much for which Unionists could justifiably claim credit *despite* their different name, and in any case, popular Unionism was also now more 'banal' (to use Colin Kidd's description) than it had been in the past, as the salience of both the Empire and the Irish question had declined.[36] Indeed, James Mitchell has shown that popular demands from the Scottish membership for a change in name go back to 1956.[37] Yet the historiography of the party has too often interpreted this change in nomenclature as indicative of a declining Scottish distinctiveness.[38] Reading forward with the gift of hindsight instead of back, as did the Unionists in 1965, this has distorted the history of Scottish Unionism in the second half of the twentieth century by privileging organisational change as a harbinger of decline.[39] The near coincidence of what have been seen as centralising tendencies in the Conservative Party after 1965 with its tentative embrace of legislative devolution has been largely ignored in favour of reading forward from 1965 a tale of unremitting Anglicisation that pays scant attention to the more contested nature of the Conservatives' relationship with devolution in these years. The name change did not signal the resolution of Scottish Conservatism's life-long contested relationship with the Union state – quite the opposite. It masked ongoing debates on Scotland's future within the UK and within Europe.

1968–97

Memoranda presented to the Scottish Constitutional Committee established following Edward Heath's famous Declaration of Perth in 1968 are testament to the fact that while the Conservatives' interest in Home Rule in these years ought to be read as a logical organic development emerging from a long gestation within Scottish Toryism, the plans sketchily outlined by the Leader of the Opposition were not.

Bill Baker (MP for Banffshire) complained to Michael Noble that the announcement at Perth had been 'ill-timed' and 'opportunistic'. Meanwhile, in the Denny and Dunipace Conservative and Unionist Association the Declaration was 'received with complete lack of enthusiasm', and the members of the Pentlands Conservative Association, while considering 'the appointing of a Scottish Assembly in principle good', were divided as to what form it should take. Meanwhile, the Orkney and Shetland Tory Associations advised that 'Our battles are as much with St Andrew's House as with the Westminster Parliament' and that 'to Orkney and Shetland Scotland is a geographical accident'.[40]

More revealing, if admittedly from a voice outwith the party, was the memorandum from the Nationalist A. J. C. Kerr, which advised: 'In a general way I think it would be wise to consider <u>how much can be conceded without breaking up the UK, rather than how little must be conceded in order to gain worthwhile support in Scotland</u>.'[41] This was surely a truly conservative approach to the dilemmas facing the Conservatives in the mid-1960s, but one that was not to be entertained by the party.

The 1970 report of the Scottish Constitutional Committee, chaired by Sir Alec Douglas-Home, recommended that the party support the establishment of a directly elected assembly that would take responsibility for the second reading and committee stages of Scottish bills.[42] In the coming 1970 UK general election the Conservative Party manifesto would for the first time include support for a directly elected Scottish Assembly. However, despite Heath's electoral victory in 1970, by the end of his premiership legislative devolution had not actively been pursued. In any case, the SNP failed to make its electoral breakthrough in 1970.[43] Pressing economic issues alongside deteriorating industrial relations increasingly preoccupied the Heath administration. In government he argued reform of the government of Scotland should be informed by the Royal Commission on the Constitution established by the Wilson government in 1968. This would not report until 1973. By the end of the Heath government the focus of arguments began to shift from a directly elected Scottish Assembly towards the reform of local government in Scotland. But the Union question did not disappear.

While explicit references to the Union had been inconsistent in Scottish Conservatism, by the end of the twentieth century this was no longer the case. Scottish devolution and the Union would be recurring issues for the Scottish party in this period. The electoral decline of the Scottish Conservative Party from October 1974 to 1997 fuelled both its pro- and anti-devolutionist wings. In 1975 the Conservative Party elected a new leader, Margaret Thatcher. Officially party policy continued to reflect the stance adopted under the Heath leadership to support the establishment of a Scottish Assembly; the following year, at the Scottish Conservative conference, a pro-devolution motion was passed, with both Mrs Thatcher and her devolution spokesman William Whitelaw voting in favour. However, the party's stance was becoming less clear, with Thatcherite scepticism beginning to make its mark. Any doubts about how the Thatcher leadership viewed Scottish devolution were set aside in 1976 when the Wilson government's Scotland and Wales Bill brought the issue back onto the political agenda. In December 1976 the Shadow Cabinet decided to oppose the bill. This split the party, with Alick Buchanan-Smith, the then Shadow Scottish Secretary, and his deputy Malcolm Rifkind resigning. The party, if not all its Scottish members, had entered a new anti-devolutionist period.

Some twenty years later, in 1997, tensions between Scottish Burkean Toryism and Thatcherism deeply divided the party in Scotland. At the root of these tensions lay the question of how Scottish national identity should be accommodated within the Union, especially how Scotland should be governed. As Conservative governments of the 1980s pursued an ideologically driven agenda which sought to bring about 'radical change', Conservatives in Scotland found themselves increasingly unable to accommodate their Scottish identity. As discussed, previous Conservative governments had been willing to facilitate the development of a distinctive central administration in Scotland as a way of appeasing Scottish Nationalism. This willingness to reform the government of Scotland not only enabled Scottish Conservatives to highlight their Scottish identity but also gave the party a distinctive Scottish image. By arguing against the need for further reform to the government of Scotland the Thatcher government fuelled the politicisation of national identity in Scotland.

The Thatcherite approach to change was to see it as a way of pursuing ideological and political motives rather than preserving and maintaining stability. This would have profound consequences for the party in Scotland and mark a new phase in the Unionism adopted by the British party. It would be unfair to argue that Thatcherism had a disregard for all established institutions and practices but it was selective in terms of which institutions and practices it sought to preserve. The Union would be defended on ideological grounds to maintain central control throughout the UK. Here it was parliamentary sovereignty rather than popular sovereignty that was the defining practice. A different kind of Unionism was advocated by Thatcherites. Thatcherites were comfortable framing the Union to achieve ideological ends. Ideological ends which drew upon the ideas of the New Right.

For Thatcherites the importance of the Union did not lie in the provisions that it included for the continued existence of a distinctive civil society in Scotland. Rather, the Union offered UK central government the opportunity to implement its policies *throughout* Britain. These sentiments were reflected in a paper published by the Centre for Policy Studies following the 1987 UK general election, *Making Unionism Positive: Proposals for a Tory Agenda for Scotland*. Its authors – Liam Fox, Mark Mayall and Alistair Cooke – argued that the Conservative Party should reaffirm its commitment to Unionism, having performed poorly at the 1987 election. Fox et al. wrote in their introduction: 'It is the ambivalence of the Conservative Party towards its own Unionist philosophy in relation to Scottish affairs which lies behind this decline.'[44] The Union would be used to offer Scotland the benefits of Thatcherism. Scotland had, in the views of Fox et al., diverged from 'mainstream' British politics. Here the claim was that Scotland needed *more* Thatcherism rather than less, and that Unionism ought to be seen within that context.

From 1987, despite Thatcherites claiming it was not politically salient, how Scotland was governed by the Conservative administrations increasingly dominated the Scottish political agenda. The diverging electoral fortunes of the party across Britain provided the political backdrop of arguments that there was a 'democratic deficit' in the government of Scotland. The cross-party Scottish Constitutional Convention formed in 1988 argued in its final report:

> This is a democratic deficit which runs contrary to Scotland's distinct political identity and system. It is affecting relations with the rest of a United Kingdom in which most Scots wish to remain, and hampering Scotland's ability to make its voice heard in the world, particularly within a fast-developing European Union well attuned to such voices. Redressing the deficit is a matter of fairness and justice, and also of better government.[45]

Across the political spectrum, including pro-devolutionists within the Scottish Conservative Party, tensions between parliamentary and popular sovereignty were increasingly leading to strains in Unionist thinking. The falling electoral support for the Conservative Party in Scotland was matched by a rise in the political salience of Scottish national identity,[46] a trend increasingly apparent to some Scottish Tory activists. Following the 1987 general election, the then leader of the Conservative group on the Convention of Scottish Local Authorities, Struan Stevenson, argued that 'Scottish Tories remained in an identity crisis'. The ability of the Scottish Conservative Party to reconcile the 'dual' British and Scottish identities, according to Stevenson, was becoming increasingly compromised by the approach of the Thatcher governments:

> Scottish Tories who have always thought of themselves as 'British first and Scottish second' have discovered that this philosophy in no way accords with the feelings of the average Scot. While the Opposition parties find it easy to identify and discuss the grievances of the Scottish people, Scottish Tories remained trapped by a national identity crisis.[47]

The politicisation of Scottish national identity from the 1980s brought an added edge to arguments about how the party in Scotland should respond to its declining electoral support. Malcolm Mackenzie, vice-chair of the Scottish Tory Reform Group, alluded to the 'two way process' which was needed between the party's British and Scottish agendas:

> Scottish Toryism must equate itself with Scottish culture and con-
> sciousness. This does not mean abandoning the ideology and the
> policies of Conservatism defined in the UK basis. It does mean trans-
> lating Conservative principles into Scottish conditions . . . It also
> means a two way process whereby Scottish thinking clearly influ-
> ences Conservative thinking at the UK level.[48]

It would take the electoral defeat of 1997 and the establishment of the devolved Scottish Parliament in 1999 before the party in Scotland could begin to move beyond these internal tensions between Thatcherite views of Unionism and the older Burkean view of Scottish Toryism. There was, inevitably, a generational dynamic to all this. As David McLetchie has noted:

> For my parents' generation, their Unionism was forged quite liter-
> ally in the heat of the battle, in the defining experience of the Second
> World War when our United Kingdom stood together and alone . . .
> For my generation . . . we have witnessed a Scotland in transition.
> We have seen the rise of political nationalism side by side with a
> stronger cultural nationalism. The political dilemma for the Scottish
> Conservatives has been how to reconcile the Unionism of our
> upbringing with this mood swing within Scotland, and our political
> failure has been a failure to adapt quickly enough to that change.[49]

By the end of the twentieth century the Scottish Conservative Party leadership was facing a very different political environment. The 'dual identities' of Scots did not sit easily together. The politics of Unionism had entered another distinctive phase. The question for the party was whether in the devolved Scottish Parliament it could, in McLetchie's phrase, develop a 'pragmatic Unionism' which would allow Scottish and British identities to coexist rather than be in conflict.

The Union, it might be argued, was the undoing of Scottish Conservatism in the twentieth century. At different times and in dif-ferent ways, a determined attachment to constitutional precedent and a lack of clarity on how Unionism and Conservatism interfaced in the Scottish – as opposed to British – environment disabled the articu-lation of a genuinely 'native' Scottish Tory voice. Pacts, alliances and coalitions made a complex situation further fraught, enforcing limiting parameters on what was possible for Scottish Tories who increasingly were, after 1987, in thrall to a centralising party bureaucracy and a growing intolerance of ideological heterodoxy.

Notes

1. While Peter Lynch has noted that 'as the old Union with Ireland died as an issue, it was gradually replaced by the Union of 1707 with Scotland', he failed to address why this might have been. Peter Lynch, 'The Northern Ireland peace process and Scottish constitutional reform: managing the Unions of 1800 and 1707', *Regional and Federal* Studies 6 (1996), p. 54.
2. James Mitchell, *Conservatives and the Union: A Study of Conservative Party Attitudes to Scotland* (Edinburgh, 1990), p. 9.
3. Alex Tyrrell, 'The Earl of Eglinton, Scottish Conservatism, and the National Association for the Vindication of Scottish Rights', *The Historical Journal* 53 (2010), pp. 87–107.
4. Michael Keating, 'The strange death of Unionist Scotland', *Government and Opposition* 45 (2010), pp. 365–85. *Conservative Century* is the title of Anthony Seldon and Stuart Ball's 1994 history of the Conservative Party in the twentieth century.
5. T. M. Devine, 'In bed with an elephant: almost three hundred years of the Anglo-Scottish Union', *Scottish Affairs* 57 (2006), p. 16.
6. J. F. McCaffrey, 'The origins of Liberal Unionism in the west of Scotland', *Scottish Historical Review* 50:1 (1971), pp. 47–71. See also Michael Fry, *Patronage and Principle: A Political History of Modern Scotland* (Aberdeen, 1987) and I. G. C. Hutchison, *A Political History of Scotland, 1832–1924* (Edinburgh, 1986).
7. I. G. C. Hutchison, *Scottish Politics in the Twentieth Century* (Basingstoke, 2001), p. 12; D. W. Urwin, 'The development of the Conservative Party organisation in Scotland until 1912', *Scottish Historical Review* 44 (1965), pp. 89–111; Catriona Burness, *'Strange Associations': the Irish Question and the Making of Scottish Unionism, 1886–1918* (East Linton, 2003), p. 212. Wesley Ferris dates the declining influence of Liberal heritage before merger. See Wesley Ferris, 'The candidates of the Liberal Unionist Party, 1886–1912', *Parliamentary History* 30:2 (2011), pp. 142–57.

8. National Library of Scotland [hereafter NLS], Acc 10424/27i, National Union of Conservative Associations of Scotland, Annual Reports, 1895, pp. 5–6.
9. Michael Dyer, 'The evolution of the Centre-Right and the state of Scottish Conservatism', *Political Studies* 49 (2001), pp. 30–50.
10. NLS, Acc 10424/122, Election Addresses, 1921–22. Horne famously refused to join the incoming Conservative government under Andrew Bonar Law.
11. NLS, Acc 10424/121, Election Addresses, 1918–20, 1918. Murray won the 1918 contest and remained the Dumfriesshire MP until 1922.
12. NLS, Acc 10424/121, Election Addresses, 1918–20, 1918.
13. NLS, Acc 10424/121, Election Addresses, 1918–20, 1918.
14. NLS, Acc 10424/27 iv–v, Annual Reports, Scottish Unionist Association.
15. Richard Finlay, 'Pressure group or political party? The Nationalist impact on Scottish politics, 1928–1945', *Twentieth Century British History* 3 (1992), pp. 274–97.
16. NLS, Acc 10424/121, Election Addresses, 1929–31, 1929.
17. NLS, Acc 10424/121, Election Addresses, 1929–31, 1929.
18. Richard Finlay, 'National identity in crisis: politicians, intellectuals and the 'end of Scotland', 1920–1939', *History* 79 (1994), pp. 242–59.
19. Christopher Harvie, 'Second thoughts of a Scotsman on the make: politics, Nationalism and myth in John Buchan', *Scottish Historical Review* 70 (1991), pp. 31–54, and G. Ward-Smith, 'Baldwin and Scotland: more than Englishness', *Contemporary British History* 15 (2001), pp. 61–82.
20. NLS, Acc 10424/27 vi, Annual Reports, 1933.
21. Finlay, 'Pressure group or political party?', pp. 284–7.
22. NLS, Acc 10424/127, Election Addresses, 1935–38, 1937.
23. NLS, Acc 10424/127, Election Addresses, 1935–38, 1935.
24. As David Seawright has noted: 'Scots were . . . relatively more right wing [than the English] in the 1950s and did not take the substantive move to the left . . . until the 1970s'. See David Seawright, 'The Conservative and Unionist party: 'the lesser spotted Tory'?', Annual Conference of the Political Studies Association, April 2002, p. 4.
25. Dyer, 'The evolution of the Centre-Right and the state of Scottish Conservatism', pp. 31–2.

26. M. Cragoe, '"We like local patriotism": the Conservative Party and the discourse of decentralisation, 1947–1951', *English Historical Review* CXXII (2007), pp. 965–85.

27. NLS, Acc 10424/130, Election Addresses, 1950.

28. NLS, Acc10424/130, Election Addresses, 1950.

29. NLS, Acc10424/131, Election Addresses, 1951.

30. NLS, Acc10424/131, Election Addresses, 1951. McLean was also supported by the Liberals in Greenock.

31. James Mitchell, 'Conservatives and the changing meaning of Union', *Regional and Federal Studies* 6:1 (1996), pp. 30–44.

32. Cragoe, '"We like local patriotism"', p. 971.

33. NLS, Acc 10424/132, *United for Peace and Progress 1955*, p. 29.

34. NLS, Acc 10424/134, Election Addresses, 1964.

35. NLS, Acc 10424/134, Election Addresses, 1964.

36. Colin Kidd, *Union and Unionisms* (Cambridge, 2008).

37. Mitchell, *Conservatives and the Union*, pp. 9–10.

38. Most notable in this regard is David Seawright, 'The Scottish Unionist Party: what's in a name?', *Scottish Affairs* 14 (1996). Here he notes: 'It is my contention that . . . its Unionist image was comfortable within the Scottish electoral environment [and] it adroitly used the negative connotations of "alien socialism" to reinforce that image, and that this advantage was lost in the mid-sixties.'

39. Scottish Tory organisation has been subject to an uncharacteristic level of historical scrutiny. See D. W. Urwin, 'The development of the Conservative Party organisation in Scotland until 1912'; D. W. Urwin, 'Scottish Conservatism: a party organization in transition', *Political Studies* 14 (1966), pp. 145–62; J. T. Ward, *The First Century: A History of Scottish Tory Organisation, 1882–1982* (Edinburgh, 1982); David Seawright, 'Scottish Unionism: an East West divide?' *Scottish Affairs* 23 (1998), pp. 54–72.

40. NLS, Acc 11368/167, Scottish Constitutional Committee, Copies of Memoranda, 1968–9.

41. Ibid.

42. Conservative Party, *Scotland's Government: The Report of the Scottish Constitutional Committee* (Edinburgh, 1970).

43. The SNP secured 11.4 per cent of the vote in Scotland and one seat, the Western Isles. The 1967 gain of Hamilton was lost to Labour.

44. Fox et al., *Making Unionism Positive: Proposals for a Tory Agenda in Scotland* (London, 1988), p. 1.
45. Scottish Constitutional Convention, *Scotland's Parliament, Scotland's Right* (1995).
46. For further discussion of the politicisation of Scottish national identity in the 1980s and 1990s see Alice Brown et al., *The Scottish Electorate: The 1997 General Election and Beyond* (London, 1999); Bromley et al., *Devolution – Scottish Answers to Scottish Questions?* (Edinburgh, 2003).
47. Struan Stevenson, *The Governing of Scotland* (unpublished paper, 1987).
48. Malcolm MacKenzie, *Scottish Toryism, Identity and Consciousness: a Personal Essay* (London, 1988), p. 5.
49. David McLetchie, *The Hampden Declaration 28th January 1999* (Edinburgh, 1999), pp. 6–7.

CHAPTER 5

Smithians, Thatcherites and the Ironies of Scottish Conservative Decline
Colin Kidd

Introduction

Historians recognise that there was no single factor that explains the decline of the Scottish Conservatives from their electoral high point in 1955, when they took more than half the vote in Scotland, to 1997, when they were left without a single seat north of the border.[1] Some long-term changes were beyond the control of the party. Processes of secularisation, for example, meant that economic rather than religious factors became more important in determining the allegiance of the Protestant working class. Similarly, with the retreat from Empire, common standards of welfare, rather than any shared pride in the projection of power, provided the most compelling basis for British unity, a social narrative that was much easier for Labour to exploit. Arguably, however, the Conservatives also made decisions that harmed their own cause. Most obviously, there was the rebranding in 1965 of the Scottish Unionist Party, a convenient banner under which Liberal Unionists had willingly voted alongside Conservatives, as the Scottish Conservative and Unionist Party. Nationalism imposed its own problems. Notwithstanding some earlier tactical versatility in the late 1960s, Conservatives did not react adroitly to the rise of the SNP from the 1970s, and increasingly the electorate came to identify the Conservatives as an English party determined to thwart the constitutional will of the Scottish people. Above all, there was the Thatcher factor, which took two forms, both a visceral dislike of Margaret Thatcher as a shrill, bossy Englishwoman, and a more substantive hostility to Thatcherism as an ideology markedly out of step with the traditional ethos of Scottish life. It is the latter objection that provides the matter of this chapter, for the rise of Thatcherite political economy was more complex and rich in ironies than the cartoonish version presented to the Scottish public. Indeed, a case can be made that Thatcherism, though widely rejected by the Scottish electorate at large, was not, as caricature had it, simply an attempt to impose the values of the south-east of England on an unwelcoming Scotland; rather, several of its central policy prescriptions – from the poll tax to the privatisation of public services – were first devised in Scotland.

This is not to question the fact that free-market economics alienated Scots of various political stripes from Conservatism. While the ideal of the night-watchman state and the tight control of monetary targets were anathema to socialists, they were also the cause of some anxiety to traditional Tory supporters, not excluding Tory paternalists, among whom was Thatcher's first Secretary of State for Scotland, George Younger, a diffident pragmatist who was as comfortable with Scottish trade unionists and the leaders of Labour-dominated local authorities as with monetarist zealots. The existence of such concerns – however muted – within the ranks of Scottish Conservative MPs reflected the worries of the Scottish middle classes. There was, for example, little support for laissez-faire policies from the pews of the established Kirk. The Church of Scotland had formerly resembled the Scottish Conservatives at prayer, but an abyss opened up during the 1980s between the Kirk's corporatist vision of a godly commonwealth and the ideals of Thatcherite individualism. Thatcher's notorious address to the General Assembly in 1988, quickly termed 'the Sermon on the Mound', provoked a stinging response from the Reverend Duncan Forrester, Professor of Practical Theology at Edinburgh, who termed her version of Christianity 'a false gospel', founded as it was on the 'the oldest idolatry in the world, mammon-worship'. The Bible, according to Forrester, 'knows nothing of an individualist's paradise'.[2] However, even the Edinburgh financial sector became alarmed at the unregulated casino capitalism of the 1980s, as corporate takeovers threatened to remove company headquarters from Scotland, and in turn the fees that were the lifeblood of the professional classes.

Electoral results bore witness to Scottish estrangement from Thatcherism. By 1987 the Conservatives – though easy victors in the UK general election of that year – were reduced to 24 per cent of the Scottish vote, and only ten out of seventy-two constituencies. Thatcher herself had some inkling of a broad irony in this situation. In her speech to the Scottish Conservative conference in May 1988 she invoked the legacy of David Hume and Adam Smith in a clever, though unsuccessful, attempt to dislodge the widespread public perception that hostility to Thatcherism was grounded in traditional Scottish values: 'I'm sometimes told that the Scots don't like Thatcherism. Well, I find that hard to believe – because the Scots invented Thatcherism, long before I was thought of.' This notion found a strong echo in a section of her memoirs entitled 'Thatcherism Rebuffed – The Case of Scotland'. Thatcher found it 'strange', given that the Scottish Enlightenment had 'produced Adam Smith, the greatest exponent of free enterprise economics till Hayek and Friedman', that there had been 'no tartan Thatcherite revolution'.[3]

There were, however, more specific ironies. Scots and Scottish institutions, it transpires, played a massively disproportionate role in the emergence of laissez-faire economics as the dominant doctrine in the modern Conservative Party, however much Scotland as a whole rejected the dogma. In particular, the triumph of free-marketeering in the party at Westminster owed a great deal, ultimately, to Scottish admiration for the legacy of Adam Smith, a fond appreciation of a native son which withstood, in some quarters at least, the near-universal fashion for the economics of J. M. Keynes during the 1950s and 1960s. At this point, when Keynesianism reigned supreme throughout British academia and laissez-faire was generally discredited, the University of St Andrews was a redoubt of free-market principles. A cadre of bright and zealous young Smithians was raised in this anti-Keynesian environment, many of whom made their way into the upper reaches of the Conservative Party during the 1980s. Adam Smith was also taken very seriously in his own alma mater, the University of Glasgow, which had its own – less nakedly ideological – Smithian tradition of political economy. Outside Scotland Adam Smith was a figure of mere antiquarian significance for post-war economists. At a time when free-market ideas were marginal within the discipline, and well beyond the 'Butskellite' consensus that prevailed within the Conservative Party quite as much as within Labour, the Scottish universities –

and St Andrews most especially – provided a protective womb for proto-Thatcherite economics.

In the two decades that preceded Thatcher's rise to the Conservative leadership in 1975 the party was far from committed to the disciplines of the market. Indeed, in the late 1950s free-market ideas, as we shall see, were as influential among the Liberals as among the Tories. At that stage the Conservative Prime Minister Harold Macmillan favoured a paternalist 'One Nation' approach and full employment at all costs, a policy whose laxity and indiscipline provoked the resignation in 1958 of his Treasury team, including one Enoch Powell. Among the most prominent paternalists of the early 1960s was Sir Keith Joseph, who would later, as a convert to the free market, recant what he now regarded as his earlier political follies. While Edward Heath's Selsdon platform of 1970, on which he won that year's general election, highlighted the party's conversion to a free-market regime, the Prime Minister soon performed a U-turn when he perceived the social consequences of sticking to a non-interventionist policy. Pragmatism, paternalism and the fashion for Keynesianism all contributed to limit the influence of laissez-faire political economy among Conservatives, a fault line that would persist in the party for some time after Thatcher became leader.

Nisbet and 'the great Adam'

If St Andrews was a more congenial environment for Smithian ideas than the pre-Thatcher Conservative Party, then this was largely owing to James Wilkie Nisbet, Professor of Political Economy at St Andrews from 1947 to 1970, an avuncular figure who set up a Political Economy Club for his students. Nisbet had started academic life as an assistant lecturer at Glasgow University in 1927, where he had been a pupil of W. R. Scott, the Adam Smith Professor of Political Economy. After publishing *The Case for Laissez-Faire* in 1932, Nisbet moved to St Andrews in 1935 as a lecturer in political economy. In his lectures Nisbet regularly referred to 'the great Adam',[4] though his private papers reveal that his real hero was another Scots champion of laissez-faire economics, Thomas Chalmers, an early-nineteenth-century St Andrews-educated theologian with a distrust of public welfare provision who had imagined – somewhat optimistically, even in the early nineteenth century –

that Christian charity could supply the deficiency.[5] Unsurprisingly, it did not take long for St Andrews students to pick up free-market ideas. Sir John Cowperthwaite, who had read classics at St Andrews and Cambridge, studied economics at St Andrews for a very brief period while awaiting his military call-up, but it was enough to inspire a Smithian approach to economic questions. Cowperthwaite went on to join the Hong Kong administrative service, becoming Financial Secretary to the colony between 1961 and 1971, when he implemented the free-market reforms that underpinned Hong Kong's economic miracle. In turn, the St Andrews-derived market reforms of Hong Kong exercised their own fascination upon Western politicians, Thatcher included.

Of course, Nisbet was not entirely alone in the mid-twentieth century as a champion of the free market. Hayek's *The Road to Serfdom* (1944) engaged a wide readership, and John Jewkes, the Professor of Organisation at Oxford, also criticised the obsession with central planning. One of Nisbet's former students recalls that he encouraged students to read Jewkes's *New Ordeal by Planning* (1948).[6] Nor should Nisbet be misconstrued as an intellectual giant. Eminent former colleagues have described him as 'a cheerful rogue, comically unaware of his own transparency,'[7] and suggested that Nisbet was a relic of a bygone era who succeeded in encouraging a Smithian environment largely because he was himself out of touch with recent advances in economics.[8]

As great an influence on the Conservative attitudes of St Andrews graduates – many of whom took joint degrees in Modern History and Economics – was Norman Gash, the Professor of History at St Andrews between 1955 and 1980. Born in India and educated in England, Gash was the leading authority on Sir Robert Peel, and a figure of greater intellectual substance than Nisbet. Yet, by a further irony Gash, who had a pronounced commitment to the Conservative Party and helped to nurture many future Thatcherites, was himself uncomfortable with Thatcherism. Indeed, he wrestled with the problem of how to reconcile Thatcher's radicalism with the traditions of the Conservative Party. His soul-searching was evident in his Swinton Lecture of 1989 to the Conservative Political Centre, 'The Radical Element in the History of the Conservative Party', where he struggled to assimilate Thatcherite daring with Conservative norms.[9]

Nevertheless, it was Nisbet's department at St Andrews that provided Thatcherism's John the Baptist: Ralph Harris, the long-serving co-director of the Institute of Economic Affairs (IEA), who proselytised for market-based ideas to anyone who would listen during the late 1950s and 1960s, and eventually won influential converts in Joseph and Thatcher, on whose recommendation he was ennobled in 1979 as Lord Harris of High Cross. Born in London and educated at Cambridge, Harris was a lecturer in Political Economy at St Andrews from 1949 to 1956, during which time he stood unsuccessfully for the Unionists in two Parliamentary seats, at Kirkcaldy in 1951 and at Edinburgh in 1955. He then spent a short period as a leader writer on the *Glasgow Herald* before joining Arthur Seldon in 1957 in the running of the newly founded IEA. The organisation had been set up by Antony Fisher, an enthusiast for Hayek, who supported the new think tank with the fortune he had made from Buxted Chickens. Although Harris was a Conservative, his co-director at the IEA, Seldon, was a Liberal, and together they promoted free-market ideas in an ecumenical manner wherever they found a receptive audience across a bleak Keynesian-dominated political landscape. Harris did not forget his St Andrews connection, becoming a frequent speaker at the St Andrews Political Economy Club in the 1960s and 1970s;[10] by the same token, Nisbet brought the publications of the IEA onto his reading lists, at a time when the IEA was at the very margins of academic economics.

Origins of the Adam Smith Institute

The cult of Adam Smith was not only fostered by the academic staff of St Andrews; in the mid-1960s it also took root among the student body, as a kind of youthful iconoclasm against the Keynesian orthodoxies of the day. Ironically, an offshoot of the St Andrews Conservative Association, known as the Reform Group, laid the foundations for one of the most significant think tanks in modern British politics. The key figures in the rise of the St Andrews Reform Group were its president, Madsen Pirie, a philosophy student who would complete his doctorate at St Andrews in 1974, and Douglas Mason, the group's secretary and treasurer, whose first degree at St Andrews was in Geology, but who also took courses in Economics. Pirie and Mason were soon joined by the Butler brothers, Stuart, who followed an undergraduate degree in Physics and Maths at St Andrews with postgraduate work there

in Economics and Economic History, and Eamonn who took his
first degree at St Andrews in 1973, and then his PhD in 1978. The
Reform Group started to produce its own pamphlets on economic
questions. The first by Pirie and Mason, published in August 1966,
was *Make it Legal*, which denounced the BBC's monopoly on radio
broadcasting. There followed an attack on the Potato Marketing
Board by Mason and Allan Stewart, under the amusing call to arms,
Plough them Under! Stewart, then on the staff of the Department of
Political Economy at St Andrews, was a recent graduate. A year or
so later, John Marshall, another high-flying graduate, launched an
attack on the British Egg Marketing Board with a parodic echo of
its own slogan, *Go to Work on the Egg Board!* The Tories' bonfire
of the quangos was prefigured in the free-market counterculture
of St Andrews in the late 1960s and early 1970s; and so too was
privatisation. In 1967 the Reform Group's fourth pamphlet, *Sold*,
co-authored by Stuart Butler and Richard Henderson, called –
prophetically – for the sale of council houses and the 'eventual abo-
lition of local authority housing'. A similarly judicious blend of the
prophetic and the politically practicable surfaced in another Reform
Group pamphlet of 1967, *The Worst They Can Get Away With*, in
which Pirie and Stuart Butler called for the privatisation of the telephone service. In *Return to Lender*, Henderson and Stephen Eyres,
who was taking Political Economy and Philosophy at St Andrews,
made the case for student loans. Indeed, the Reform Group was
deliberately provocative and iconoclastic. Its libertarianism was at
a remove from the buttoned-up Conservatism of bourgeois con-
ventionality, and its questioning of policy taboos owed something
to the satire boom of the 1960s. Pirie and the Butlers produced a
comic book featuring the adventures of Free Market Man, a super-
hero modelled on Superman and Batman, who performed more
prosaic feats, including abolishing wage and price controls, floating
exchange rates and taking care of the money supply. This satirical
outlook was apparent in the mock-up *Daily Telegraph* for 18 June
1981, which the Reform Group produced for the Conservative
Party conference in 1971. By 1981 they predicted, with wild opti-
mism, that Ralph Harris was Chancellor of the Exchequer and that
the Secretary of State for Education, Dr Rhodes Boyson, presided
over a privatised education system. Nevertheless, the mock-up also
anticipated, with greater accuracy, the sale of council houses and
the election of Ronald Reagan as President of the United States.[11]

The Reform Group at St Andrews was an early embodiment of

what became the Adam Smith Institute (ASI).[12] However, for Pirie and the Butlers there was a vital American interlude between the informal mimeographed outpourings of the St Andrews libertarians and the formal establishment of the ASI as a London-based think tank in 1977, with Pirie as its president and Eamonn Butler as its director from 1978. In particular, the Heritage Foundation, established in Washington, DC in 1973 by Ed Feulner, who had studied at the London School of Economics and worked part-time for Harris at the IEA, provided a template for a free-standing policy-based organisation. Pirie and the Butlers were also exposed to new developments in market-led economic theory, in particular the Virginia school of public choice economics, associated with the Nobel Laureate James Buchanan and also with Gordon Tullock. Public choice theory exposed the central fallacy of state planning, namely the notion that officials acted in the public interest; rather, officials – whether politicians or bureaucrats – acted in their own political and bureaucratic interests. Ostentatious political compassion, by the lights of public choice theory, tended to involve buying votes with other people's money. Thus the public choice school attempted to construct institutional arrangements in the structures of government that replicated the mechanism of price competition. The founders of the Adam Smith Institute applied the insights of public choice economics to the delivery of public services in the United Kingdom. In particular, Pirie's focus on microeconomic solutions was underpinned by public choice analysis. Close links persisted between the ASI and the Heritage Foundation. Stuart Butler remained in the States and became vice-president at Heritage for Domestic Policy Studies, while Eamonn co-authored a Heritage Foundation pamphlet, *Forty Centuries of Wage and Price Control*, with Robert Schuettinger in 1979. Although the network of St Andrews Smithians stretched from London to Washington, DC, it retained its roots in Fife. Mason led the Conservative group on Kirkcaldy District Council, where he chaired its Housing Committee and oversaw Scotland's first 'right to buy' council house sale. However, his career was not confined to parish-pump obscurity, for he acted as a domestic policy adviser to the ASI, leading its Omega Project which called for the contracting out of local government services. Indeed, it was Mason who made the serious case for a poll tax in his ASI pamphlet, *Revising the Rating System* (1985).

Networks and influences

There were two distinct generations of Smithian Conservatives educated at St Andrews, the first, in the late 1950s and early 1960s, nurtured in the environment created by Nisbet and Gash, and the second, in the late 1960s and early 1970s, as much a product of the countercultural libertarian network established by the student Reform Group. The political heavyweight in the first wave, John MacGregor, who took a First in Modern History and Political Economy at St Andrews,[13] would serve Thatcher as Chief Secretary to the Treasury, Minister of Agriculture and Education Secretary. Two other members of the early generation attained academic distinction in economics before moving into politics. After his degree in political economy at St Andrews, during which he was president of the Political Economy Club, John Marshall held lectureships at Glasgow and then Aberdeen between 1962 and 1970 and authored pamphlets for Aims of Industry. Although unsuccessful in his attempts to contest Dundee East at the elections of 1964 and 1966, he became a Conservative MEP for London North between 1979 and 1989, and became a Westminster MP for Hendon South between 1987 and 1997. Allan Stewart, who also distinguished himself as a student at St Andrews, became a Lecturer in Political Economy there. He became MP for East Renfrewshire in 1979, and successfully held the seat and its successor constituency Eastwood, until the Labour landslide of 1997. In the interim, Stewart served as Under-Secretary of State for Scotland from 1981 to 1986, and again from 1990 to 1995. Stewart authored an ASI pamphlet, *Landing Rights*, which favoured open skies and the deregulation of the airline industry. Ronnie Dundas, who studied History and Political Economy at St Andrews and became president of the University Conservative Association in 1962–3, did not manage to forge the career in politics for which he had hoped. He lost at Greenock in 1966, and in 1970 failed to win Glasgow Kelvingrove by a matter of 832 votes. Nevertheless, Dundas was an influential figure on the Scottish scene, joining the *Glasgow Herald* in 1964, and becoming its Business Editor in 1973.[14]

In the second wave, there was a mixture of MPs and figures whose aspirations focused as much on the backroom work of policy formation within the Smithian network as on high politics at Westminster. The career of Michael Forsyth, indeed, exhibits elements of both. Forsyth, who took his degree at St Andrews in 1976, served as the President of the St Andrews University Conservative Association between 1972 and 1975. By the early 1980s he sat on Westminster City Council, and had become a prolific pamphleteer. In 1980 Forsyth published *Re-servicing Britain* and in 1983 *The Myths of Privatisation*. Forsyth sat as MP for Stirling between 1983 and 1997 and held various high offices in the party and government, including the chairmanship of the Scottish Conservative Party from 1989 to 1990, and the post of Secretary of State for Scotland from 1995 to 1997. Stephen Eyres, a Reform Group stalwart, became a tutor at the Conservative Party's training establishment, Swinton College in Yorkshire. He also became deputy chairman of the Selsdon Group which was set up in 1973 as a free-market conscience to nag Edward Heath about his recent abandonment of market principles. Among other St Andrews graduates, Richard Henderson became Treasurer of the Selsdon Group and authored the Group's report on council house sales, while Mark Call became a special adviser at the Treasury.

St Andrews attracted many students from England, several of whom became involved in Conservative politics at the University and eventually became Tory MPs south of the border, not uncommonly as part of the Smithian network. These included Christopher Chope, the MP for Southampton Itchen and junior minister at the Departments of Environment and Transport, and Michael Fallon, the MP for Darlington, serving as an assistant whip and then as a junior minister, who took his degree at St Andrews in 1974. While for several ambitious young Englishmen St Andrews was a mere staging post towards a career in English public life, others participated in grassroots politics in Scotland. Robert Jones was born in Bedford and came to St Andrews to study Modern History. He stayed on after graduation, winning election to St Andrews Burgh Council and then to Fife County Council. However, his bid to become MP for Kirkcaldy failed at the October 1974 general election. Thereafter Jones moved to England, but he retained close connections with the ASI. He achieved some prominence on the national stage with a pointed Thatcherite barb in his speech at the Conservative Party conference in 1981: 'Margaret Thatcher has a vision that Britain will be great again one day. Ted Heath has a vision that Ted Heath will be great again one day.'[15] He went on to win the safe Tory seat of Hertfordshire West in 1983, becoming a junior minister at Environment in 1994.

Scots outside the St Andrews nexus also contributed significantly to the rise of free-market economics in pre-Thatcherite Britain. Sir Frank (later Lord) McFadzean, a Glasgow graduate, successful businessman and Visiting Professor of Economics at Strathclyde, where he sat on the steering board of its new business school, authored two pungent attacks on the economics of J. K. Galbraith;[16] and Jock Bruce-Gardyne, the financial journalist who sat as MP for South Angus between 1964 and 1974, also popularised free-market ideas. The works of both McFadzean and Bruce-Gardyne[17] – along with Adam Smith's *Wealth of Nations* and *Theory of Moral Sentiments* – appeared on the notorious reading list that Sir Keith Joseph circulated to his leading civil servants at the Department of Trade and Industry in an attempt to wean them off dirigisme.[18]

However, by a further irony, enthusiasm for the free market in Scotland also went beyond the Conservative Party. In 1985 the David Hume Institute (DHI) was set up in Edinburgh as an undoctrinaire quasi-academic think tank which would explore market-based solutions to problems in law and economics.[19] Among the DHI's projects were Professor Hector MacQueen's exploration of intellectual property and Professor Brian Main's work on corporate governance. The leading figure in the DHI was Sir Alan Peacock, an estranged-Liberal-turned-free-thinking-radical-anti-collectivist. Born and raised in Dundee, Peacock graduated from St Andrews in 1947 and was appointed to a lectureship there in Economics. He rapidly moved on to the London School of Economics, but in 1956 returned to Scotland as Professor of Economics at the University of Edinburgh. In the meantime, he had become involved in party politics as a Liberal, joining the Liberal Party's anti-statist Unservile State Group, set up in 1953. By the early 1960s Peacock was interrogating the rationale of welfare policy and promoting the privatisation of council housing, while his advocacy of 'the principle of consumer sovereignty' led him to suggest the introduction of education vouchers. At this point he found himself swimming counter to the statist drift among the Liberals and left the party. Although he tended to be associated thereafter with what came to be thought of as Conservative causes, such as the private University of Buckingham, set up by the Liberal academic (later Conservative peer) Max Beloff, Peacock remained a non-partisan figure, even serving for a time as an adviser to Tony Benn at the Department of Industry in the mid-1970s.[20]

Although Peacock fell out with the Liberals, his anti-statist ideals were shared with the then leader of the party, Jo Grimond, the MP for Orkney and Shetland from 1950 to 1983. Toward the end of his political career Grimond revealed a certain queasiness about involvement with the SDP, precisely because as a traditional Liberal he valued non-statist answers, when possible, to social problems. For, although Grimond supported realignment on the Left of British politics, he was anti-collectivist in principle. He was, for instance, sympathetic to vouchers in the fields of education and health as an alternative to impersonal nationalised behemoths. Grimond particularly admired the ideas of Norman Macrae of *The Economist*, who advocated a kind of internal market whereby large nationalised corporations would be broken down into smaller entities each contracting with one another. Self-reliance was a vital component of Grimond's non-statist communitarianism, and he acknowledged that 'much of what Mrs Thatcher and Sir Keith Joseph say and do' was 'in the mainstream of liberal philosophy'.[21]

Conclusion

The Scottish relationship with Thatcherite political economy, it transpires, was far from straightforward. Any chance that Scotland might have come to embrace a populist strain of free-marketeering probably evaporated at the 1979 election with the defeat of Thatcher's first choice as Scottish Secretary, the engagingly demotic MP for Glasgow Cathcart, Teddy Taylor. Thereafter the leaders of Scottish Conservatism, Younger and Malcolm Rifkind, though affable communicators, lacked both Thatcherite zeal and Taylor's common touch. As a result, a mixed message was delivered in a toff's accent. The widespread and enduring rejection of Thatcherism at the ballot box in Scotland has its ironic counterpoint in Smithian networks and webs of influence which stretch from North America to Hong Kong, and have their focus as much among Anglo-Scots in London as in Scotland itself. Not that St Andrews has any claim to being the sole or even the primary begetter of Thatcherism. The origins of Thatcherite policy can, of course, be traced to various different sources in Britain and the United States, not least the Chicago of Milton Friedman and Hayek. Scotland played a significant part nevertheless in its emergence, dissemination and implementation. Indeed, there were pockets of Scottish Conservatism – and, by a deeper irony, Liberalism too – that contained ardent champions of privatisation long before Thatcher herself became an open exponent of Thatcherism.[22]

Notes

1. See for example David Seawright and John Curtice, 'The decline of the Scottish Conservative and Unionist Party 1950–92: religion, ideology or economics?', *Contemporary Record* 9 (1995), pp. 319–42; Seawright, *An Important Matter of Principle: The Decline of the Scottish Conservative and Unionist Party* (Aldershot, 1999).
2. Duncan Forrester, 'Sermon on the Mound', *Third Way* (August 1988), p. 13.
3. Margaret Thatcher, *The Downing Street Years* (London, 1993), pp. 618–24.
4. Interview with John Marshall, 24 July 2010.
5. Nisbet Papers, St Andrews University Library, MS 38055, 38313, 38272.
6. Interview with John Marshall.
7. Kenneth Dover, *Marginal Comment* (London, 1995), p. 100.
8. Interview with Sir Alan Peacock, 30 November 2010.
9. Norman Gash, *The Radical Element in the History of the Conservative Party* (London, 1989), pp. 5–6, 12.
10. Richard Cockett, *Thinking the Unthinkable: Think-tanks and the Economic Counter-revolution, 1931–1983* (London, 1995), p. 189.
11. I should like to acknowledge my thanks to Dr Madsen Pirie for lending me copies of these materials.
12. Richard Heffernan, 'Blueprint for a revolution? The politics of the Adam Smith Institute', *Contemporary British History* 10 (1996), pp. 73–87.
13. Lorn Macintyre, 'St Andrews crucible of revolution', *Glasgow Herald*, 6 October 1989.
14. *Herald*, 16 June 2001 and 19 June 2001; private information from John Marshall.
15. *The Times*, 19 April 2007.
16. Frank S. McFadzean, *Galbraith and the Planners* (Glasgow, 1968); McFadzean, *John Kenneth Galbraith: A Study in Fantasy* (London, 1977).
17. Jock Bruce-Gardyne, *Meriden: Odyssey of a Lame Duck* (London, 1978).
18. Nick Bosanquet, 'Sir Keith's reading list', *Political Quarterly* 52 (1981), pp. 324–41.
19. Interview with Hector MacQueen, 16 July 2010; Nick

Kuenssberg and Gillian Lomas (eds), *The David Hume Institute: The First Decade* (Edinburgh, 1996).

20. Alan Peacock, *Anxious To Do Good* (Exeter, 2010), pp. 94–6, 140, 164, 167, 176–9.
21. Jo Grimond, *The Liberal Future* (London, 1959), pp. 19–20; Grimond, *Memoirs* (London, 1979), pp. 262–3; Grimond, *The Future of Liberalism* (London, 1980), pp. 11–12; Grimond, *A Personal Manifesto* (Oxford, 1983), pp. 24, 90–1, 95, 117–19; Grimond, 'Who wants economists?', *Journal of Economic Affairs* 3 (1983), pp. 205–8.
22. I should like to thank Hector MacQueen, John Robertson, Chris Smout, Archie and Kathleen Rennie, Madsen Pirie, Hamish Scott, Michael Fry, John Marshall and Sir Alan Peacock for help with this topic.

CHAPTER 6

'It's only a Northern Song': The Constant Smirr of Anti-Thatcherism and Anti-Toryism

Gerry Hassan

Introduction

Once upon a time the Scottish Tories were proud, popular and at the same time perceived as Scottish, while confidently proclaiming their national credentials. This story is well known and well worn. Not only did the Tories win a majority of the popular vote and Parliamentary seats in 1955, but during the period from the late 1920s to the late 1950s, Unionist, Tory Scotland was the predominant counter-narrative to socialist, collectivist Scotland; 'Blue Scotland' in opposition to 'Red Scotland'. This chapter aims to explore:

- What happened to this Unionist, Tory Scotland? Why did it become perceived as a force at odds with majority Scottish sentiment, as 'alien' and 'unScottish'?
- What happened post-1979 and what vision of Scotland came to the fore in the forces of anti-Thatcherism?
- What was the role of a number of pivotal national and cultural figures and their influence on the creation of myths and folklore about Scottish Tories and society?
- Finally, what are the contemporary consequences of this prevailing sense of Scottish politics as being anti-Tory?

Anti-Toryism is of course not just a Scottish phenomenon, but something found across the UK. Anti-Thatcherism similarly was articulated across Britain, particularly in the alternative music scene of the 1980s. Two spokespeople for the 'anti-Thatcher generation', Morrissey and Elvis Costello, wrote songs in that decade looking forward to the day of her death, 'Margaret on the Guillotine' and 'Tramp the Dirt Down' respectively. And even recently, Labour leader Ed Miliband got into trouble for standing next to someone wearing a T-shirt stating 'Dance on Thatcher's Grave'.[1]

But in Scotland anti-Toryism and anti-Thatcherism are still the current defining political narratives, with a backstory about the 1980s, what Scotland is, why we are different and what our politics and values are today. An equivalent comparison to Morrissey and Costello would be that the protest songs of the 1980s, of the Proclaimers and others, have not been forgotten, but have become marching cries and part of today's popular culture. This chapter aims to look at why this happened, its consequences and what it means for us today.

The strange story of Scottishness and Toryism

Scottishness and Toryism are not, as some now assume, unnatural bedfellows. In the late 1940s Churchill and other Tories stood up against Labour centralisation and the insensitivities of London rule, thus marking out their Scottish credentials.[2] The slow unravelling of the assumption that it was natural to be Scottish and Tory can be traced back to the period of the late 1950s and Harold Macmillan's 'you've never had it so good'. In the 1959 general election, as the Tories won their third UK election in a row, Scotland began its long embrace of Labour – which was to see it have an unchallenged hold over Scottish politics for most of the next fifty years.[3]

A further rupture occurred with the arrival of Ted Heath's Tory government in 1970 which was elected on a right-wing 'Selsdon Man' agenda to challenge the post-war consensus.[4] This jarred with powerful vocal elements of Scottish society which saw this as an assault on some of the most important characteristics it cherished such as municipal statism, trade union partnership and quasi-corporatism.[5] This was then amplified and wrapped round the political environment of the time which had seen Labour returned with a significant lead over the Tories north of the border (forty-four to twenty-two seats), while Heath won an overall majority of thirty on English (and Northern Irish) seats.

The first mainstream utterances of concern about what would later be called the Scottish 'democratic deficit' begin to be heard in this period in the gatherings of the Scottish Trades Union Congress's (STUC) 'People's Assemblies' in 1972–3[7] which were set up at the time of Upper Clyde Shipbuilders to primarily address economic concerns and then linked to the democratic and constitutional with Jimmy Jack, General Secretary of the STUC, strongly advocating a 'workers' parliament'.[8] This agenda was one that was influenced by a Left outside the Labour Party and SNP, involving the still powerful Communist Party, but at the time it did not have a potent enough reach to define Scottish Left politics, let alone those of further afield; it was, however, the slow lighting of a spark that would ignite around the anti-Thatcher coalition.[9]

'Tories no more': the making of the anti-Tory nation

When the Thatcher government was elected in 1979 it had a narrower electoral base in Scotland than that of Heath both in terms of seats (forty-four Labour to twenty-two Tory) and votes (31 per cent). It also had a more abrasive, ambitious right-wing agenda and faced across the UK a weaker Labour Opposition in an economic, political and ideological climate conducive to its ideas.[10] Scottish majority opinion did not like the Thatcher government and saw it as uncaring, harsh and uncompassionate, but crucially and more emphatically as the 1980s wound on, it began to see Toryism and the Thatcher government as distinctly 'anti-Scottish'.[11] Scotland during the 1980s fused the following perspectives:

- The Tories had 'no mandate' to govern Scotland, leading to 'the Doomsday Scenario' of Scots voting one way (Labour) and getting another result, i.e. a Tory government;
- The construction of an anti-Tory set of ethos and 'anti-Tory Scotland';
- The prominence of the belief that Scotland was distinctly Centre-Left and different from the rest of the UK;
- The Tories increasingly became seen as something 'external' and 'unScottish' that should be repulsed from the Scottish body politic like a virus;

- This led to Scots increasingly denying something in themselves and their very DNA; Scots were intrinsically egalitarian and compassionate and not greedy or individualistic;
- An essentialist, unified political community emerged with clear boundaries of who was inside and outside; it was characterised by a number of clarion calls such as the 'we are the people' of Canon Kenyon Wright.

The 'mythmakers' of the anti-Thatcher consensus

This chapter looks at a number of prominent mythmakers in the 1980s, from contemporary writers and published sources of the era, before assessing whether the passing of time has allowed a more rounded, nuanced perspective. A whole host of prejudices and opinions rolled up into the instinctual, gut Scots reaction to Thatcher the person, her government and her philosophy. There was her right-wing policies, her Englishness, the fact she was a woman challenging the norms of a then very male, masculinised society, and then there was the voice. Historian A. D. R. Dickson commented:

> The public persona of Mrs Thatcher appears to many Scots to capture all the worst elements of their caricature of the detested English – uncaring, arrogant, always convinced of their own rightness ('there is no alternative'), possessed of an accent that grates on Scottish ears.[12]

Neal Ascherson, looking back, observed 'aspects of Englishness got on people's nerves in that decade . . . people hated that voice'.[13]

The anti-Thatcher consensus view of Thatcher and Scotland has been aptly summarised by Denis Canavan, former MP and MSP: 'Scotland was simply part of the United Kingdom and she proceeded to foist upon the people of Scotland policies which were perceived by many Scots as the diktats of an alien government.'[14] Canavan reflected that in Thatcher's first years, 'George Younger, the Secretary of State for Scotland, was like a Governor-General with no electoral mandate from the people he governed'.[15] These comments articulate the views of much of the anti-Thatcher rhetoric of the period. First, Scotland faced a government that had 'no mandate' because a majority of Scots had not voted for it. This missed the fact that all of Scotland's political parties were minorities in the 1980s, and aggregated the non-Tory vote into an 'anti-Tory majority' of 76 per cent by 1987. Second, there was the language of 'foisting', bringing to the forefront the lack of democratic process which came to a head with the poll tax. Third is the language of calling the UK government 'alien' and seeing it as 'unScottish'. All of this contributed to what many Scots perceived as a decline in the legitimacy not just of the Thatcher government but also of the British state. In 1989 10 per cent of Scots agreed that Thatcher had 'the best interests of Scotland at heart', while 77 per cent thought she treated 'the Scots as second class citizens'.[16]

William McIlvanney was one of the most prominent cultural voices in the 1980s and 1990s to articulately oppose Tory rule, call for the anti-Tory forces to cooperate and paint an inclusive picture of Scotland and its identity as a 'mongrel nation'. In his 'Stands Scotland Where It Did?' lecture, an influential, defining speech which he delivered to the SNP conference in September 1987 he stated: 'We live under a government which has wiped out whole areas of Scotland and then cynically carved on the headstones: "Regeneration". Aye. Maybe in the next world.'[17]

This was not just a government that people like McIlvanney opposed, but something unprecedented:

> we have never, in my lifetime, until now had a government whose basic principles were so utterly against the most essential traditions and aspirations of Scottish life. We have never until now had a government so determined to unpick the very fabric of Scottish life and make it over into something quite different ... Under this government, it is not the quality of our individual lives that is threatened. It is our communal sense of our own identity.'[18]

McIlvanney's argument was about philosophy and politics. And it was personal:

> For Margaret Thatcher is not just a perpetrator of bad policies. She is a cultural vandal. She takes the axe of her own simplicity to the complexities of Scottish life. She has no understanding of the hard-earned traditions she is destroying. And if we allow her to continue, she will remove from the word 'Scottish' any meaning other than geographical.[19]

The speech was made in the shadow of Thatcher's third election victory of 1987 and at a point when a significant part of Scotland felt it and its values were threatened, and under attack from her and her government. In this political environment, many Scots agreed with McIlvanney's thesis that Scotland's existence as a nation, political community and its difference were in peril and could be lost. He wrote: 'At such a time we should at least consider what it is we are in danger of losing.'[20]

Owen Dudley Edwards, in the conclusion to the collection of essays inspired by 'A Claim of Right for Scotland', also wrote: 'Thatcherism has done everything it can to bribe, bully and blackmail Scotland into bowing down before its gods of materialism and British chauvinism, self-enrichment and self-regard, community destruction and beggar-your-neighbour.'[21] Dudley Edwards believed that 'Thatcherism is in an extreme stage of alcoholism', and then, discussing comparisons between Scotland and Ireland, took the view that the 'SNP abhors violence; Thatcherism worships it'.[22]

Such views could be found all across the political spectrum of non-Tory Scotland. Brian Wilson, arch-anti-devolutionist in the 1970s, upon his election as Labour MP for Cunninghame North in 1987, reflected after speaking to a group of constituents in a pub in Ardrossan:

'You've got to do something for us,' I was told repeatedly. It was a plea from friends which only a fool would disregard or misinterpret. By 'you' they meant the Labour in which they have just invested such a massive vote of confidence. By 'us' they meant Scotland which had declared a near-total rejection of the Thatcherite evil.[23]

These accounts can be given some leeway for being understandable, if over-the-top, reactions at the time, but they became the dominant narrative. McIlvanney has not gone back and qualified what he said all those years ago, or offered any kind of more nuanced reasoning. Scots seem to want to refuse to put the Thatcher government in proper perspective and engage in any kind of historical revisionism as is occurring across the UK.[24]

How Thatcherism is viewed twenty years after her exit from Downing Street shows that the above has remained the unchallenged received wisdom. Neal Ascherson wrote in *Stone Voices* that 'Mrs Thatcher demolished Scotland's steel, engineering and mining industries'.[25] Neil Oliver in his book of the BBC series *A History of Scotland* commented: 'Moribund dinosaurs like shipbuilding, coalmining and steel, living on state finance, starved to death in no time.'[26] Thatcher's 'Sermon on the Mound' speech to the Church of Scotland in 1988 is dismissed by Ascherson as 'notorious' and characterised by 'impudence';[27] while Oliver states it had 'a breathtaking display of arrogance and deluded self-belief'.[28]

Another cultural overview of Scotland's journey to the present summarises Thatcher and her 'ism' in the following: 'Hers was a gospel of greed, and she never disguised it', talked of her 'notoriety' and nickname as 'Snobby Roberts', before remarking, 'Her patriotism was a noisy creed demanding defence of all the loot accumulated by "us" to date'.[29] There is then a passing swipe at her 'pride' in her Oxford degree, which puts this in context: this is liberal snobbery and anger of the kind we saw in Hampstead England, and just as unattractive; a Scots form of 'the personal is political'.

Even Carol Craig in *The Scots' Crisis of Confidence*, which attempts to set out a counter-analysis to some of the prevailing orthodoxies, does not avoid this. When it comes to Thatcherism and the poll tax, Craig draws from the well of Scots myths: 'Many Scots were outraged that a government with no electoral mandate in Scotland was muscling through a policy which ran against the grain of Scottish values.' She went on: 'Here was a government which did not believe in society, putting a tax on democracy itself and taking little account of householders' ability to pay.'[30]

The BBC Scotland programme *Thatcher and the Scots* offered an interesting take on the subject, with presenter Allan Little observing: 'When you think of the Thatcher years, you think of the dole queues, the mass unemployment, the industrial dereliction, and the despair of it.' 'She remains unforgiven here,' he commented, observing that 'we have built her into our national mythology'. Neal Ascherson, while recognising the lack of differences between the Scots and English in numerous value surveys, stated, 'Scotland has a much greater belief in the importance of equality'.[31]

'We are the People' politics and the limits of Scots communitarianism

Anti-Thatcherism in Scotland was then and now influenced by this. Canon Kenyon Wright at the inaugural meeting of the Scottish Constitutional Convention stated: 'What happens if that other voice we all know so well responds by saying, "We say No and we are the State?" Well, we say Yes and We are the People', and in the last analysis, 'Scotland believes not in the "Royal We" but in "We the People".'[32] Kenyon Wright reflected later on one of the most famous soundbites of the period: 'It was effective because it succeeded in encapsulating the central challenge that the Convention was making to the authority of the British state.'[33]

Writers such as Neal Ascherson and Patrick Wright conceded to Thatcher the idea of 'the nation', and claimed that Labour and the Left could not counter it with an alternative version of that nation; Ascherson stated: 'this is a game which the Tories will always win'.[34] What of his alternative credo? 'Not in the name of the nation, but not in the name of one class either. How about in the name of the people? It is not a nation or a class which demands Liberty, Equality, Fraternity, but the living.'[35]

Patrick Wright in his thoughtful mediation, 'On Living in an Old Country', wrote:

> 'the nation' to which Thatcher has learned to appeal is full of adventure, grandeur, ideas of freedom, ceremony and conscripted memories (of childhood or war for example) . . . There are indeed 'two nations' in the symbolism of Thatcher's Britain . . . Empire and War on the one hand and the bureaucratic imagery of the welfare state on the other.[36]

This is a significant element of the Left's failure across Britain: its retreat from any British idea of 'the nation' and its populist counterposing with 'the people'. This was ahistoric, unworldly politics, ignoring the long rich progressive tradition on these isles, one of which was 'the Labour nation' of the forward march of a people via the state and collective action towards egalitarianism, planning and rational order.[37]

This political rejection of 'the British nation' in the 1980s became even more obvious north of the border, although interestingly writers such as Ascherson who were so dismissive south of the border of 'the nation' seemed more than happy in Scotland to contribute towards the making of the myths of a northern nation, standing splendidly in opposition to Thatcherism and the absolutism of the Westminster state. As David McCrone wrote at the height of Thatcherism: 'Essential to current Conservative appeal south of the border was an appeal to "the nation" . . . But Scots had a nation of their own'[38]

The Scottish rejection of Thatcherism led to the clear demarcation of a Scottish moral community and sense of distinctiveness.

McIlvanney in the lecture quoted above wrote, 'I know nowhere less defined by materialism than Scotland'. And he went on to reflect on speaking to a French friend in Paris:

> 'I like to meet you, Willie', he said. Then he shook his head. 'But you are so Scottish. Always the moral issue. The demand for justice. The world is not like that.' Many Scots have always felt that it should be.[39]

McIlvanney then emphatically stated, 'There is a deeply ingrained tradition in Scotland that we will not judge one another by material standards' and the need to question the orthodoxies of 'measurement' and 'performance', and instead celebrated the belief in 'the deep humanity of the Scottish people'.[40] This latter sentiment is

> not a hard system to apply. Its principles are simple enough. You want a measurement of people? Then, if you wish to remain Scottish, here it is. You will measure them by the extent of their understanding, by the width of their compassion, by the depth of their concern and by the size of their humanity.[41]

This is, lyrically and poetically put, the Scottish tradition of communitarianism, a set of values with a longer pedigree than socialism or social democracy, which have defined the Scottish narrative of difference for several centuries.

McIlvanney's power as a writer and populiser does justice to what is a scant, threadbare programmatic vision contemporaneously built on a few homespun homilies and supposedly self-evident truths. These were to become the kernel of anti-Thatcher Scotland, the property of 'Labour Scotland' and the terrain over which Labour and SNP were to fight for political dominance in devolved Scotland.[42] The Scots communitarian tradition, some have argued, comes from different political traditions compared to similar ideas in England with consequences for contemporary politics,[43] yet it has not delivered any detailed policy prospectus beyond opposition to Thatcherism and New Labour.[44]

'What Margaret Thatcher did to Scotland' and its legacy

Scotland increasingly told itself a set of comforting narratives throughout the 1980s, through the stories, songs and theatre of the time, of a desire to construct and imagine a sense of a romanticised, sentimentalised, collectivist golden age, where men were men, women were women and everyone looked out for each other. In this view, the reason for what is wrong with contemporary Scotland – its inequality, exclusion, dislocation, lack of aspiration and hope – is all due to one factor: the malign influence and shadow of the Thatcher-era Tories.

This perspective led to a distortion of the landscape of debate, and to some notable exclusions in political debate. A study of the cross-party Home Rule magazine, *Radical Scotland*, from 1983 to 1991 finds a host of articles on how to achieve a Scottish Parliament and why Scotland is different, but there was scant coverage of why Scotland's health record was worse than that of the rest of the UK, or the limitations of its state education sector; it was simply assumed that Scotland's public services were an embodiment of our collectivist values.[45]

Scotland, a familiar argument goes, learned in the 1980s what it was *against*, but not what it was *for*. This is too simple an argument; what did happen was the delegitimisation of the Conservatives which allowed Scottish politics to feel good about itself, and to wrap itself in a warm, comforting, suffocating blanket. Scottish politics became defined by a set of popular narratives shaped around the politics of class and nation, of calling ourselves Centre-Left and anti-Tory, while our rhetoric disguised the fact that – as in most places – there had been a decline of that Centre Left.[46] A complex account of the fundamental change that the Scottish economy and society faced post-1979 became reducible to, in many accounts, the politics of Thatcherism;[47] a powerful sense of loss filled the Scottish atmosphere in the 1980s, and a denial by some of the basic facts that many of the old industries and ways had been crumbling for decades.[48] The world came to be shaped by what Michael Gove, the Scots-born Tory MP and Cabinet minister, described as the belief that 'you could only be a good Scot if you were pro-Parliament and anti-Thatcher: the three became one'.[49]

All of this was reinforced by a set of elite narratives by writers, commentators, politicians and institutional actors who adopted the mantra of Scotland as an anti-Tory nation.[50] This became the fig leaf of the Scottish political establishment, aiding it to define its difference, distinction and *raison d'être*; thus over this period Scottish politics and culture became more imbued by a gradual 'tartanisation' and Scots civic Nationalism which explicitly emphasised its inclusiveness (although not its exclusionary anti-Toryism).

This has had huge consequences, many unforeseen all those years ago. Scottish politics have become dominated by a narrow spectrum of political debate around a social democratic politics centred on Labour versus the SNP which has not been vibrant, pluralist or challenging. Instead, it has celebrated and evoked a self-congratulation that has consciously avoided asking tough questions or developing a politics of renewal, debate and practice around the supposed values of its main actors. This has allowed Scottish politics to settle for an atrophied social democracy led by elites, shaped by elites and for elites. The lexicon and veneer of anti-Tory rhetoric has allowed all of this to be given a popular, radical cover, disguising the inadequate state of our body politic.

The prospect for radical Scotland: after anti-Toryism

The sad state of Scottish Toryism is not one for which many people outside the dwindling rank of Conservative Party membership will weep; the dominant Scots response will be indifference and a cold contempt, thinking 'it serves them right', from politically active Centre-Left Scotland. Yet, this state of affairs has wider repercussions. This is not to make the case for the Tories; instead it is a call for having boundaries on the pursuit of delegitimising, dehumanising and caricaturing the Scottish Tories, which has removed them from the mainstream and weakened the breadth and health of our politics.

In this, the world of the 1980s has become the defining set of events for a generation that has grown up; they remember a simplified version of that decade: the miners' strike, the poll tax, 'the Doomsday Scenario', the 'Sermon on the Mound' and Ravenscraig. This set of mobilising myths has become as important to contemporary Scotland as the folklore of a selective memory of the 1930s based on mass unemployment, Jarrow marches and Tory appeasement of Hitler to an earlier generation, omitting the collusion of the entire political classes – including Labour – in all of the above. What happens when the 1980s pass, as they have to, into the mists of history, when children stop being raised on their parents' knees with tales of the poll tax, warrant sales and the Scots being treated as 'guinea pigs'? Unless we are very careful, all we will be left with will be detesting Tories for reasons that no one will be able to remember. The false collective memory syndrome of Thatcherism allowed part of Scotland to place the blame for our problems on one factor, to paint a black-and-white past (and, thus, present and future) and luxuriate in the power of victimhood. What it did not address was that part of Thatcherism's revolution, which oversaw the disappearance of a certain kind of Scotland: of 'big men', their industries and that way of life which dominated towns, communities and families (for good or ill). Scotland became more feminised in work, culture and politics, maybe not enough for some, but the changes were far-reaching and uncomfortable for many.[51] The transition from McIlvanney's 'the big man' to the 'walking wounded' of post-industrial central belt Scotland spawned a whole cultural genre called miserablism centred on loss and displacement.

Critically, and this has become more important, first with the establishment of the Scottish Parliament, and then with the global crash and crisis from 2008 onwards, anti-Toryism and the threadbare nature of social democracy have disguised the way the right political rhetoric has been used to disguise the influence and debt all Scotland's parties and politicians have to Thatcherism. It is not just Tony Blair and Gordon Brown who have knelt at the court of Margaret Thatcher; Alex Salmond famously got into trouble for saying of Thatcherism:

> The SNP has a strong, beating social conscience, which is very Scottish in itself. One of the reasons Scotland didn't take to Lady Thatcher was because of that. It didn't mind the economic side so much. But we didn't like the social side at all.[52]

Beyond individual politicians, all of Scotland's mainstream parties have been influenced and reshaped by Thatcher and Thatcherism; the pervasive nature of anti-Thatcherism has been used to feed crumbs to people and prevent a serious debate about the condition of Scotland's radical imagination. In this New Labour proved just as useful as a foil and a secondary set of pantomime villains that all Scottish politics could define itself against, including Scottish Labour. No need to have a serious debate on the scale of New Labour's successes on child and pensioner poverty in the good times and what this told us about reducing poverty, when you could just bandy about the term 'neo-liberalism' as an insult.[53] Gordon Brown in his complex journey from supposed firebrand to 'the Iron Chancellor' was just 'a second-wave neo-liberal'; no other analysis was needed.

Scottish Labour rode this tiger in the 1980s, then when the Scottish Parliament came about, the political anti-Tory tide shifted and then the baton passed to the SNP. And yet at the same time there was a myopia, a kind of Alice in Wonderland world which saw both parties shaped by the legacy of Thatcherism, the Scotland her philosophy had created, their adherence to the consensus of the post-Thatcher agenda while trying to pretend otherwise. This is not a very healthy state of affairs. Anti-Toryism will in due course be challenged by new faultlines and fissures, and new myths and stories will arise which will create new defining points and folklores. Anti-Tory Scotland served Scotland well at points in the 1980s. However, in many respects it aided a mass deception exercise which has continued to the present day. We choose to tell ourselves, buy into and believe a set of narratives that made us feel good, special and unique: we were different, distinct and under attack and needed to cherish our values and traditions. We have lived with the consequences and damage for too long now. The not very strange story of the death of Tory Scotland and the creation of anti-Tory Scotland has to become just one among many stories in contemporary Scotland.

Ian Hamilton, someone with a special place in recent Scottish history, has written that what matters is, 'The people who make the songs of a country have a habit of making the laws also'. This changed over the last half of the twentieth century from people singing songs that were 'foreign and what they sang was only an alien copy of other peoples' ways of life' to a situation where 'Now everyone sings Scottish songs'.[54] This is romantic mythmaking, but the songs and stories we tell are important and defining, as long as we pay careful attention to what stories emerge and which are marginalised and silenced, and whose voices and accounts we are listening to.

Anti-Tory Scotland and the stories of the 1980s need to become just one part of our history. They have been mythologised and bowdlerised to the extent that we have done serious damage to the language of politics, the body politic and Scottish democratic debate. There has to be at some point a moving on, but for that to happen there needs to be some acknowledgement of the over-reach of the 1980s, of the damage done by McIlvanney's Scotland with its romantic myths and creation of a kind of modern-day Scottish utopia of anti-materialism and universal compassion, one that denies the messy complexities of having to face the difficult choices of living in the 'real' Scotland. This is not a luxury diversion: it is a prerequisite in our journey of growing up and maturing; that we stop telling ourselves the tale of the Tory bogeyman and the white knights coming to rescue us. That's if we want to be serious about developing a distinct, radical, relevant Scottish politics which lives up to the hopes and dreams of self-government. Isn't it time to scotch one of the most enduring 'Scotch myths' that has grown up in modern Scotland, after kailyardism, tartanism and Clydesidism: the myth of anti-Tory Scotland?

Notes

1. *Daily Mail*, 8 May 2011.
2. James Mitchell, *Conservatives and the Union: A Study of Conservative Party Attitudes to Scotland* (Edinburgh, 1990); David Seawright, *An Important Matter of Principle: The Decline of the Scottish Conservative and Unionist Party* (Aldershot, 1999).
3. Gerry Hassan and Eric Shaw, *The Strange Death of Labour Scotland* (Edinburgh, 2012).
4. The phrase 'democratic deficit' was first used by the Young European Federalists in their 1977 manifesto and subsequently used by David Marquand in his 1979 'Parliament for Europe', referring to the then European Economic Community (EEC).
5. Dominic Sandbrook, *State of Emergency. The Way We Were: Britain, 1970–74* (London, 2010).
6. Jim Phillips, *The Industrial Politics of Devolution: Scotland in the 1960s and 1970s* (Manchester, 2010).
7. The first STUC People's Assembly held on 14 February 1972 was a huge and impressive gathering of Scottish society and much larger and representative than the later Scottish Constitutional Convention. The Assembly brought together more than 1,500 participants comprising representatives from all the main political parties including the then Conservative government and the SNP, along with business, unions, local authorities, churches and many other sectors.
8. *Tribune*, 18 February 1972.
9. James Mitchell, *Strategies for Self-Government: The Campaigns for a Scottish Parliament* (Edinburgh, 1996); Keith Aitken, *The Bairns O'Adam: The Story of the STUC* (Edinburgh, 1997).
10. Hugo Young, *One of Us: The Life of Margaret Thatcher*

(London, 1989); John Campbell, *Margaret Thatcher: Volume Two, The Iron Lady* (London, 2003).

11. On an early questioning of the mandate of the Tories and the use of Nationalist language outside the SNP, see George Galloway, 'Devolution challenge', *New Socialist* 3 (January–February 1982).

12. A. D. R. Dickson, 'The peculiarities of the Scottish: national culture and political action', *Political Quarterly* 59:3 (July–September 1988), p. 3.

13. *Thatcher and the Scots*, BBC Scotland, 1 January 2009.

14. Dennis Canavan, *Let the People Decide: The Autobiography of Dennis Canavan* (Edinburgh, 2009), p. 203.

15. Ibid. p. 203.

16. James Mitchell and Lynn G. Bennie, 'Thatcherism and the Scottish Question', in C. Rallings, D. M. Farrell, D. Denver and D. Broughton (eds), *British Elections and Parties Yearbook* (London, 1995), pp. 96–7.

17. William McIlvanney, *Surviving the Shipwreck* (Edinburgh, 1992), p. 241.

18. Ibid. pp. 245–6.

19. Ibid. p. 246.

20. Ibid. p. 246.

21. Owen Dudley Edwards, 'Birth without beauty or terror', in Owen Dudley Edwards, (ed.), *A Claim of Right for Scotland* (Edinburgh, 1989), p. 187.

22. Ibid. pp. 188, 191.

23. *Glasgow Herald*, 15 June 1987.

24. John Campbell, 'The DNA of a generation', *Prospect* 190 (January 2012).

25. Neal Ascherson, *Stone Voices: The Search for Scotland* (London, 2002), p. 107.

26. Neil Oliver, *A History of Scotland* (London, 2009), p. 364.

27. Ascherson, *Stone Voices: The Search for Scotland*, p. 238.

28. Oliver, *A History of Scotland*, p. 365.

29. Mitch Miller, Johnny Rodger and Owen Dudley Edwards, *Tartan Pimps: Gordon Brown, Margaret Thatcher and the New Scotland* (Colonsay, 2010), p. 109.

30. Carol Craig, *The Scots' Crisis of Confidence* (Glasgow, 2003), pp. 106–7.

31. *Thatcher and the Scots*.

32. *Glasgow Herald*, 31 March 1989.

33. Canon Kenyon Wright, *The People Say Yes: The Making of Scotland's Parliament* (Colonsay, 1997), p. 52.
34. Neal Ascherson, *Games with Shadows* (London, 1988), p. 156.
35. Ibid. pp. 156–7.
36. Patrick Wright, *On Living in an Old Country: The National Past in Contemporary Britain* (London, 1985), pp. 187–8.
37. Arthur Aughey, *Nationalism, Devolution and the Challenge to the United Kingdom State* (London, 2001), Chapter 5.
38. David McCrone, 'Thatcherism in a cold climate', *Radical Scotland* 39 (June/July 1989).
39. McIlvanney, *Surviving the Shipwreck*, p. 247.
40. Ibid. p. 248.
41. Ibid. pp. 248–9.
42. Hassan and Shaw, *The Strange Death of Labour Scotland*, Chapter 1.
43. Lindsay Paterson, 'Scottish Social Democracy and Blairism: difference, diversity and pluralism', in Gerry Hassan and Chris Warhurst (eds), *Tomorrow's Scotland* (London, 2002).
44. Michael Rosie and Ross Bond, 'Social Democratic Scotland?', in Michael Keating, (ed.), *Scottish Social Democracy: Progressive Ideas for Public Policy* (Oxford, 2007).
45. *Radical Scotland* was first edited by Kevin Dunion and then Alan Lawson and existed from 1983 to 1991, running for a total of fifty-one issues. It was cross-party and non-party, pro-Home Rule while being open-minded and ecumenical in tone, and drew from a wide range of sources challenging mainstream political orthodoxies.
46. Gerry Hassan, 'The last revolutionary? After the left and the coming gathering storm', in Gregor Gall, *Tommy Sheridan: From Hero to Zero? A Political Biography* (Cardiff, 2012).
47. Ewen A. Cameron, *Impaled Upon a Thistle: Scotland since 1880* (Edinburgh, 2010), Chapter 13; David Stewart, *The Path to Devolution: A Political History of Scotland under Margaret Thatcher* (London, 2009), Chapter 6.
48. Carol Craig and Tom Devine, 'Scotland's Velvet Revolution', in Gerry Hassan, Eddie Gibb and Lydia Howland (eds), *Scotland 2020: Hopeful Stories for a Northern Nation* (Edinburgh, 2005).
49. David Torrance, *'We in Scotland': Thatcherism in a Cold Climate* (Edinburgh, 2009), p. 264.
50. Murray Stewart Leith and Daniel P. J. Soule, *Political Discourse*

and National Identity in Scotland (Edinburgh, 2011), Chapter 7.

51. Catriona M. M. Macdonald, *Whaur Extremes Meet: Scotland's Twentieth Century* (Edinburgh, 2009), Chapter 6; Hilary Young, 'Being a man: everyday masculinities', in Lynn Abrams and Callum G. Brown (eds), *A History of Everyday Life in Twentieth Century Scotland* (Edinburgh, 2010).

52. http://www.opendemocracy.net/article/ourkingdom-theme/thatcher-s-shadow-over-salmond; David Torrance, *Salmond: Against the Odds* (Edinburgh, 2010), p. 256.

53. See as an example of this Neil Davidson, Patricia McCafferty and David Miller (eds), *Neoliberal Scotland: Class and Society in a Stateless Nation* (Cambridge, 2010).

54. Ian Hamilton, *The Taking of the Stone of Destiny* (Colonsay, 1991), p. 203.

CHAPTER 7

The Wilderness Years

David Torrance

Introduction

This chapter will explore the Scottish Conservative Party's 'wilderness years' from electoral wipeout in 1997 to further steady decline at the May 2011 Holyrood election. How did the party respond to electoral decline in terms of organisation and campaigning? What happened to the party's membership during this period? And, more broadly, this chapter will examine the party's approach to its new role within the Scottish Parliament, and its strategy for revival beyond Holyrood. How did the party adapt its political narrative and communicate its ideas to the electorate? Common themes are the party's identity, its relationship with London, its personalities and, perhaps most importantly, its approach to devolution.

Wipeout: 1997–9

It was a moment of light relief following a troubled general election campaign. Arriving late for a post-election press conference on 2 May 1997, Michael Forsyth, the former Conservative MP and defeated Secretary of State for Scotland, joked to the assembled media: 'So sorry for being late. The traffic was awful. Frankly, I blame the government.'[1]

Forsyth's wry humour could not disguise the extent of his party's defeat. All eleven Scottish Conservative MPs had lost their seats, including several Cabinet ministers, and its share of the vote had fallen to just 17.5 per cent. (The fact that the swing against the party in Scotland had been smaller than that in England provided scant comfort.) As Scottish Secretary, Forsyth had set the party north of the border on a more independent footing by publishing a separate Scottish manifesto and adopting a lion rampant as the party's emblem, but it all amounted to too little, too late.

Radical responses were immediately aired, such as breaking the link with London, finding a new name and even urging a 'yes, yes' vote in the devolution referendum due that September. The Scottish Tory Reform Group, chaired by Arthur Bell, had already called for an autonomous Scottish party, under a new name, to drop its opposition to a Scottish Parliament. 'We have been perceived, wrongly in many cases, as an English party with a branch office in Scotland,' explained Bell. 'I think that has got to go. There are fundamental changes coming in Scotland which will not allow us to survive at all if that perception is maintained.'[2]

Senior party figures, however, rejected the idea. 'We can have a substantial degree of autonomy,' commented Scottish Conservative and Unionist Association (SCUA) president David McLetchie, 'but the idea of an independent breakaway party is a complete nonsense.'[3] Also agitating for a more thoughtful response was the journalist and one-time candidate Michael Fry. In the late 1980s he had proposed – in a pamphlet called *Unlocking the Future* – a full tax-raising Scottish Parliament within a federal UK, but there had been little appetite for such schemes in the Thatcher era, never mind now.

The Scottish Conservative Party conference in Perth the following month amounted to a post-mortem on the election result. New UK party leader William Hague (elected only by MPs and therefore with no direct Scottish Tory support)[4] attacked what he called a 'flawed referendum', but conceded that, if created, a Scottish Parliament would exist 'for quite a long time to come'.[5] When delegates debated a motion condemning devolution, only two speakers challenged the party line. Ian Buchanan, a former Edinburgh councillor, said it was clear Scots wanted a parliament and those who opposed it were 'deluding themselves'. But Paul Burns, a former office bearer, spoke for the majority when he declared: 'If we were right in May we remain right now.'[6] When it came to a vote, only twelve delegates were opposed.

With David McLetchie and party chairman Annabel Goldie having roundly condemned talk of a separate party, delegates instead backed a special review commission to be chaired by Lord Strathclyde, then the Opposition Chief Whip in the House of Lords. Its remit was organisational rather than political, but nevertheless some activists were cynical. 'When you're going down the tubes, what do you do?' asked former Scottish Tory MP Anna McCurley rhetorically. 'You form a committee.'[7] Hague, meanwhile, urged party discipline and unity, promising that Scotland could once again be 'fertile ground' for Conservatives. 'It has been in the past and will be again,' he said. 'In 1983 we won twenty-one seats in Scotland. Forty years ago we held over half the seats in Scotland. We can win again.'[8]

Hague had already appointed Liam Fox (a Scot representing an English constituency) his Scottish Affairs spokesman,[9] and after the conference chose former Scottish Office minister Raymond Robertson as chairman of the Scottish Conservative Party (an appointment in his gift as UK leader). Meanwhile, a coherent 'no, no' referendum campaign gradually took shape which was supported by the vast majority of members. Under the banner 'Think Twice', the party ignored calls to do a volte-face on devolution and instead maintained its anti-devolution stance. Its director was Brian Monteith, soon to be an MSP and, ironically, a convert to full fiscal autonomy for Scotland. On 11 September 1997 the Scottish Conservative Party suffered another heavy defeat when Scottish voters overwhelmingly endorsed a Scottish Parliament (74.3 per cent) with tax-varying powers (63.5 per cent) on a 60.4 per cent turnout.

Again, there were pleas from certain quarters to do something radical in response. Edinburgh councillor Brian Meek said the party could not 'wait for the political tide to turn; we have to shape our own destiny'. That meant following Labour's lead in 'ditching the ideological baggage, establishing a modern political structure, and not being afraid to pinch a policy or two'.[10] And Michael Fry again urged fiscal autonomy, arguing that the 'obvious field for radicalism is the fiscal one, of taxing and spending, where Labour's scheme is weakest, where the danger of a shambles is greatest'.[11] A year later, Fry co-authored a Tuesday Club pamphlet entitled *Full Fiscal Freedom for the Scottish Parliament* with Peter Smaill and – not yet an MSP – Murdo Fraser. This was the first mention post-1997 of a concept that would increasingly dominate the political discourse of a devolved Scotland, and significantly it started life as a Conservative idea.

The Strathclyde Commission, however, avoided recommending anything so bold and instead urged – as expected – a merger of the party's voluntary and professional wings and the creation of a Scottish executive as its new governing body.[12] Scottish Tory members were consulted ahead of a special party conference in Dundee on 7 March 1998, at which Sir Malcolm Rifkind – the party's new president – promised a root-and-branch review of Scottish Conservative policies, adding that it should 'dare to differ' from those in England and Wales.[13] A month later, Rifkind was urging Unionism to develop new language.[14]

The Dundee conference marked the last stage in the party's post-election shake-up, and attention then shifted to selecting candidates for the first elections to the Scottish Parliament in May 1999 (the June 1998 Glasgow conference having put the devolution issue to rest), and also finding the party its first 'Scottish' leader. There were two candidates, the former Ayr MP Phil Gallie and the former SCUA president David McLetchie. From a curious electorate of prospective candidates and constituency association chairmen, McLetchie won by a whisker, with ninety-one votes to eighty-three. The closeness of the result surprised many, and reflected concerns – expressed at the conference in a 'whispering' campaign – that McLetchie lacked the necessary experience and charisma to do the job. Although he identified with the Right of the party, his election was nonetheless welcomed by pro-devolutionists such as Christine Richard and the Scottish Tory Reform Group.

With just months to go until the election, the party did all it could to emphasise its 'Scottishness'. William Hague declared 'you are truly a Scottish party' at a Hampden Park rally,[15] while McLetchie extended the footballing analogy by saying that the Scottish Parliament election gave his party 'an opportunity to get back on the pitch' and away from the 'side lines'.[16] Significantly, this was McLetchie's first formal acceptance of devolution. 'It was meant to be a big, bold statement,' recalled Michael Fry, who drafted the declaration. 'As a matter of fact, the big bold statement was made, only for the party to pretend it had not made it.'[17] Based on 1997 voting figures, the Scottish Conservatives ought to have won twenty-two MSPs, although opinion polls suggested the total might be as low as twelve. In the event, the party managed eighteen, while coming third in terms of vote share. Nevertheless, the failure to win any seats first past the post and 15.56 per cent of the vote was disappointing. Ironically, an electoral system opposed by Conservatives had ensured their survival in an institution most of its members did not want. 'For the first time in a generation, there are Conservatives representing every region in Scotland,' said McLetchie, putting a positive spin on the outcome. 'We will be the Unionist Opposition at Holyrood.'[18]

Rebirth: 1999–2003

An important factor aiding the Scottish Conservatives' new lease of life was the financial backing of the Monte Carlo-based business-man Irvine Laidlaw. As well as providing the party with more than £250,000 before the first Scottish Parliament elections, Laidlaw (later Lord Laidlaw) facilitated a new HQ on Princes Street for a peppercorn rent. Significant amounts of money, for example, were spent on high-profile advertising designed by the Yellow M agency, including a controversial poster depicting SNP leader Alex Salmond as a Teletubby living in 'Scot-laa-laa-land'.

In the new Parliament itself, McLetchie quickly found his feet as a confident and credible performer despite having the least political experience of the four main party leaders. He essentially pursued a core vote strategy, highlighting the new Parliament's failings – not least a growing row about the cost of a new building at Holyrood – and appealing to social conservatives by arguing that Scottish Executive priorities, such as the repeal of Section 28, were out of kilter with most Scots. But although McLetchie's attacks on the Scottish Executive were often effective, it masked the absence of a clear, positive Conservative approach to a post-devolved Scotland.

Reversing a Thatcherite ban on the 'promotion' of homosexual-ity in schools also played a part in the first by-election to the new Parliament, in Ayr on 16 March 2000. Having narrowly missed taking that seat first past the post in May 1999, the Scottish Conservatives had high hopes of recapturing it, vindicated when John Scott took the seat with a majority of more than 3,000. In truth, the Tory share of the vote had barely increased on the 1999 figure, but it provided a valuable psychological boost to a party keen to detect any signs of an electoral recovery. Similarly, when the party won a Stirling Council by-election from the SNP, the press was full of further 'revival' claims.[19]

There were, however, also setbacks. In June 2000 the Scottish Tory candidate Tasmina Ahmed-Sheikh, hailed as the 'new face' of

Scottish Conservatism the year before, defected to the SNP citing the 'rightward switch in Tory policy' under William Hague's leadership.[20] A bout of infighting sparked by an internal election for the post of deputy chairman, the Scottish Conservative Party's representative on the UK party's governing board, appeared to confirm this rightward drift. The former Tayside North MP Bill Walker (an arch anti-devolutionist) won a convincing victory, but his victory was overshadowed by a spate of resignations – Sir Adrian Shinwell as chairman of the candidates' board, Jacqui Low from the party's executive, likewise with Gordon McIntosh (husband of Lyndsay, a Tory MSP) – all a result of discontent with Raymond Robertson's performance as party chairman.

Indeed, Bill Walker's election highlighted an unusual situation – created by the Strathclyde Commission recommendations – whereby ordinary party members directly elected the Scottish party's deputy chairman but not its chairman. Robertson's position, commented Brian Meek in his *Herald* column, was 'weakened by the fact that he is appointed and not elected'.[21] At around this time, the Scottish Conservative Party also initiated an ideological shift, although one motivated more by electoral considerations than political philosophy. Sir Stewart Sutherland's report on long-term care for the elderly had recommended making the 'personal care' aspect of support for elderly Scots free, and the party's health spokespeople, Mary Scanlon and Ben Wallace, wrote to Sir Stewart in support of this finding. 'The number of elderly people in Scotland is set to rise this century,' they wrote, 'and we are rising to the challenge of safeguarding their future.'[22] The adoption of this policy was driven by the concern Tory voters had of having to use their savings or sell their homes to pay for care, in contrast to others who would be cared for by the state and therefore 'rewarded' for not saving.

It was no coincidence that the majority of Tory voters in Scotland were, of course, elderly themselves, but Scanlon confirmed this apparently statist slant when, in August 2000, she indicated that 'as a general principle'[23] the party did not want the private sector to play a bigger role in healthcare provision north of the border. Similarly, in early 2001 the party promised to 'sweeten the pill' of university tuition fees by raising the threshold under which Scottish students had to pay into a compulsory endowment fund from annual earnings of £10,000 to £20,000, while in June 2001 David McLetchie unexpectedly sent a message of support to the organisers of Scotland's Gay Pride festival, all the more surprising given the party's recent stance on the repeal of Section 28.

Not every Scottish Tory, however, was convinced by the general thrust of this strategy, many of whom believed their MSPs had gone 'native'. Those in the party who wanted to see less state spending on welfare rather than more were perturbed by the long-term care for the elderly pledge, and when Scanlon suggested banning sweet cigarettes, one 'prominent activist' said: 'That's not a Conservative policy. We're the party of individual freedom – we don't go around banning things.'[24] But with half an eye on the next UK general election, party chairman Raymond Robertson said the Scottish Conservatives had 'listened and learned'. 'The Scottish Conservative Party is rejuvenated,' he said, 'and welcomes the chance to show the people of Scotland just how much we have changed.'[25] Indeed, several figures involved in the party during this period remembered, among MSPs, a 'desperate desire to cease to be pariahs and be liked; accepted within the Scottish political mainstream, which was dominated by broadly social democratic attitudes'.[26] Attempts to reposition – or indeed 'detoxify' – the party were confused and sporadic: there was no coordinated or ideologically consistent strategy.

UK party leader William Hague, however, was apparently comfortable with this divergence from his own, more traditionally right-wing, policy agenda in the rest of the UK. 'Something called devolution has happened,' he observed as he launched the Scottish party's manifesto for the 2001 general election. 'Policies that only relate to Scotland are determined in Scotland by the Scottish Conservative party.'[27] Hague's pragmatism, however, had a limited impact on Scottish voters. The apparently 'rock-bottom' vote share of 1997 – 17.5 per cent – fell to 15.6 per cent in June 2001, although that electoral cloud had a silver lining in the form of Peter Duncan, the Scottish party's sole victor in Galloway and Upper Nithsdale (Raymond Robertson, contesting Eastwood, did not come close, while Sir Malcolm Rifkind failed to regain Edinburgh Pentlands).

The twin refrains of name-change and fiscal autonomy resurfaced in the wake of the election result and Hague's resignation as leader. David Davis, one of those bidding to succeed him, advocated not only fiscal autonomy for Scotland but devolution for England. Curiously, Brian Monteith at this point opposed any moves in this direction, arguing that the party needed 'more division, disruption and divorce like we need a collective hole in the head'.[28] The latter half of the Scottish Parliament's first term, however, played witness to plenty of division and disruption for the Scottish Conservatives. Not only did Mid-Scotland and Fife MSP Nick Johnston resign, alleging by way of a parting shot that David McLetchie had 'no idea how to lead',[29] but the spring of 2002 was dominated by another row about candidate selection, the party's Scottish executive (which did not want to give members a vote) seemingly at odds with most of the nineteen-strong MSP group (who wanted a one-member-one-vote system for the selection process). All this from a party that, as one source told a journalist in late 2001, found 'politics rather vulgar and ungentlemanly'. The Scottish Conservatives, observed Douglas Fraser, were simply 'struggling to find a role in the new terrain of Scottish devolution and Tony Blair's occupancy of a wide swathe of the political centre ground'.[30]

The high-profile scalp claimed by McLetchie at the end of 2001 did at least offer some respite. His relentless attacks on Henry McLeish over the Officegate affair finally provoked Henry McLeish's resignation, although the Scottish Tory leader still felt the need to write to every Conservative association in Scotland to explain what had happened. 'In bringing the facts of this case to public attention,' he wrote, 'the Scottish Conservative Party was performing the proper role of an opposition party, which is to hold the executive and ministers to account.'[31] The trouble came in converting that 'opposition' into electoral support, particularly in the absence of a clear message about what the party stood for in Scotland. As the party's sole Scottish MP Peter Duncan admitted in the run-up to the 2003 Scottish Parliamentary elections: 'Our failure is that we haven't yet tapped into that [Centre-Right] market. We haven't yet made ourselves the obvious home for that [potential] 35% support.'[32]

That campaign brought new troubles when two sitting Tory MSPs (Keith Harding and Lyndsay McIntosh), both ranked too low on their respective lists to win re-election, defected to the fledgling Scottish People's Alliance, but it had minimal impact on the election result. In a personal triumph for David McLetchie, he won Edinburgh Pentlands from Labour, while the party also held Ayr and took Galloway and Upper Nithsdale from the SNP, giving the party a trio of first-past-the-post seats. Its 16.6 and 15.5 per cent of the vote in the constituency and list votes respectively, however, represented only modest progress on the 1999 result.

As Alexander Smith argued in his study of the Dumfries and Galloway Conservative Association during the 2003 election, post-devolution Scottish Tories had buried themselves in 'banal activism' to avoid facing up to the deeper and more difficult questions about their future.[33] This malaise was mirrored at Central Office in Edinburgh. 'We said we accepted devolution but appeared very grudging about it,' recalled a key figure. 'We'd simply demonised it too much, talking about the tartan tax and all that. So at some point we needed a big, bold statement to show people we had changed as a party, but we kept putting it off.'[34]

Stagnation: 2003–7

The second term of the Scottish Parliament saw David McLetchie continue his core vote strategy while making modest attempts to engage more generally, although the next four years would be dominated by resignations and further party infighting. He also appeared to be warming to the idea of enabling the Scottish Parliament to have greater 'fiscal responsibility', endorsing the idea of a Royal Commission to investigate the issue, although this was not a view shared by the new UK party leader Michael Howard.[35]

MSPs such as Brian Monteith and Murdo Fraser (not to forget Michael Fry from the media sidelines, although he would declare support for Scottish independence in October 2006) continued to press their leader to view fiscal autonomy as a game-changer for the Scottish Conservative Party (the SNP having backed fiscal autonomy in 2001), and in May 2004 the notion was at least discussed at an away day for the eighteen MSPs at the Huntingtower Hotel in Perth. McLetchie, however, said he remained 'utterly opposed' to the idea of giving the Scottish Parliament full fiscal powers, but conceded that it was 'unhealthy' for the Parliament and Scottish Executive to be seen 'wholly as a spending institution with limited financial responsibility'.[36] Conscious of party opinion and keen to avoid division, he shied away from making what some MSPs viewed as much-needed strategic decisions. McLetchie also began developing an idea floated during the election campaign of working with Labour on an issue-by-issue basis in order to imprint Conservative influence on legislation.

In October 2004 Peter Duncan, by then the Scottish Conservative Party's sole MP and Shadow Secretary of State for Scotland in Howard's Shadow Cabinet, also succeeded David Mitchell as Scottish party chairman. Despite being the Scottish party's 'link' with London, tension remained between unreconstructed elements at Westminster and those trying to make devolution 'work' on the Mound. Speaking in the House of Lords, Michael Forsyth suggested getting rid of all 129 MSPs and instead sending Scottish MPs north to sit in the Scottish Parliament on specified days, spending the money saved on 'more useful' employees such as doctors, nurses and teachers. When James Gray, the Scots-born MP for North Wiltshire, made the same point a week after being appointed Shadow Scottish Secretary following the 2005 general election, he was compelled to resign by furious MSPs. That election, in which the party's share of the vote rose slightly (0.2 per cent) to 15.8 per cent, also produced just one Scottish Tory MP, although not the same one as in 2001. Peter Duncan lost the newly redrawn constituency of Dumfries and Galloway, having arguably tried to wear too many hats over the previous few months, while in the new seat of Dumfriesshire, Clydesdale and Tweeddale, the South of Scotland MSP David Mundell overturned a notional Labour majority (Derek Brownlee, who was next on the list, replaced Mundell at Holyrood).

Indeed, an interesting feature of the Scottish Conservatives post-1999 was an apparent frustration with the limitations of devolved politics. Ben Wallace, the North-East list MSP, had been the first to indicate his intention to contest a Westminster constituency less than a year after his election to the Scottish Parliament (he eventually became the MP for Lancaster and Wyre in 2005); Phil Gallie stood in Ayr in 2001; while in addition to Mundell in 2005, Jamie McGrigor contested Argyll and Bute, while Alex Johnstone and John Lamont stood in West Aberdeenshire and Kincardine and Berwickshire, Roxburgh and Selkirk respectively, both of them trying again in 2010. Political opponents consistently argued that this demonstrated the Conservatives' lack of commitment to Scottish devolution.

Furthermore, the general election result – in which the Conservatives gained more votes than Labour in England – served to highlight the lack of any tangible recovery north of the border (unlike in Wales, where the party gained three MPs having won no seats in 1997 and 2001). Murdo Fraser argued that the anti-Holyrood view of some Tory MPs meant a debate on 'the links between the Scottish Tories and the UK party is required', citing the German CDU/CSU relationship as a possible model. 'It would entail a separate party, separately funded, with separate responsibility for policy,' explained Fraser. 'There would be two parties united by conservatism.'[37] Although swiftly dismissed by McLetchie and other senior party figures, this was essentially the prospectus on which Fraser would fight the 2011 Scottish Tory leadership contest.

Fraser chose to bide his time when, in November 2005, McLetchie resigned as leader after it emerged he had claimed more than £5,000 for taxi expenses without properly filling in expenses claim forms, making him perhaps the first victim of Scotland's new Freedom of Information legislation. He had already been weakened by a conflict-of-interest claim earlier that year, which compelled him to quit his legal work at the Edinburgh firm of Tods Murray. Annabel Goldie, his deputy, took over as interim leader and, within a matter of days, had been confirmed as leader in a 'coronation' arranged by party managers to avoid a prolonged leadership contest. Murdo Fraser withdrew from the non-race in return for the deputy's post, with speculation that he would assume the leadership following the 2007 Holyrood poll.

The rise of Murdo Fraser, meanwhile, coincided with the fall of another fiscal devolver, Brian Monteith. Exposed (as a result of questionable journalistic ethics) as having aided McLetchie's downfall, he at first lost the Scottish Tory whip and then voluntarily resigned his party membership. Fraser certainly kept the fiscal autonomy flame burning, although less ostentatiously than before. And while admitting doubts about such a plan, the new UK Conservative leader David Cameron said he 'certainly did not rule out' full fiscal autonomy should the Scottish party choose to follow that path.[38] Whatever doubts Cameron had about his northern troops were probably confirmed when, in March 2006, the eccentric right-wing former MP Bill Walker won re-election as the Scottish Tory Party's deputy chairman. As Cameron's Conservatives moved to the centre ground, Goldie's Scottish Conservatives appeared to be drifting in the opposite direction. 'I'm not really sure we know what to make of them, really,' said one senior London Conservative. 'They're certainly not very close to what we're trying to do here.'[39]

There was much criticism of Annabel Goldie in her first six months as leader, although she was in many respects McLetchie mark II. Both were good performers and more interested in tactics than grand ideological exercises (i.e. fiscal autonomy), while both were also cautious and diligent when it came to internal party management. In June 2006 Goldie appointed Douglas Osler, a former civil servant, to lead a nine-strong policy advisory group charged with developing ideas for the next Holyrood manifesto.

Interestingly, the advisory group recommended fiscal autonomy, although the Tory MSP group quickly ruled this out. Goldie also built upon McLetchie's plan of cooperating with Labour by floating the idea of a more formal 'stability pact' with Jack McConnell's party should it lack Liberal Democrat support after polling day.

Beyond that subtle positioning, Goldie simply reiterated that just 'as Scotland has changed, the Scottish Conservative party has changed and is changing'.[40] But Brian Monteith, now free of the formal party machine, argued that words were not enough; only by 'advocating what is loosely called fiscal autonomy' could Scottish Conservatives 'end any doubts once and for all that they are taking part in the devolution process grudgingly'. He wrote:

> The party should develop its semi-autonomous relationship with London so that it is truly independent, able to have its own identity, maybe a new name, certainly a new logo of its own choice, appointing its own party chairman and raising its own money. Once people are able to see that the party is willing to put Scottish interests before party interests, then they should be willing to listen to what it has to say.[41]

These were all familiar refrains, but at this stage in the game moves were actually afoot in London to do precisely what Monteith set out. The context was one of obvious frustration with the Scottish party, not unlike that a century before. 'The organisation up there was completely ramshackle,' recalled George Bridges:

> They didn't understand what we were trying to do at all, and I had absolutely no control up there as Director of Campaigns. It was a complete struggle, so they employed an extra person [John Read] for us to liaise with, but it didn't make much of a difference.'[42]

The decline of professional agents, who were important in maintaining local organisation and membership, continued apace after 1997.

Despite several high-profile forays north of the border, David Cameron had failed to make much of a connection with Scottish voters, his perceived 'poshness' one of many barriers. Initially reluctant to make anything of his Scottish ancestry, he declared, to no avail: 'I'm a Cameron, there is quite a lot of Scottish blood flowing through these veins.'[43] When Cameron asked David Mundell, his Shadow Scottish Secretary since late 2005, for his thoughts, he said in a memo leaked to coincide with the party's May 2006 conference that there was a 'simple lack of thinkers' among Scottish Tory MSPs at Holyrood, and that while Goldie had made a reasonable start as leader she possessed a 'lack of activity and strategic thought'. The Scottish party, meanwhile, simply did not 'get' the new moderation of the UK party.[44]

At some point during 2006, therefore, Cameron authorised Francis Maude to draw up plans for what the *Spectator* called a 'velvet divorce' between the Scottish and UK Conservative parties. Several senior Conservatives – including Shadow Chancellor George Osborne – saw the logic of this position, while it attracted grassroots support via the influential ConservativeHome website. 'With independence, a new name and new personnel, the Scottish Conservatives can break free in one leap,' judged Tim Montgomerie. 'They will no longer be seen as stooges of a London establishment.'[45] It would provide, in summary, a win-win situation for Cameron: if it worked, he would enjoy greater Scottish support; if it did not, then he would not be tainted by its failure. Naturally, Annabel Goldie denied reports of the plan. 'We're the Scottish Conservative and Unionist Party; I'm the leader of that party,' she told journalists. 'There is no divorce. It's just not going to happen.'[46] The Scottish Tory leader had, meanwhile, demonstrated a flair for publicity on the campaign trail, riding quad bikes, going ten-pin bowling and delivering fruity one-liners. Come polling day, the Scottish Tory result was not quite as bad as some in London expected, the constituency vote holding steady at 16.6 per cent but the list vote sinking yet further to 13.9 per cent. The party lost just one MSP and therefore the 'velvet divorce' did not happen, another snag being Goldie's apparent reluctance to become Holyrood's third Presiding Officer.

Detoxification: 2007–11

If one moment in the Scottish Parliament's eight-year existence required a strong Conservative and Unionist Party it was the point at which the SNP formed its first, albeit minority, Holyrood administration. Initially, however, the Scottish Conservatives – in common with the defeated Labour and Liberal Democrat coalition partners – floundered, unsure of how to respond. Murdo Fraser, who had expected to be leader by the summer of 2007, was the only senior figure to articulate a coherent solution to what he characterised as a constitutional 'mess'. 'Perhaps the end point will be a federal, or quasi-federal, United Kingdom,' he wrote in October 2007. 'A reformed House of Lords might act as a pan-UK "senate" binding the UK together.'[47]

The initiative, however, actually came from the new Scottish Labour leader Wendy Alexander who, like Fraser, had previously toyed with fiscal autonomy for the Scottish Parliament. In a speech on St Andrew's Day 2007 she set out the case for a review of the devolution settlement, and a week later the three 'Unionist' parties at Holyrood had agreed a cross-party commission, later chaired by Sir Kenneth Calman. Annabel Goldie appeared enthusiastic. 'It is the start of devolution phase two,' she said, 'a process which will chart the direction of this parliament and the future of Scotland in the 21st century.'[48] But some MSPs were unhappy at this tack, fearing it would play into Nationalist hands. Margaret Mitchell, for example, later described the Calman Commission as 'a knee-jerk reaction' to the election of a minority SNP government.[49] Most Scottish Tory members, meanwhile, reacted to Calman much as they had to Edward Heath's Declaration of Perth in 1968, with a mixture of muted enthusiasm and scepticism.

Labour and Liberal Democrat hopes of a coordinated anti-SNP front at Holyrood were, however, short-lived. Derek Brownlee, the Scottish Conservatives' finance spokesman had, since the election, been urging Annabel Goldie to take advantage of the SNP's minority status and put into play what she and David McLetchie had previously hinted at in relation to the Scottish Labour Party. Convinced the party had to do something to demonstrate its political 'relevance' in legislative terms (and conscious that either alternative, a Labour minority government or an early election, was not 'good' for the Conservatives), Goldie allowed Brownlee to establish a working relationship with Finance Secretary John Swinney. This paid dividends early the following year when the Conservatives secured three concessions from the SNP's first Budget, namely 500 new police officers over three years, more money for drug rehabilitation and an accelerated scheme of tax relief for small businesses.

There were obvious risks in a staunchly Unionist party keeping the SNP afloat, not least among Scottish Tory voters, but the party was playing the long game, judging that by 2011 this ongoing constructive relationship would enable candidates in 2011 to say: 'Look, this is what we achieved in Opposition; if you give us more power and more MSPs we will achieve even more.' After the Budget deal, one Tory MSP even claimed the party had achieved more in one vote than during the previous eight years.[50] Reflecting on these events in 2011, Derek Brownlee said

> What we got out of that budget was credibility; it was the first time we'd led the news in ages, and it was seen as quite a coup. Yes, John Swinney was using us for numbers, but we were using him to get stuff we could punt at an election. What better way to decontaminate than to align ourselves with the SNP?'[51]

In early 2009, the party sought to augment this strategy with the appointment of a new director of communications and strategy, the former STV journalist Michael Crow. Reporting to both London (UK director of communications Andy Coulson) and Edinburgh (new Scottish party chairman Andrew Fulton), Crow's task was to slicken the party's presentation while preparing an electoral strategy for a UK general election expected in mid-2010. David Cameron, meanwhile, promoted the so-called 'respect agenda' (the brainchild of David Mundell), promising that, as Prime Minister, he would 'govern the whole of the United Kingdom, including Scotland, with respect'.[52]

The Calman Commission, meanwhile, reported in June 2009, prompting a mini-crisis in the Scottish Conservative Party as Annabel Goldie appeared to distance herself from its recommendations to extend some financial and other powers to Holyrood. Her problem, as ever, was reconciling several factions of the party, those uncomfortable with greater devolution, those anxious to go much further and those in between who did not much care either way. 'There is nothing in our manifesto that says we have to back Calman,' complained one sceptical Tory MSP. 'We must be very careful. A lot of our people do not like the way the party is travelling.'[53] Eventually Goldie endorsed Calman's findings (rather than merely 'taking note', as had been mooted by the rebels), but it appeared grudging.

There were high hopes as the party prepared for the 2010 general election, with some (including Crow) predicting gains of around ten seats. These proved wide of the mark. Although the Scottish Conservative vote share increased by a modest 0.9 per cent, it still emerged with just one seat despite spending significant sums of money in around a dozen target seats, a victim of anti-Tory tactical voting and the effective deployment of Mrs Thatcher's legacy by Labour. Its legislative prowess in the preceding three years also appeared to have made little impact on voters. Unabashed, Annabel Goldie made it clear she intended to lead her party into the 2011 Holyrood elections. 'There was praise for the campaign we fought for the general election in Scotland' was her rather positive spin on the election result, 'and there was praise for my role within it'.[54]

As far as the new Prime Minister was concerned, Scotland was a Liberal Democrat responsibility, David Mundell (who held on in Dumfriesshire, Clydesdale and Tweeddale) having been compelled to deputise for a Scottish Secretary drawn from the coalition's junior party. Reports suggested David Cameron had given up on the Scottish party, which was compelled to relocate to a more modest HQ as Lord Laidlaw withdrew funding. Post-election events followed a predictable pattern: a bout of infighting and the formation of a commission to review the party's organisation.

This, chaired by former SCUA president and Scottish party chairman Lord Sanderson (whose appointment prompted media derision, including a *News of the World* graphic depicting him as 'Torysaurus'), reported later that year. *Building for Scotland: Strengthening the Scottish Conservatives* painted a bleak picture of 'moribund' local associations at the bottom and 'weak' leadership structures at the top. A party that could boast 40,000 members in 1992 now had only 10,000 (although that figure was probably optimistic), many of whom did not rate either the party's HQ staff or elected representatives very highly. More widely, the review admitted that Scots remained unclear as to 'what the Scottish Conservatives stand for', except that the party was still considered to be 'anti-Scottish'.

Importantly, in light of the later leadership election, Sanderson considered but ruled out a change of name or a change in the relationship with the UK Conservative Party. It noted that the Scottish Conservatives 'obtain numerous benefits from being part of the UK party, including opportunity to access resources, training and expertise and for members to vote for the UK leader'. Therefore, 'given the Conservative commitment to Scotland remaining within the United Kingdom, it is both appropriate and beneficial that there should be an integrated relationship between the Scottish Conservatives and the UK party'.

Although Sanderson's remit – like Lord Strathclyde's in 1997/8 – had not included policy matters, his report could not 'ignore the quantity of submissions on whether or not Scotland should have greater fiscal accountability' and recommended it be 'discussed fully between both the Scottish Conservatives and the UK party, as well as forming the basis of a fully informed debate within the party membership'. Sanderson's key recommendation, however, was that a 'distinctly Scottish leader' ought to command the whole Scottish party rather than just its MSPs.[55]

This put Annabel Goldie in a difficult position, forced to counter speculation that she would not survive re-election following the 2011 Holyrood election (a timetable stipulated by Sanderson). Ironically, polling suggested Goldie was a popular and respected figure on the Scottish political scene; it was just that she – and her party – struggled to turn this obvious personal appeal into votes. Gearing up for the Holyrood election, Goldie said there was 'going to be no bullshitting'. 'Give me more and we will deliver more for Scotland,' she added, reminding voters that her party had delivered more police officers, help with business rates and a town centre regeneration fund.[56]

Visiting Inverness during the 2011 Holyrood election campaign, David Cameron did his best to remain upbeat about the Scottish Conservative Party's prospects, conceding it had 'tragically' been some time since his party had enjoyed majority support north of the border. 'We have to emphasise three things,' he told journalists following his keynote speech. His comments are worth reprinting in full:

> First, the Scottish Conservative Party is a party of the United Kingdom, that we – head, heart and soul – would never put at risk. We're always the real, true believers in strengthening our union.
>
> Second, that the Scottish Conservative party is Conservative, yes, but it's Scottish, run by Scots, for Scots. It makes decisions for Scotland. It does not take orders from Westminster. The judgements it reaches about policy, about manifestos, about who to partner with after the election, all that will be decided by Scots. It is, if you like, more Unionist but also more Scottish.
>
> The third thing, absolutely crucially, and it will take some time to get to 50 per cent [of the vote], is that the values that Scottish Conservatives stand for, the values of supporting families and backing enterprise, or looking after those who need to be looked after, of helping people get on. Classic Conservative, Centre-Right, strong, patriotic, family, pro-enterprise values are the values that millions of people in Scotland share. And if we can get people to link

their values with their voting behaviour, seeing a party that is both absolutely for the United Kingdom but fundamentally Scottish, that to me is the long-term answer to getting back to that magic number.

Now it will take time but I've always said I'll be patient. I've been banging this drum for five years as the leader of the Conservative Party in the United Kingdom, and I will be banging this drum as long as there's breath in my body, whatever role I play in this party.[57]

The Prime Minister appeared to be engaged with the condition of his party in Scotland, but voters were not. On polling day, the Scottish Conservative and Unionist Party – a party which in 1955 had secured a majority of both votes and MPs – registered its worst ever result, 13.9 and 12.4 per cent of the constituency and list votes respectively, enough to elect just fifteen MSPs (five fewer than anticipated following positive boundary changes). In Labour's worst Scottish result since 1931 it spoke volumes that in the two key Labour-Tory marginals, Eastwood and Dumfriesshire, there were marked swings to Labour. Internal critics of the SNP engagement strategy also expressed concerns that this had sent a signal to Tory-inclined voters that it was 'safe' to vote SNP.

Having initially indicated that she would remain as leader (unlike her Labour and Liberal Democrat counterparts), Annabel Goldie threw in the towel. 'I believe that the time has come for the torch to pass,' she told reporters a few days after the result, 'and I can confirm that I will not be a candidate.' Alex Salmond, triumphantly re-elected as First Minister, this time at the head of a majority administration, paid the outgoing Tory leader a compliment of sorts. 'Although her party lost ground,' he said, 'I believe they would have lost more had she not been leader.'[58]

Conclusion

The Scottish Conservative Party described by David Seawright in his 1999 study, *An Important Matter of Principle*, as predominantly old, 'the party of cabal and clique, too prone to the internecine skirmish'[59] and in desperate need of new blood and new thinkers, remained a pertinent sketch more than twelve years later, although with even fewer members.

There had, since those first elections to the Scottish Parliament in May 1999, been modest progress.[60] The party had not become extinct – a reasonable prospect following the Labour landslide of 1997 – and aided by the generally credible leadership of David McLetchie and Annabel Goldie had managed to maintain political relevance if not electoral recovery. But frequently positive press coverage and apparently popular leaders had not translated into extra votes for the party, indeed quite the reverse.

And there had also been missed opportunities. Social attitudes surveys indicated that in the period 1999–2011 Scotland had become a less socially democratic and even more conservative country, a context from which any reasonably adept Centre-Right party might have benefited.[61] There was also the prospect, mooted by several figures from 1997 onwards, of embracing devolution by taking it to its logical next step: full fiscal responsibility. Cast alongside structural changes such as an autonomous organisation and a name change, the historically flexible Scottish Tory Party might have convinced greater numbers of Scots that it had changed enough to play a serious part in the new Scottish political landscape.

In retrospect, 1997–9 might be considered a crucial period of flux in which fundamental change had been possible, and, in many ways, the Scottish Conservatives in 2012 still lived with decisions taken, or rather not taken, during that pre-devolutionary window. Ironically, a package of reforms first proposed by the left-leaning Scottish Tory Reform Group (STRG) at that time was, in 2011, taken up by a former leading right-winger called Murdo Fraser and vehemently opposed by the new STRG chairman John Lamont. The leadership election of that year left a whole series of issues – from the party's identity, its relationship with London and, still, its stance on devolution – essentially unresolved.

Notes

1. http://news.stv.tv/election-2010/174200-i-blame-the-government/
2. *Scotsman*, 19 May 1997. Arthur Bell later quit the party, accusing it of 'blindness to reality' over the devolution issue (*Herald*, 7 July 1997).
3. *Herald*, 20 June 1997.
4. Reports suggested the majority of Scottish Tory activists – including eight out of ten constituency association chairmen – had backed Ken Clarke.
5. Conference report (BBC Scotland, 27 June 1997).
6. *Scotsman*, 28 June 1997.

7. Conference report (BBC Scotland, 27 June 1997).
8. *Local Government Chronicle*, 30 June 1997.
9. Liam Fox argued at the 1998 conference that the Scottish Conservatives had been mistaken in 'cavorting with the language of nationalism for the last twenty years'. David Seawright, *An Important Matter of Principle* (Aldershot, 1999), p. 205.
10. *Scotsman*, 17 September 1997.
11. *Herald*, 24 September 1997.
12. *The Strathclyde Commission: Made in Scotland – The Final Report* (Edinburgh, 1998).
13. Press Association, 7 March 1998.
14. *Scotland on Sunday*, 5 April 1998.
15. *Scottish Daily Mail*, 29 January 1999.
16. *Sunday Times*, 4 April 1999.
17. Michael Fry to the author, 12 May 2012.
18. *Scotsman*, 8 May 1999.
19. *Herald*, 14 April 2000.
20. *Scottish Daily Mail*, 15 June 2000.
21. *Herald*, 28 June 2000.
22. *Herald*, 30 June 2000.
23. *Health Service Journal*, 17 August 2000.
24. *Sunday Herald*, 18 March 2011.
25. *Scotsman*, 27 September 2000.
26. Private information.
27. *Guardian*, 12 May 2001.
28. *Edinburgh Evening News*, 25 June 2001.
29. *Scotsman*, 11 August 2001.
30. *Sunday Herald*, 2 September 2001.
31. *Scotsman*, 12 November 2001.
32. *Herald*, 3 February 2003.
33. Alexander Smith, *Devolution and the Scottish Conservatives* (Manchester, 2011).
34. Private information.
35. *Sunday Herald*, 7 December 2003.
36. *Scotland on Sunday*, 9 March 2004.
37. *Scotsman*, 23 May 2005.
38. *Scotsman*, 21 December 2005.
39. *Scotsman*, 12 July 2006.
40. *Daily Express*, 28 October 2006.
41. *Sunday Times Scotland*, 8 November 2006.
42. Peter Snowdon, *Back from the Brink* (London, 2010), p. 247.

43. http://news.bbc.co.uk/1/hi/programmes/how_euro_are_you/51 14618.stm
44. *Daily Record*, 8 March 2007.
45. *Spectator*, 7 April 2007.
46. *Scotsman*, 6 April 2007.
47. *Scotsman*, 31 October 2007.
48. *Scotsman*, 7 December 2007.
49. Official Report, 25 June 2009.
50. *Scotsman*, 7 February 2008.
51. Interview with Derek Brownlee, 1 December 2011.
52. *Daily Express*, 13 February 2010.
53. *Daily Telegraph*, 19 June 2009.
54. *Scotsman*, 17 May 2010.
55. http://www.scottishconservatives.com/downloads/building-for-scotland.pdf
56. *Scotland on Sunday*, 2 January 2011.
57. Press Association Scotland, 20 April 2011.
58. http://www.bbc.co.uk/news/uk-scotland-13340641
59. Seawright, *An Important Matter of Principle*, p. 202.
60. Local government and European elections are often over-looked. In 1999 and 2003 and in some new areas in 2007 thanks to proportional representation (PR) the Scottish Conservatives made modest progress in local government, once again controlling some local authority areas. At the 1999 and 2004 European Parliament elections, meanwhile, the party secured two MEPs again because of PR, an electoral system the Conservatives opposed, and one in 2009 following the reduction in Scotland's MEPs.
61. http://www.scotcen.org.uk/media/788216/scotcen-ssa-report.pdf

CHAPTER 8

Why no Tory Revival in Scotland?

John Curtice

In 1997 Scottish Conservatives suffered a disaster. At 17.5 per cent, not only did the party's share of the vote fall to its lowest level ever since the introduction of the universal franchise, but in addition it failed to win any constituencies at all. However, at least it was not alone in its distress. Across Britain as a whole Tory support fell by nearly twelve percentage points compared with five years earlier – against which the eight-point drop in Scotland seemed almost respectable – and at 31.5 per cent the party's share of the vote was lower than at any election since 1832. True, a long-term decline in the party's support north of the border between the 1950s and the 1990s meant that it was particularly vulnerable to any tsunami of disaffection such as that which engulfed the party in 1997, but the immediate source of its travails at least appeared to be John Major's divided and derided government rather than any new home-grown source of disaffection specific to Scotland.

However, south of the border the party has gradually recovered from its 1997 drubbing. In 2001 and 2005 it registered small advances in both England and Wales. Then in 2010 much more substantial progress was achieved. The Conservatives advanced to 39.5 per cent of the vote in England, nearly six points up on their tally in 1997, while much the same level of increase was achieved in Wales too. Between them these advances were sufficient to see the party return to power at Westminster, albeit in coalition with the Liberal Democrats.

In Scotland, by contrast, the Conservatives have, if anything, slipped back even further. Although the party did manage to win one constituency in 2001, its share of the Scotland-wide vote actually fell back further to just 15.6 per cent, while at 15.8 per cent it was little better in 2005. Then in 2010 the party registered no more than a modest advance. At 16.7 per cent, its share of the vote was still below what it had been in the disaster of 1997. Meanwhile, at nearly twenty-eight percentage points, the difference between the party's share of the vote in Scotland and that in England was wider than ever before in the modern era. Whatever conclusion might have been drawn in 1997, there could now be little doubt that the Scottish party's difficulties were all too close to home.

Elections to the Scottish Parliament, newly created in 1999, have not proved any more fruitful a hunting ground for the party either. At each of the first three elections, the party's share of the constituency vote lay between 15.6 and 16.6 per cent, that is at much the same level as at Westminster elections. On the list vote, where smaller parties are able to perform relatively well, the party's vote in the first three elections was even lower – between 13.9 and 15.4 per cent. Then in 2011 Conservative support slipped to yet another new record low of 13.9 per cent on the constituency vote and just 12.4 per cent on the list, at a time when the party was largely holding its own in devolved elections in Wales and in local elections in much of England.[1] But for the use of proportional representation, the party would never have had more than a handful of MSPs in the Holyrood chamber either.

In this chapter we investigate why the Scottish Conservatives have failed to achieve any kind of recovery since 1997. We do so by utilising survey data to examine key trends in public opinion in Scotland and to ascertain the kinds of people who do still vote for the party in Scotland, and thus by implication who does not. In addition, we look for clues as to why the Scottish party has performed far worse than its English cousin by comparing the pattern of support on the two sides of the border. To begin with, however, we need to consider the possible explanations for the Scottish Tories' misfortunes on which we might focus.

Explanations

There are two possible main explanations for the absence of a Tory revival in Scotland. One suggests the reason for failure lies in the character of Scottish society, and the way in which the political environment north of the border is thought to be (increasingly) non-conducive to Conservative electoral success. The other explanation suggests we need to look instead at the political strategy that has been pursued by the Scottish party during the last twenty or thirty years and how this might have militated against any prospect of a revival north of the border.

The Conservatives are, of course, a party on the Centre Right of British politics and one that has come to be regarded as the party of the country's 'middle classes', in contrast to Labour, which is both a social democratic party and was founded specifically to advance working-class representation. One might well imagine that Scotland would not take readily to a party with such an ideological stance and social image. Part of the engine house of the British industrial revolution, Scotland was once home to much heavy industry, and thus of a manual working-class labour force that fostered a strong and sometimes radical trade union movement, not least in 'Red Clydeside'. This legacy still seems to live on in the claim that is often made that, unlike England, Scotland is a social democratic country that values equality and supports government action to create a more just society.[2] Some of the iconic policy differences to have emerged since the advent of devolution, such as free personal care and free university education, are sometimes touted as evidence of the country's distinctive adherence to a social democratic outlook. Certainly it is an image that Nationalists as well as those on the Left have been willing to promote. The SNP First Minister, Alex Salmond, has referred in speeches both to 'our Scottish social democracy' and to 'our social democratic contract with Scotland'.[3]

Thus, we might well wonder whether there is simply not the same appetite for a Centre-Right party in Scotland that there is in England. Moreover, perhaps that is even more so the case now that devolution is in place. After all, politics at Holyrood has been dominated by two parties that both claim to be on the Centre Left, and consequently the voice of the Centre Right is less likely to be heard in the debates about public policy that now take place north of the border independently of whatever is being discussed in England.[4] The less the message of the Centre Right is heard, the less likely perhaps that people are persuaded of its merits. At the same time, we might wonder whether the growth of white-collar employment in London and the South East prior to the financial crisis of 2008 has meant that the differences in the social profile of Scotland and

England have widened too. In short, perhaps devolved Scotland has become an even more difficult environment in which to promote the cause of a Centre-Right party than was the Scotland of the 1980s and 1990s.

But, of course, whatever may be the position in England, politics in Scotland is not just about class and questions of Left and Right. It is also about identity and Scotland's constitutional status. And the latter is an issue on which the Conservatives have taken a distinctive stance. Although the 'Unionism' in the party's full title, the Scottish Conservative and Unionist Party, originally referred to the Union between Great Britain and Ireland rather than that between Scotland and England, concern to preserve the integrity of the British state meant that the party was imbued with a strong wish to defend the Anglo-Scottish Union too. Although this did not stop the party dallying with the idea of devolution for a while under the leadership of Edward Heath, in the 1980s and 1990s the party nailed its colours very firmly to the mast that the creation of a Scottish Parliament would put the Union at risk. The party had no truck with the Scottish Constitutional Convention and, uniquely amongst Scotland's major parties, called for a 'no' vote in the 1997 devolution referendum.

In short, the Scottish Conservatives found themselves on what proved to be the wrong side of the devolution debate. To that their opponents added a wider critique, that it was an 'English' party intent on imposing inappropriate 'English' policies on a Scotland in which it lacked a democratic mandate. It was a critique that reached its height with the introduction of the ill-fated poll tax a year earlier than in England. So as well as appearing unattractive to those who wanted some kind of Scottish Parliament, the Conservatives would also seem to be at risk of looking unappealing to those with a strong sense of Scottish national identity. As a result, perhaps the party struggles even to win the support of those in Scotland who are middle class or are on the ideological Right, let alone anyone else. Moreover, although the party may now have come to accept devolution, perhaps it has failed to shake off the image that it acquired as a result of its stance in the 80s and 90s.

Struggling with social democracy?

The first proposition we have to consider then is that Scotland is a more working-class and more social democratic country than England, and that this feature has made it increasingly difficult for the Conservatives to win votes north of the border. In truth, this argument is difficult to sustain. Table 8.1 shows how people in Scotland and England have reacted during the course of the last decade to two propositions that might be thought to lie at the core of a social democratic outlook: concern about the degree of inequality in Britain and a belief that the government should take action to make it less unequal.

The table shows that people in Scotland do indeed seem to be somewhat more likely than those in England to express a social democratic outlook. In most years during the course of the last decade, people in Scotland have been more likely than those in England to agree that 'ordinary people do not get their fair share of the nation's wealth' and that 'government should redistribute income from the better-off to the less well-off'. But the differences have typically not been large ones. On average people in Scotland have been four points more likely than those in England to agree that ordinary people do not get their fair share of wealth and just six points more likely to feel that government should redistribute income. Moreover, there is no consistent evidence that the gap between Scotland and England has widened since the advent of devolution. Rather, if anything, there appears to have been something of a drift away from a social democratic perspective in both countries in recent years.

So ideologically Scotland is somewhat less congenial territory than England in which to promote the cause of a Centre-Right party. But the difference of outlook between Scotland and England is far smaller than the difference in Conservative performance in the two countries. Moreover, there is no evidence that promoting a Centre-Right message has become any more difficult now than it was a decade ago. In short, the ideological culture of Scotland is not a sufficient explanation either of the much lower level of Conservative support in Scotland than in England or of the party's failure to restore its fortunes north of the border since 1997.

Much the same is true of the class composition of Scottish society. Scotland is a little less middle class than England, but not dramatically so. According to the 2010 Scottish Social Attitudes

Table 8.1   Trends in attitudes towards inequality, Scotland and England, 2000–10

Ordinary working people do not get their fair share of the nation's wealth

	2000	2002	2004	2005	2006	2007	2009	2010
Scotland	%	%	%	%	%	%	%	%
Agree	71	64	63	56	56	62	55	59
Neither agree nor disagree	18	22	23	26	29	22	29	28
Disagree	9	11	12	15	13	14	13	11
England	%	%	%	%	%	%	%	%
Agree	61	61	53	55	54	58	58	55
Neither agree nor disagree	23	23	28	27	29	26	25	28
Disagree	13	13	17	17	14	13	14	15

Government should redistribute income from the better-off to those who are less well off

	2000	2002	2004	2005	2006	2007	2009	2010
Scotland	%	%	%	%	%	%	%	%
Agree	50	45	40	31	39	37	37	43
Neither agree nor disagree	24	25	30	29	26	25	30	28
Disagree	24	27	28	37	33	36	31	26
England	%	%	%	%	%	%	%	%
Agree	38	37	31	32	34	32	36	34
Neither agree nor disagree	24	25	28	27	26	29	27	27
Disagree	36	35	39	40	38	37	35	37

Sources: Scottish Social Attitudes, British Social Attitudes (respondents living in England only)

Survey, 42 per cent of people in Scotland currently belong to one of the occupational groups amongst whom we would expect Conservative support to be highest, that is employers, managers, professionals or own account workers (as defined by the National Statistics Socio-Economic Classification), only a little below the 47 per cent proportion in England. Moreover, there is no evidence that this difference in class composition has widened during the course of the last decade.

Struggling with identity?

Our second possible explanation for the party's difficulties is that Scottish Tories have proved unable to escape from their association with opposition to devolution and the charge that they are an 'English' rather than a Scottish party. Of this there is plenty of evidence.

First of all, the party is relatively unsuccessful in securing support among those with a strong sense of Scottish identity. According to the Scottish Social Attitudes Survey, only 11 per cent of those who say they are 'Scottish, not British' or 'More Scottish than British' voted for the party in the 2010 UK general election. In contrast 24 per cent of those who feel they are 'Equally Scottish and British' or who feel that their sense of being British is stronger than their sense of being Scottish (if they feel Scottish at all) voted for the party. Meanwhile, crucially, the former group (constituting 58 per cent of all those resident in Scotland) is much larger than the latter (34 per cent). At the same time there is widespread scepticism among the Scottish public about the willingness of Scottish Tories to stand up for Scotland's interests. According to the 2007 Social Attitudes Survey, only 34 per cent believe that the party looks after Scotland's interests 'very' or 'fairly' closely, far fewer than the proportion who feel the same way about the Liberal Democrats (54 per cent) let alone Labour (64 per cent) or the SNP (71 per cent).

But even more dramatic than the Scottish Conservatives' failure to overcome their lack of association in the public mind with the identity and interests of Scotland is the degree to which the party's support is concentrated among those who are doubtful about the merits of having a Scottish Parliament.[5] According to the Scottish Social Attitudes Survey, on the occasion of the 2010 UK general election no fewer than 42 per cent of those who do not believe that there should be any kind of Scottish Parliament voted for the party. In contrast, just 16 per cent of the advocates of devolution did so, and unsurprisingly only 2 per cent of those who favour independence. Similarly, no fewer than 37 per cent of those who feel that the UK government should have most influence over the way that Scotland is run backed the party in 2010, compared with just 11 per cent of those who feel that the Scottish Government should have most influence. Meanwhile, unfortunately for the Conservatives, the vein of scepticism about the idea of Scotland having its own political institutions is now a very thin one indeed. Only one in ten

Table 8.2 Patterns of Conservative support, Scotland and England, 2010

% voted Conservative 2010 general election	Scotland	England
Gender		
Men	16	41
Women	16	41
Age group		
18–34	13	34
35–54	13	39
55+	19	46
Social class		
Employers, managers and professionals	21	42
Intermediate	12	40
Small employers and own account	28	48
Lower supervisory and technical	9	41
Semi-routine and routine	7	36
Religion		
Protestant	19	49
Catholic	8	25
None	15	38
National identity		
British	26	38
Scottish/English	13	47
Ideological stance		
Left	7	27
Centre-Left	8	40
Centre-Right	15	41
Right	37	57

Note: not all categories are shown in all instances. Social class is based on the National Statistics Socio-Economic Classification schema. Details of the derivation of ideological stance are given in note 6 at the end of this chapter. All figures are based only on those respondents who voted and declared how they voted, of whom there were 959 in Scotland and 595 in England.
Sources: Scottish Social Attitudes, British Social Attitudes (respondents living in England only)

do not want any kind of parliament at all (little more than half the equivalent proportion in 1997) while only 16 per cent think that the UK government should be more influential than the Scottish Government north of the border.

What we should also note, however, is that such scepticism as does exist north of the border is concentrated in particular sections of Scottish society. As many as 19 per cent of those on the Right of the ideological spectrum in Scotland[6] do not feel that there should be any kind of Scottish Parliament, around twice the proportion in the rest of Scottish society. Similarly, opposition to the Parliament is more common amongst small employers and own account workers (15 per cent) and those who are employers, managers or in a professional occupation (12 per cent). In other words, scepticism is relatively (albeit only relatively) common amongst those kinds of voters who might be thought most likely to support the Conservatives anyway. Consequently, the link that seemingly still exists in the public mind between the party and reticence about devolution would appear to be a potential barrier to the ability of the Scottish party to reach out much beyond its traditional sources of core support.

It is with that insight in mind that we should examine the figures in Table 8.2. The table shows the level of Conservative support in the 2010 UK general election among various different demographic and political groups. This information is presented separately for Scotland and for England, thereby enabling us to compare systematically the pattern of support for the party on the two sides of the border.[7] Some of the conclusions we have already reached are confirmed by the table. Thus, we can see that although the level of support for the Conservatives is higher amongst those on the Right in Scotland than it is amongst those on the Left, it is still lower than it is among those on the Right in England. More generally, the level of support for the party is lower in Scotland than it is in England across all demographic groups in the table. The party does not fare less well in Scotland because the social composition or ideological orientation of Scotland is different from that in England, but rather because it is less successful at winning the support of all sections of society in Scotland than it is in England.

At the same time, however, we should also note that the party's relative lack of success in Scotland in 2010 was greater among some groups than others. For example, the difference between the two countries in the party's level of support amongst employers, managers and professionals was, at twenty-one points, rather less than the equivalent figure of twenty-nine points among those in routine and semi-routine occupations. Similarly, at twenty points the difference in the level of support amongst those on the Right is greater than the thirty-two-point gap amongst those on the Centre Left. In other words, it looks as though in respect of social class and ideological orientation at least, Scottish Conservative support is more heavily concentrated than is its English counterpart among what would be usually regarded as the party's core constituency.[8] This is just what

Table 8.3   Patterns of Conservative support, Scotland and England, 1997

% voted Conservative 1997 general election	Scotland	England
Age group		
18–34	8	29
35–54	15	28
55+	18	37
Social class		
Salariat	26	38
Junior non-manual	10	34
Petty bourgeois	25	43
Foremen and technicians	9	18
Working class	3	19
Religion		
Protestant	18	39
Catholic	5	21
None	9	23
National identity		
British	28	32
Scottish/English	10	35
Ideological Stance		
Left	3	4
Centre-Left	3	15
Centre-Right	14	32
Right	46	67

Note: not all categories are shown in all instances. Social class is based on the Goldthorpe-Heath class schema;[9] the categories shown here are roughly analogous to those of the National Statistics Socio-Economic Classification schema used in Table 8.2. Details of the derivation of ideological stance are given in note 9 at the end of this chapter. All figures are based only on those respondents who voted and declared how they voted, of whom there were 686 in Scotland and 1,845 in England.
Source: British and Scottish Election Studies 1997

we would expect to find if the party's continued association with scepticism about devolution is indeed an impediment to its ability to secure electoral support.

Further evidence in support of that argument comes if we compare the position in 2010 with that in 1997 when the party was as its lowest ebb. Table 8.3 thus analyses the pattern of Conservative support on both sides of the border in 1997 in as similar manner as possible to the analysis of what happened in 2010 in Table 8.2. It suggests that at that election support for the party in England varied just as much, if not more, by class and ideological orien- tation[10] as it did in Scotland.[11] The party was struggling to win support outside its core constituency on both sides of the border. In contrast, by 2010 the revived English party had managed to garner support more broadly, whereas the Scottish party, encumbered by its perceived scepticism about devolution, remained largely within its traditional ghetto.

Conclusion

Scotland is certainly not particularly natural Tory territory. Overall its class composition and ideological orientation mean that it is always going to be somewhat harder for the party to win votes and seats north of the border. But that is not the principal problem facing the party, and it certainly does not account for its failure, in contrast to the position in England, to have enjoyed any measure of revival since 1997. Rather, the party has an image that is at odds with the predominant sense of Scottish identity that has long prevailed north of the border,[12] and, above all, appears to have little appeal for the vast majority of Scots who feel not only that the devolved institutions are here to stay, but also that they should constitute the pre-eminent layer of government in Scotland. That latter quality in particular appears to have made it very difficult for the Scottish Conservative Party to reach out beyond its core constituency and thereby share in the revival that its English counterpart enjoyed in 2010 south of the border. Given that the party's newly elected leader, Ruth Davidson, appears to share her party's traditional lack of enthusiasm about devolution, it is also hard to see how the Scottish Tories are going to manage to restore their fortunes any time soon.

Notes

1. J. Curtice, 'A return to two-party politics? Lessons of the 2011 local and devolved elections', *Public Policy Research* 18 (2011), pp. 88–96.
2. G. Mooney and L. Poole, 'A land of milk and honey'? Social policy in Scotland after devolution', *Critical Social Policy* 24 (2004), pp. 458–83; M. Keating, 'The territorialisation of interest representation: the response of groups to devolution', in J. Curtice and B. Seyd (eds), *Has Devolution Worked?* (Manchester, 2009); G. Scott and G. Mooney, 'Poverty and social justice in the devolved Scotland: neoliberalism meets

social democracy', *Social Policy and Society* 8 (2009), pp. 379–89.

3. Alex Salmond, Speech to SNP Conference, 13 October 2006; available at http://www.scotsindependent.org/features/alex_ salmond_perth_06.htm; Alex Salmond, Speech to SNP Conference, 18 March 2007; available at http://www.scot-sindependent.org/features/alex_salmond_glasgow_07.htm

4. Keating, 'The territorialisation of interest representation'; J. Curtice and R. Ormston, 'On the road to divergence? Trends in public opinion in Scotland and England', in A. Park, E. Clery, J. Curtice, M. Phillips and D. Utting (eds), *British Social Attitudes: the 28th Report* (London, 2011).

5. Multivariate analysis demonstrates, among all the associations considered in this chapter, that the association between attitudes towards Scotland's constitutional status and Conservative support is second only in strength to the association between Conservative support and a Left–Right ideological stance.

6. The 'ideological stance' variable used in the analysis of voting patterns in 2010 is a Likert scale based on the two items in Table 8.1, together with responses to the following three items: big business benefits owners at the expense of workers; there is one law for the rich and one for the poor; management will always try to get the better of employees if it gets the chance. The resulting interval level scale has values ranging from 1 (the most left-wing possible stance) to 5 (the most right-wing). This scale was then collapsed into four categories of roughly equal size as follows: Left = score of between 1 and 2; Centre-Left = score of more than 2 but no more than 2.5; Centre-Right = score of more than 2.5 but no more than 3; Right = score of more than 3. For further details about the scale see A. Park, J. Curtice, E. Clery and C. Bryson (eds), *British Social Attitudes: the 27th Report: Exploring Labour's Legacy* (London, 2010), pp. 235–7.

7. It will be noted that the number of cases on which the data for England are based is relatively small (595). We have therefore replicated as closely as possible the analysis in Table 8.2 using data from the 2010 British Election Study, which has a larger sample of voters in England (1,950) but a much smaller one in Scotland (458). The results are consistent with our argument here that the association between Conservative support and both social class and ideological stance was stronger in Scotland than in England.

8. This comment is confirmed by the results of logistic regression analyses of voting Conservative versus not-voting Conservative against all the variables listed in Table 8.2 and conducted separately for Scotland and England. For Scotland this analysis (conducted using a stepwise inclusion method) resulted in a Nagelkerke R^2 of 32 per cent, whereas for England the equivalent figure was only 16 per cent.

9. See J. Goldthorpe and A. Heath, *Revised Class Schema 1992* (Oxford, 1992).

10. Ideological stance is again measured here using a Likert scale, but some of the component items are different as is the derivation of some of the categories. The component items are: ordinary people do get their fair share of the nation's wealth; there is one law for the rich and one for the poor; there is no need for strong trade unions to protect employees' working conditions and wages; private enterprise is the best way to solve Britain's economic problems; major public industries ought to be in state ownership; it is the government's responsibility to find a job for everyone who wants one. The direction of the scores on the first, third and fourth items has been reversed before constructing the Likert scale. Left and Centre-Left are then derived as in the analysis for 2010, but Centre-Right = a score of more than 2.5 but less than 3, while Right = a score of 3 or more.

11. This comment is supported by the results of a logic regression analysis of the relationships illustrated in Table 8.3 conducted along similar lines to the analysis reported in note 8. At 45 per cent and 44 per cent respectively, the resulting Nagelkerke R^2 for Scotland and England are almost identical.

12. J. Curtice and B. Seyd, 'The citizens' response: devolution and the Union', in Curtice and Seyd, *Has Devolution Worked?*

CHAPTER 9

Refashioning Welsh Conservatism – a Lesson for Scotland?

David Melding AM

Introduction

The results of the first Scottish and Welsh general elections in 1999 were broadly similar. Labour failed to win outright in either country but was comfortably the largest party. A Labour–Liberal Democrat government followed immediately in Scotland and within seventeen months in Wales. The Nationalist parties came second, predictably enough in Scotland but the cause of some surprise in Wales. Indeed, just as 2011 was seen as a climacteric result for the SNP, so did the 1999 outcome seem for Plaid Cymru as it smashed through Labour bastions from Llanelli to the Rhondda and even Neil Kinnock's old constituency of Islwyn. Welsh Tories limped in third, in better shape than their Scottish cousins admittedly, but still well out of contention for government. The 2011 results could not have been more dissimilar, with Plaid failing comprehensively to match the SNPs vitality, Labour recovering substantially and the Welsh Conservatives securing a credible and comfortable second place. How did the Conservative and Labour parties tame the Nationalist menace and restore Wales to more regular, bi-polar politics? And will this success, if one views it as such, be sustained? This chapter will focus on the role played by Welsh Conservatives in devolved politics and how well they have adapted to a nationalist-lite political culture.

When examining the change in the relative fortunes of Plaid Cymru and the Welsh Conservative Party, a clear hypothesis is immediately apparent. Welsh Conservatives have become more small 'n' nationalist while Plaid has become less eclectic as a result of its attempt to make Labour obsolete. Few Tories drift into Plaid's column; there is no equivalent of Stirling in Wales. In fact the most striking result in 2011 was perhaps the Conservative gain in Aberconwy – a seat formerly held by one of Plaid's few Centre-Right members, Gareth Jones, who chose to retire. More generally, as Plaid vainly chased Labour in the old industrial heartlands, the Conservative vote increased in West and North Wales where Plaid has traditionally been strongest.

The path to Welsh Conservatism

Things did not start well for the Welsh Conservative Party. Its 1999 election manifesto was thin and strident, infamously containing a commitment to end 'linguistic apartheid'[1] in Wales. This was the work of the party's first campaign leader, Rod Richards. Richards is one of the intriguing 'what ifs' of Welsh politics. He seemed to have all the vital ingredients for inspired leadership: fierce intelligence, charisma and the ability to debate fluently in English and Welsh. But he was also strangely adrift of the popular mood and his style soon appeared needlessly aggressive and at odds with the more con-sensus-driven nature of devolved politics. Richards quickly left the scene as a result of misfortune and ill health, but not before his lead-ership had confirmed the Welsh Conservatives as archly sceptical on devolution. Richards had beaten his successor, Nick Bourne, in the first member-elected leadership contest in 1998. Party members all over Wales had enthusiastically endorsed the firm and unrepent-ant style that Richards instinctively embodied. Far from trying to detoxify the brand, Richards doubled the dose. Bourne's style was very different: urbane, academic and more at ease with the new political culture. The party's sceptical attitude to devolution did not change overnight but the need to change tone was immediately recognised by the new leadership.

As in Scotland, Conservative activists in Wales had found it difficult to warm to devolved politics. While hostility was gradu-ally replaced by mild acquiescence, Tory modernisers in Wales had rarely been able to push at an open door. The strong dependence culture within the party had been hard to shake off, making greater autonomy difficult. This was hardly surprising given that the Conservative Party in Wales, as it was so aptly named, had been led for ten years by a succession of English politicians prior to the referendum in 1997. After the crushing election defeat of 1997 there was a call for reform from some quarters, and strangely enough a similar call had been made with great force in the 1950s. Then the party had taken the first bold step in its Cymrification by adopting a well-thought-out and detailed policy platform for Wales (the first major party to do so). Other reforms were suggested but not implemented, including the establishment of stronger Welsh institutions, a distinct Welsh Conservative organisation and even a change of name.[2] This vivid picture of what a Welsh Conservative Party could look like suddenly attracted new admirers with the dawn of devolution.

Welsh devolution was very much a house half built in 1999. From the start the executive model of devolution was lopsided and broke the basic rules of British constitution building. Wales had a fairly powerful devolved government, but the Assembly's legislative powers were feeble and in no way adequate to check and scrutinise the executive. It was a bizarre convolution of the Westminster model where executive and legislative powers are closely matched. The National Assembly bore more resemblance to a tame legislative council of the colonial era. Had Labour sought to contain Welsh devolution by reversing this formula and devolving legislative but not executive powers, the ruse might have worked or at least endured for longer. Instead the Government of Wales Act 1998 never looked like a proper settlement and this created an opportunity for the Welsh Conservative Party to join the devolution-building project. The key moment came in 2004 when the Richard Commission published its authoritative report on the future of the National Assembly.[3] This recommended brisk progress to full legislative powers by 2011[4] (exactly what eventually transpired) and was signed by the Welsh Conservative Party's commissioner. It was true that the party never formally adopted a policy in favour of full legislative powers; the 2007 manifesto, however, promised to work within the provisions of the Government of Wales Act 2006 (hereafter GOWA 2006)[5] which paved the way for a stronger National Assembly. When the referendum provision was exercised under the Act in March 2011, it recorded two-thirds support for an Assembly with primary law-making powers. The party declared itself neutral in the referendum campaign but allowed members to support either side. Without doubt this was a major achievement for the pro-devolution wing of the party as the majority of Conservative Assembly Members actively supported a 'yes' vote, and none campaigned against. For a party with a stubborn English image, this shift in attitude helped to detoxify Welsh Conservatism.

This second chance on devolution was not really afforded Scottish Tories because the decision the people of Scotland were asked to make in 1997 was far more decisive and complete. After 2003 in particular, the Conservative group in the National Assembly adopted a more confidently pro-devolution line. In turn this helped the party defend much of its softer ground against Plaid Cymru. Had Plaid maintained its clear lead over the Welsh Conservatives, a leakage of Tory support to the Nationalist alternative would have been possible. Arguably this occurred to a considerable degree in Scotland where the distance between Scottish Conservatives and any prospect of government was an electoral barrier and encouraged some of a Tory disposition to vote SNP in order to keep Labour out. In 1999 Plaid beat the Welsh Conservative Party into third place by a considerable margin and just kept its nose in front in 2003. In 2007 there was a near dead heat between the parties in terms of votes cast, although the quirks of the electoral system ensured that Plaid won several more seats than the Welsh Conservatives.

A rainbow coalition – nearly

Well before the 2007 election Nick Bourne launched a campaign to detoxify the party and make it a potential coalition partner with the Liberal Democrats and Plaid Cymru. Extensive behind the scenes cooperation was sanctioned in the Assembly, and these confidence-building measures started to pay off when the Labour Welsh Assembly government became increasingly obdurate despite lacking a working majority. Labour suffered one of its worst ever results in a Welsh election in 2007 when its vote fell to 32 per cent. Again, the quirks of the electoral system saved Labour from the full consequences of this reverse, but it was lucky to hold twenty-six seats. Nevertheless, the scene was set for the formation of a non-Labour coalition.

At first, most thought the 'rainbow' coalition an utterly fanciful prospect. Labour certainly underestimated its viability and played its cards badly in the weeks immediately after the election. When the All Wales Accord[6] emerged – a full agenda for government agreed by Plaid, the Welsh Conservative Party and the Liberal Democrats – many observers were surprised and the Labour Party seemed utterly bewildered. How could a Welsh government not have the Labour Party at its heart? And, only slightly less shocking, how could the Tories get into government in Wales? Rather more easily than Rhodri Morgan was inclined to think! The Welsh Conservative Party's management board agreed the rainbow deal after consultation with David Cameron. Nick Bourne had been at his masterful best in persuading both the Shadow Welsh Secretary, Cheryl Gillan, and the Leader of the Opposition, of the need to grasp this historic moment. Within an hour of the management board's endorsement, however, the Liberal Democrats failed to back their leaders' judgement and the rainbow's chances were eclipsed. By the time the Liberal Democrat leadership had reversed this blunder, Plaid had decided the whole enterprise was too flaky and had agreed a deal with Labour. While there was bitter disappointment among Welsh Conservatives, there was satisfaction also that the party had shown itself ready to enter a coalition government and hence become a serious player in Wales.

Plaid probably suffered as a result of the rainbow's collapse too, although that was not clear at the time. It is difficult on the one hand to believe that Labour is obsolete and no longer fit to hold the mantle of Welsh radicalism, and on the other to join a Labour-led coalition. Furthermore, with the SNP taking on the challenge of minority government in Scotland, many were disappointed that Plaid did not take its opportunity to lead a government and send Labour into Opposition. Some murmured that Alex Salmond would have acted very differently from Plaid's leader, Ieuan Wyn Jones. More positively, after eighty years in the wilderness, Plaid became a party of government and most observers praised its ministers for the way they performed in office. The outstanding achievement from Plaid's point of view was the One Wales[7] coalition's commitment to hold a referendum on full legislative powers – a referendum that was comfortably won two months before the 2011 Assembly election. It was also striking that Labour and Plaid worked well together and the One Wales government appeared a coherent Left-of-Centre alliance. Yet this too came at a cost for Plaid as it seemed to be Labour's natural but junior partner. During the 2011 election campaign the Plaid leadership tried to keep the prospect of a Plaid-led government alive but, as this would inevitably have entailed an alliance with the Welsh Conservative Party, it was a strategy few believed in and those who did feared its consequences in seats such as Llanelli. Plaid did try to occupy the left flank of the One Wales government – notably by insisting on no market involvement, nor even any significant private sector involvement, in the NHS – but this drew fierce criticism from business groups and made it ever more difficult for Plaid to make inroads into soft Tory territory.

The Welsh Conservative Party's attempts to become a more autonomous force were only partly successful during this period; even so this paid dividends, at least among the politically engaged. While some senior figures considered the Scottish model of a distinct organisation desirable, the reforms introduced in 1998[8] only established a Welsh management board to exercise limited functions. More radical options – including the suggestion of a name change – were dismissed as fanciful as the Welsh Conservative Party was dependent on funding from Central Office. Rather lamely, the fiction that the head of the Welsh Conservative Party is the UK leader was maintained. Of course this meant that the Welsh Conservatives did not have a leader at all and the party appeared a derivative, not an indigenous, political force. Unsurprisingly this anomalous situation blunted the party's effectiveness when quick and bold decisions were necessary. This is best illustrated in the way the Welsh Conservative Party responded to calls for a referendum under the GOWA 2006. The Act allowed for a referendum on primary legislative powers if there was a two-thirds vote in favour in the Assembly and a simple majority at Westminster. Plaid had insisted on a referendum pledge as a condition of entering the One Wales coalition. There was no doubt that the call for a referendum would clear the two-thirds hurdle in the Assembly as there were not enough Welsh Conservative Assembly Members to block it had they wanted to (which they did not). It seemed a simple proposition, then, for the 2010 UK general election manifesto to state that a Conservative government would allow any request for a referendum to proceed. However, the Shadow Secretary of State for Wales, Cheryl Gillan, came under strong pressure from some senior party members to explore ways to block or deflect such a request for at least the life of a parliament. The Conservative group in the Assembly remonstrated strongly against any such machination, pointing out that it would massively confirm the image of

Welsh Tories as the English party. Eventually, David Cameron held a meeting with the main players and made it very clear that denying the people of Wales their say in a referendum would spell disaster. That the leader in the Assembly could not act with such authority confirmed the limits of decentralisation within the Conservative Party's structure.

Labour bounces back

The results of the 2011 election had profound implications for all of the major parties in Wales. Labour did best and succeeded in reversing some of the secular decline which seemed to have set in with devolution. Welsh Labour had assumed its dominance of Welsh politics would continue under devolution and a new political dynamic would not be created. By 2007 this complacent attitude was in shreds and even the charismatic Rhodri Morgan seemed to have few answers. However, in convincing his party to hold on to power through an alliance with Plaid, Morgan demonstrated foresight and great leadership. His successor, the reassuring and affable Carwyn Jones, reaped the benefits. Labour's share of the vote leapt by 10 per cent to 42 per cent and it gained four seats to reach a total of thirty. Close but no cigar – it now appeared unlikely that Labour could ever expect to win a working majority in a Welsh general election. However, Labour's grip on its heartland had been secured – remarkably it won every constituency in Glamorgan[9] (sixteen seats) and in particular its advance in Cardiff bode ill for its opponents.

Fourteen seats secured the Welsh Conservative Party second place. This was a gain of two seats on 2007 and surely confirmed the wisdom of Nick Bourne's decision to detoxify the brand and make it more visibly Welsh and pro-devolution. Despite this, first-past-the-post gains in constituencies ensured the loss of Nick Bourne's own list seat in Mid and West Wales. This inadvertent decapitation was accompanied by defeat of the dauphin, Jonathan Morgan, in Cardiff North. The party was now very much under new management. Plaid's poor performance – it lost four seats and finished on eleven – ensured the departure of its veteran leader Ieuan Wyn Jones. Leanne Wood convincingly won Plaid's leadership contest in March 2012. A self-proclaimed socialist–feminist–republican politician, she won on a strongly pro-independence ticket. The Liberal Democrats somehow held five of their six seats but the margins were very thin indeed and for a while it looked as if only Kirsty Williams, the leader, would win re-election.

And so this was the state of play as the parties engaged in what will probably be a challenging and definitive fourth Assembly term. It was likely that the Welsh Conservative Party and Plaid would face the same challenge – how to establish themselves as Labour's principal opponent. Labour felt that its position as the leading force in Welsh politics would not be overturned soon, and the Liberal Democrats merely hoped for survival. It was the Welsh Conservative Party/Plaid contest that was most intriguing, and one that might be most influenced by parallel political events in Scotland. As a party that still suffered the stigma of an English image, Welsh Conservatives would be well advised to look to Canada for inspiration when conducting the next stage of the party's development. In Canadian provinces it is political death to appear to be in the federal party's pocket. This would seem to suggest that the best way for the Welsh Conservative Party to develop is as an autonomous or even independent party in alliance with the UK Conservative Party. One model would be to allow the UK party to contest all Westminster elections and for the Welsh Conservative Party to contest only the Assembly elections. This would most closely follow Canadian practice and appears to be the best way to represent Welsh interests. Party members could have two membership cards: one for the UK party, one for the Welsh. Alternatively, the Bavarian option could be taken with the Welsh Conservative Party contesting all elections in Wales. Its MPs would then sit in alliance with their English colleagues in Westminster. Whichever direction is taken, the imperative is for a fully autonomous Welsh Conservative Party to operate in the Welsh Assembly. Without such organisational freedom, Welsh Conservatives will find their English image a difficult incubus to shift.

Founding a fully autonomous Welsh Conservative Party would be a highly federal development. It would also allow for federalism to emerge as the clear counter-offer to Scottish independence. In many ways this is the debate that has already started in Scotland but with great ambivalence in the Scottish Conservative Party. The repudiation of Murdo Fraser's vision for a new and independent Conservative movement in Scotland could impair the development of such a reformed Unionism. More optimistically, the election of Ruth Davidson as the *leader* of the party in Scotland was a major advance. What does seem to be true is that the Unionist reformation must be driven by Unionist parties in Scotland and Wales. The very act of rejuvenating the Union might provide the means to strengthen Conservatism in Scotland and Wales.

Meanwhile, Plaid must try to re-establish itself as the main opposition to Labour. Again the Scottish dimension is key as is the question of independence and whether Plaid mirrors the strategy of the SNP. With Plaid taking a more assertive pro-independence stance under Leanne Wood's leadership, an easy advance into the Centre-Right ground of Welsh politics is unlikely. A more nuanced approach that asserts independence as the first option but also leaves open the possibility of devo-max might yet win the day. As the SNP has found, this dual strategy would require some concept of what sort of British association might endure after 2014 or whenever the Scottish referendum is held. Devo-max would imply clear national development within the British state, while neo-independence would imply Welsh and Scottish states within some sort of British confederation. There are some voices in Plaid advocating the more subtle and flexible strategies now favoured by the SNP.

What if the people of Scotland vote for independence? Clearly Plaid would then focus on independence for Wales. Why continue in a reduced 'Little Britain', they would ask with great force. How would the Welsh Conservative Party and more generally the forces of Unionism respond? A well-balanced federal union would seem the only viable choice, but it might not appear very viable unless adopted as policy before the Scottish referendum. Otherwise, it could be dismissed as the last rather desperate throw of the Unionist dice. In abstract, federalism would seem doubly attractive to the Conservative Party as it represents the best chance to keep Scotland in the Union; and if this is not successful then the original British Union – England and Wales – might still have life in the event of Scottish independence. Yet in practice the Conservative Party has been deeply antipathetic towards federalism. This is a curious phenomenon and makes the party a rather peculiar entity in comparison to Centre-Right parties in other Western democracies. Such idiosyncrasy could now cost the party dear.

To conclude, the task facing Plaid Cymru is to combine its shift to the Left with the pragmatism needed to appeal to those in the tamer centre ground, a portion of the electorate that wants a robust alternative to Labour. For the Welsh Conservative Party the task is no less formidable. It is only by attracting more Nationalist-minded voters that it can secure its position as Labour's principal opponent. There is strong evidence in Wales, as there is in Scotland, that many Nationalist voters are prepared to accept, or even prefer, a constitutional future in the shape of a British federation of the Home Nations. Our Edwardian ancestors arrived at a similar realisation in respect of Ireland, but far too late to save the Union. By 1920 Irish Nationalist voters had despaired of changing Unionist culture in favour of a looser and more federal arrangement. If Conservatism remains a centralising constitutional ideology, history might very soon repeat itself.

On the face of it both Labour and the Welsh Conservatives have adapted well to devolution, but much work remains to be done if they hope to tame Nationalism with federalism. Labour did well in 2007 to embrace Plaid and accept much of its nation-building agenda in the One Wales government. It seemed to reap the benefits in 2011 under its avuncular and nationalist-lite leader, Carwyn Jones. The Welsh Conservative Party's success has been less vigorous in the sense that its main achievement has been to defend and recover the Centre-Right ground, ground that has been a lot more difficult for the Scottish Conservatives to defend. Through the steadfast work of its leader, Nick Bourne, the Welsh Conservative Party not only accepted the devolution 'project' but was prepared to make it stronger and more coherent. As a result, in the more Nationalist-friendly territory of North and West Wales the party has gained significant support. However, it has been less successful in direct clashes with Labour, as the results in Glamorgan demonstrated in 2011. Gains against Labour will have to be hard won but those against Plaid seem likely to endure if the party absorbs small 'n' nationalism into its culture and organisation.

Between 2007 and 2011 the Welsh Conservative Party underwent major change as its leadership attempted to detoxify the brand with a 'three Rs' remedy. The first 'R' was the putative rainbow alliance which demonstrated that the party was prepared to get its hands dirty and enter a coalition with Plaid Cymru. The party's credibility soared (at least amongst the political *crachach*). The referendum on primary law-making powers was the second 'R'. That nearly two-thirds of the electorate backed extra powers for the Assembly demonstrated just how fully devolution had been embraced by the electorate. While the Welsh Conservative Party was technically neutral, not one Conservative Assembly Member campaigned for a 'no' vote. The final 'R' is party reform. Here efforts to bring the spirit of devolution to the Conservative Party's own structures have only been partly successful. With colleagues in government at Westminster, this lack of organisational space between Welsh Conservatives and the UK party might yet prove troublesome.

Notes

1. Welsh Conservative Party, *Fair Play for All* (Cardiff, 1999), p. 12.
2. David Melding, *Will Britain Survive Beyond 2020?* (Cardiff, 2009), pp. 146–52.
3. Report of the Richard Commission on the Powers and Electoral Arrangements of the National Assembly for Wales (Cardiff, 2004). Available at http://www.richardcommission.gov.uk/content/finalreport/report-e.pdf
4. Ibid. p. 256, paragraph 23.
5. Welsh Conservative Party, *Vote Welsh Conservative for a Change* (Cardiff, 2007), p. 35.
6. John Osmond, *Crossing the Rubicon: Coalition Politics Welsh Style* (Cardiff, 2007), particularly Appendices 2 and 3.
7. Ibid.
8. Constitution of the Conservative Party (London, 1998), schedule 8.
9. The county no longer exists but if it did, it would be made up of the following constituencies: Aberavon; Bridgend; Cardiff Central; Cardiff North; Cardiff South and Penarth; Cardiff West; Cynon Valley; Gower; Merthyr Tydfil and Rhymney; Neath; Ogmore; Pontypridd; Rhondda; Swansea East; Swansea West; and the Vale of Glamorgan. This area was the heart of the South Wales coalfield and the commercial towns and ports that served it.

CHAPTER 10

The Press, National Identity and the Scottish Tories

Alex Massie

Introduction

The most important fact about the decline of the Scottish Conservative and Unionist Party is mercifully simple to grasp: it is difficult to find a successful right-wing party in Europe that is not considered, or does not consider itself, the patriotic party. Grasp this and you have grasped the heart of the matter. From this flows all the party's problems. It helps explain why the party is mistrusted by much of the electorate and why it has been ill served by its erstwhile cheerleaders in the press.

It is not, despite what is sometimes claimed, that Scotland is a land uniquely hostile to Conservatism, rather that Scotland's Right-of-Centre party boasts of a patriotism and a sense of the national interest that is at odds with the prevailing, and now long-established, trends in Scottish political life. The same might – and will – be said of much of the party's remaining support in the media.

The Tories remain a toxic brand in Scotland. There has been no active 'decontamination' project, merely the hope that the Conservatives' Scottish radioactivity will decay naturally. Alas, it seems to have a very long half-life. Though thoroughly scunnered by Gordon Brown's performance as Prime Minister, neither *The Scotsman* nor the *Herald* could bring themselves to endorse David Cameron's Conservatives at the 2010 general election, recommending instead that their readers exercise their franchise. Doubtless they did not wish to anger readers by suggesting a vote for the Tories.[1]

As matters stand in 2012, there seems every prospect that future political scientists and historians will note that the most significant development in Scottish politics in the later decades of the twentieth century was the decline in British consciousness and its gradual replacement by a renewed sense of 'Scottishness'.

This shift was evident across Scotland, even in settings that were not obviously political. It seems reasonable to suppose that few gatherings of 50,000 or more Scots are likely to contain as many Unionists as the crowd attending rugby internationals at Murrayfield. Yet even here, a revived 'Scottishness' was in evidence off the pitch: for decades, the Scotland team's anthem had been, like England's, 'God Save the Queen'. By 1990 the embarrassment of hearing home supporters boo and whistle their own anthem had persuaded the Scottish Rugby Union to switch anthems, replacing the national anthem with The Corries' maudlin 'Flower of Scotland'. This was a small but telling example of the national mood, not all of which by any means can be ascribed to the unpopularity of Margaret Thatcher's Conservative governments.

It was, rather, a longer-term process that, in some ways, accelerated after the Lady's fall. In 1974, 31 per cent of Scots answered 'British' to the question 'What nationality best describes you?'; by 2001 that figure was just 16 per cent. A more nuanced consideration reveals that while one in three Scots felt 'Equally Scottish and British' in 1992, fewer than one in four did so in 2001. Asked in that year to select 'something that is very important to you when you think of yourself', 'Being Scottish' was mentioned almost as often as 'Being a mother/father'. Forty-five per cent of respondents referenced their 'Scottishness'; just 11 per cent their 'Britishness'.

What is more, surveys reported that most Scots wanted the Scottish Parliament to enjoy greater powers. Asked the question 'Which institution(s) should have the most influence over the way Scotland is run?', 63 per cent of those who considered themselves 'Equally Scottish and British' wanted the Scottish Parliament to take the most prominent role. Even among those considering themselves 'More British than Scottish', or 'British not Scottish', Holyrood (51 per cent) bested Westminster (39 per cent).[2]

Many factors account for this change – the retreat from Empire, the fading memory of the shared sacrifices of the Second World War, the unpopularity of the Thatcher government – but what is evident is that the Scottish Conservative and Unionist Party has either ignored this shift in Scottish consciousness, preferred to deny it or, worse still, been actively hostile towards it. Whichever explanation you favour, it has ensured that the Tories are not only not the 'patriotic' party, they have come to be seen as the party most hostile to 'Scottishness' and any expressions of 'Scottishness'.

The impression, often unfair but nonetheless widespread, has been that Conservatives see Scotland and 'Scottishness' as second-best and certainly something subordinate to 'Britishness'. Or, to put it another way, any expression of a distinctive 'Scottishness' that challenges, downplays or marginalises 'Britishness' is deeply suspect and best avoided.

In this way, the Tories could not feel a current without wanting to swim against it. Before the 2007 Holyrood election, a poll[3] reported that 55 per cent of voters felt Alex Salmond could be counted upon to 'stand up for Scotland'. Just 24 per cent of respondents felt that could be said of the incumbent First Minister, Jack McConnell, and had the pollsters included the then Tory leader, Annabel Goldie, in this question, one fears she would have been found even more wanting than poor Mr McConnell.

In these circumstances the wonder is not so much that the Conservatives have lost so much support but that so many voters remain content to endorse a party that, by any sensible definition, is all but on its uppers. The Tories and, as we shall see, their supporters in the national press, have been out of step with Scottish opinion on the most fundamental parts of the national question for so long that one wonders quite how they have managed to survive at all. In their present enfeebled state, they are a reminder of what happens when a Right-of-Centre party is perceived, fairly or not, to have deserted its own country's flag.

It did not have to be this way. The Tories were once, younger readers may be astonished to discover, ahead of the devolution game. Edward Heath's Declaration of Perth, delivered in 1968, committed the party to a Scottish Assembly (though one with relatively few powers). In 1974 that pugnacious Glaswegian champion Teddy Taylor offered as one of his 'pledges to the people' his commitment to 'a Scottish Assembly to ensure that decision-making is removed from London'.[4] In 1979 the former Prime Minister Sir Alec Douglas-Home intervened in the devolution referendum, urging Scots to vote 'no' on the grounds that a Tory government would introduce a better Bill. Even when it became apparent this was unlikely, he continued to maintain that, 'I'm a decentraliser, and the more you decentralise, to my mind, the better.'[5]

The failure to act on Douglas-Home's promise helped ensure that the Tories would lose the respect of much of civic Scotland. Thatcherism might have scunnered many Scots in any case but the party's constitutional bad faith could only further erode whatever trust remained between the party and at least some of the people whose favour it sought.

The 1980s were difficult, stormy times for Conservatives in Scotland, reaching their nadir with the (Scots-designed) poll tax introduced in Scotland a year ahead of England being taken as 'proof' Scotland was as vulnerable and exploited as a sad beagle in an animal-testing lab. This was a myth, but a potent one impervious to reason or the simple explanation that a looming and dependably unpopular rates revaluation persuaded the government to introduce the Community Charge north of the border a year before it was due to come into force in England and Wales. Here, on top of all else (especially the decline of heavy industry), was 'proof' Tories could not be 'real' Scots.

The Iron Lady's defenestration offered only a short respite. Indeed, the trouble really began after John Major's unexpected victory in 1992. The Prime Minister believed his soapbox defence of 'the Union' contributed to the Tories' minor resurgence in Scotland (in which they picked up one seat). Regardless, the impression – eagerly encouraged by newspapers and, especially, the BBC – was that Scotland was governed by an alien party, hostile to Scottish interests.

The so-called 'democratic deficit' stripped Major's government of its legitimacy. George Galloway, among many others, took to the airwaves to announce the formation of a group called Scotland United, arguing the Tories had no right to govern Scotland. Voting Conservative, in this analysis, was not a matter of expressing different political preferences but tantamount to some kind of treason. Scotland was occupied by a hostile, illegitimate power and, with little exaggeration, those who supported the occupiers could be compared to Marshal Pétain's followers in Vichy France.

The Major government's response was as earnest as it was impossibly inadequate. Reconvening the Scottish Grand Committee could only be a sop. Returning the Stone of Scone to Scotland was a splendid, even romantic, piece of political theatre but scarcely relevant to the unwelcome realities of late-twentieth-century Scottish politics. These measures, and others like them, sent half a signal. They acknowledged there was something unsatisfactory about how Scotland was governed. But though the Major government, amply stocked with Scots, hinted something would have to be done to address the electorate's clearly expressed grievances, it stopped far short of doing anything that might satisfy Scots' evident desire for a measure of Home Rule.

This was not a promising place from which to campaign. Conservative opposition to devolution was often principled but Unionism's last ditch would be choked with the bodies of the honourable dead. Since the press was almost uniformly in favour of devolution, Tory hostility to what had become, whether the party accepted this or not, in John Smith's immortal phrase 'the settled will of the Scottish people' helped strip away any remaining sympathy the press might have for the Conservative perspective.

After 1997 no matter how much the party protested that it accepted the people's verdict and had made its peace with devolution, the impression persisted that there was something perfunctory about this contrition. The press, like the public, was not interested in hearing from the Tories. For many, it seemed, opposing devolution meant forfeiting the right to comment on devolution's shortcomings. Not that the party made much noise. In a crowded market place, only the pushy and the loud are heard and since 1997 the Scottish Tories have been timid creatures. There was some sense to this: the electorate told the party a period of silence on its part would be welcome. This message was heard and obeyed; a party accused of failing to listen when in government seemed, when in Opposition, only too happy to say nothing at all.

Had the purdah period been spent refashioning Toryism for a changed Scotland, this could have been a useful opportunity for taking stock. This did not happen. Writing in 2006, Michael Fry, by then a lapsed Tory converted to the independence cause, made the acid observation that 'The Scots Tories, nine years on, neither uphold their old policies nor seek new ones – they prefer to have no policies at all.'[6]

By the time Holyrood had bedded itself in, the Tories had become a party so feart and lacking in self-respect it lost the respect even of some journalists, such as Fry, who might, all other matters being equal, be expected to support it. In the first dozen devolution years few Right-of-Centre journalists ever offered the Scottish Conservative and Unionist Party their unequivocal backing. Since the party proved incapable of generating ideas for itself it was unusually dependent upon outside voices to provide some kind of spark.

Alas, few of the remaining Conservative voices in the Scottish media have distinguished themselves in recent years either. Though there are exceptions, such as Allan Massie,[7] Bill Jamieson and Andrew McKie, who have generally resisted the invitation to panic over every punch Alex Salmond throws, many of the other Right-of-Centre voices commenting on Scottish affairs appear determined to reinforce past Conservative failures with fresh failures of precisely the same kind. Contra Talleyrand, they have forgotten everything and learned nothing.

So long as Labour ruled its Scottish fiefdom this was, if you will, easily tolerated. It did not matter much. But with the Salmond Ascendancy everything changed. At a stroke it became apparent that leading Tory commentators preferred a Labour ministry in Edinburgh to one led by Salmond. That, of course, was a respectable opinion even if it also meant treating the Union as a static object of quasi-religious devotion. Nevertheless, it is hard to imagine anything worse for Scottish Conservatism than that it should be identified as the home for last-ditch Unionism and nothing else. The future of Centre-Right politics in Scotland to some extent depends upon the Tories' ability to escape that trap.

The High Priest of the Last Ditch was Gerald Warner, who wrote of the 2007 election campaign in strikingly apocalyptic tones. Tory voters, he said, must 'save the Union' and do so

> if necessary, by voting Labour on one ballot paper out of three. They should do so with a clear conscience, on the honourable principle of country before party. They owe nothing to a Scottish Tory party so lukewarm in defence of the Union it would not even mention it in its manifesto: in this single-issue election, the Tories ignored the issue.[8]

With friends like these, the Tory party had no need for enemies. Better an incompetent, disastrous Labour ministry than a semi-competent Nationalist government! Why *would* voters get the impression the Tories are 'anti-Scottish' when Tory commentators sometimes seemed uninterested in the quality of the Scottish government?

Warner might be dismissed as a mere Jacobite entertainer were it not for the fact he was hardly alone. Conservatives have been crying wolf about 'separatism' for years. In the last days of the 1997 election, John Major claimed there were only '72 hours to save the Union'.[9] Even by the debased standards of electioneering hyperbole this was dire stuff. And yet it continued: leading Conservatives such as Michael Forsyth warned against 'appeasing' the Nationalists as though it were a zero sum game. According to Forsyth, 'Any policy which appeases nationalists is damaging to the union by definition.'[10] Tory pragmatism, the core of the party's identity and success, was sacrificed to ideological demands that Conservatives still, in the phrase coined and made famous by William F. Buckley, stand 'athwart history athwart history, yelling Stop, at a time when no one is inclined to do so, or to have much patience with those who so urge it'.[11]

Unfortunately for the Tartan Buckleys, the Tories had lost the argument. Poll after poll suggested the electorate favoured the transfer of more powers to Edinburgh. Screaming 'stop' when the light is green is the kind of behaviour liable to provoke odd looks from passers-by. If Conservatives believed Scotland would be worse governed if Holyrood was responsible for raising at least some of its revenue they should have said so. They did not say so, however, though perhaps this was only because they feared being accused of 'talking Scotland down'. Instead the impression given, fairly or not, was that Tory hostility to fiscal accountability, or fiscal autonomy, or devo-max, or whatever else it was called, was based principally on the fact that Alex Salmond and the SNP approved of the idea. It was a poor and purely reactive kind of politics.

Perhaps it was axiomatic that Tory Unionists believed Scotland would be impoverished – financially and culturally – by independence, but the choice in 2012 was not a binary one between the status quo and a wholly separate Scottish state. Writing in the *Spectator* in the aftermath of Salmond's remarkable election triumph in 2011, Iain Martin usefully summarised the paleo-Unionist viewpoint thus:

> The devolutionists aimed to kill Scottish nationalism by setting up a parliament in Edinburgh. To put it mildly, this has not gone according to plan. When home rule was introduced by New Labour, it was obvious to many of us on both sides of the border that such crackpot constitutional changes would weaken the United Kingdom and imperil its survival. Wouldn't giving power to Scotland only boost the SNP and create an appetite for more concessions? So, alas, it has proved.[12]

The persuasiveness of this argument was moot since there was little benefit to be gained from rehashing pre-devolution arguments. It was one thing to say 'we told you so', quite another to offer no proposals that might ameliorate the original devolution 'settlement'. Moreover, while thwarting Nationalism – 'killing it stone dead', as George Robertson put it – was one devolutionary aim (or one aim for some devolutionists) it was hardly or rarely the principal goal. That, accurately or not, was the better and more accountable governance of Scotland. Conservative commentators spent years mocking the 'wee parliament', relentlessly dripping scorn upon its shortcomings, but they rarely offered ideas to make it work better. If Tories had chosen a form of intellectual internal exile for themselves then they could scarcely complain when matters developed in ways they considered unfortunate, distasteful and regrettable. The political game, if you will, is played by players, not by those chirping from the sidelines.

Furthermore, the Conservative obsession with constitutional issues to the exclusion of almost all else reinforced the impression that Tories feared Scottish assertiveness must inevitably weaken the Union. International comparisons should be treated gingerly but it is worth observing that Spain and Canada have arranged for Quebec and the Basque country (and Catalonia) to enjoy greater fiscal powers than those available to Holyrood without compromising the future of Greater Canada or Greater Spain. Scotland might have been a different case but that had not been proven so. Not by 2012, at any rate.

The Unionist fear that any 'concession' to the SNP must move Scotland towards independence was a symptom of a crushing lack of confidence that sometimes seemed to manifest itself as a form of schizophrenia. The *Daily Telegraph*'s Alan Cochrane, for instance, observed that 'No matter how the Nats try to massage the opinion poll figures, support for independence remains where it has been for a generation – at about one third'.[13] On one hand, Salmond was depicted as playing a minority position skilfully, while on the other he was portrayed as a political Pied Piper hoodwinking Scots into following him to independence. The 'threat' was containable yet the alert position had always to be set at DEFCON1.

Despite the fevered ravings of the Conservative commentariat, the Union was not 'at risk'. Moreover, the guarantee of a referendum on the question ensured it would be protected by the good sense and sound judgement of the Scottish people. If support for

independence had been, with some fluctuations, stable for a generation, it seemed sensible to conclude that what Scots wanted was
the ability to control a greater share of their own affairs within
the United Kingdom. Polling confirmed this: 67 per cent of voters
wanted much greater fiscal autonomy while nearly 40 per cent of
SNP supporters did not support independence.[14]

Yet, not content with having been behind the curve of history
in the pre-devolution years, the Tories seemed determined to miss
another opportunity and one that, this time, actually advanced
traditional Tory ideas. Fiscal autonomy, complex though its workings might be, was the beginning of a plausible route back to relevance for Right-of-Centre politics in Scotland. A parliament that
did not raise its own revenue could not possibly be as disciplined
or accountable as a parliament that did. The people had moved;
a political party that craved relevance should have accepted this
and moved too, especially when doing so would have advanced
Conservative principles.

Or it would have had the party not been so afraid of doing
anything that might also have pleased Alex Salmond. Nothing
more effectively illustrated the feebleness of Scottish Conservatism
than this reluctance to follow its own interests, subordinating
everything instead to a misplaced and unnecessary constitutional
hand-wringing. Paleo-Unionism may have been the easiest way of
ensuring a warm reception at the party's annual conference and the
members may have remained resistant to significant change, but
relying on the 'core vote' had ceased to be a viable strategy. At some
point, it seemed clear, that core vote would die.

The Conservative press still refused to acknowledge this. Before
Ruth Davidson assumed the party leadership, the *Daily Telegraph*
editorialised that 'the Conservatives' woes are primarily due to
personality, not identity'.[15] Nothing could be further from the
truth. David McLetchie and Annabel Goldie had each been seen
as reasonably capable figures doing their best. Goldie, especially,
won admirers for her twinkly-couthy style and occasional candour.
She was generally held to have enjoyed a 'good' election in 2011.
And a fat lot of good that had done the Scottish Conservative and
Unionist Party. Identity mattered and the Scottish Tories had lost
theirs.

What was the Conservative vision for Scotland? The constitutional obsession had crowded out all else. Since the Tories remained
wary of real fiscal autonomy they lacked the standing to make a

strong argument for a lower-taxed, higher-enterprised Scotland; since they remained timid the educational reforms Michael Gove was pushing through the English system remained too bold for Scotland. Other policy cupboards were just as bare.

There were many potential Scotlands but in 2012 the electorate was offered the choice of just two: an unimaginative Labour Party or an SNP that, however much one may have disagreed with individual Nationalist policies, evidently had a faith in Scotland and its people that too often did not appear to be shared by the Conservatives or their supporters in the press. That was a platform for permanent Conservative irrelevance. It may have been that Tory commentators were correct and that transferring further powers to Holyrood would have 'endangered' the Union. Perhaps that slippery slope was not wholly imaginary. But embracing the opportunity afforded by greater fiscal autonomy remained the best hope for a Conservative revival. It may have been that to save the Union it must first have been put at some greater risk. The future of Scottish Right-of-Centre politics, however, demanded that the Conservatives awaken from their slumber, screw their courage to the sticking place and, at last, accept that the electorate had moved and therefore so must they. They should have heeded the advice given by Giuseppe di Lampedusa in his great Sicilian novel *The Leopard*: 'Everything must change so that everything may stay the same.' Scotland was changing but remained, in 2012 at least, within the Union. This, for Scottish Conservatives, was no time to be afraid.

Notes

1. http://politics.caledonianmercury.com/2010/05/05/newspapers
   -line-up-behind-their-chosen-parties-or-not/
2. Ross Bond and Michael Rosie, 'National identities in post-devolution Scotland', *Scottish Affairs* 40 (summer 2002), pp. 34–53.
3. http://cdn.yougov.com/today_uk_import/YG-Archives-pol-stim
   es-ScotParlElections-070423.pdf
4. *Spectator*, 10 March 1979.
5. Quoted in Lindsay Paterson (ed.), *A Diverse Assembly: The Debate on a Scottish Parliament* (Edinburgh, 1998), p. 131.
6. http://www.prospectmagazine.co.uk/2006/12/scotlandalone/
7. The present author's father. Make of that what you will.

8. *Scotland on Sunday*, 29 April 2007.
9. http://www.bbc.co.uk/news/special/politics97/background/pastelec/ge97.shtml
10. http://conservativehome.blogs.com/thetorydiary/2011/09/after-twenty-years-of-scottish-tory-failure-its-time-for-a-made-in-scotland-conservative-party.html
11. http://www.nationalreview.com/articles/223549/our-mission-statement/william-f-buckley-jr
12. Iain Martin, 'How to save the Union', *Spectator*, 14 May 2011.
13. *Daily Telegraph*, 17 December 2011.
14. http://www.ipsos-mori.com/researchpublications/researcharchive/2856/Scots-back-full-fiscal-powers-but-not-independence.aspx
15. *Daily Telegraph*, 4 September 2011.

CHAPTER 11

'Handbagging' the Feminisation Thesis? Reflections on Women in the Scottish Conservative and Unionist Party[1]

Antje Bednarek

Introduction

If one believes that scholarship for its own sake is decadence then there is hardly ever a reason to investigate a subject matter unless it is perceived as at least somewhat problematic. Working with this humble premise, Scottish Conservatives, who are to date a thoroughly under-researched topic, should soon cease to be so, and indeed the present collection of essays may well be the turning point in that process. For problems abound in the Scottish Conservative Party. For instance, Scottish Conservatives have famously been likened to a rare species which, living somewhere out there in the political wilderness, is quite hard to spot.[2] This is a problematic situation sure enough, both for the rare Tory who wants to survive as well as for the social or political naturalist interested in rarities. A related and equally fascinating problem is that politics is a masculine-coded field, that the Conservative Party has a track record of not supporting positive discrimination of female candidates and that, at the same time, feminisation has been a declared goal of the Conservative Party since David Cameron became party leader. Something is clearly out of kilter here – in light of the presumed rarity of Conservatives north of the border one might even want to ask if there are any Scottish Conservative women at all. Of course there are, but what do we know about them? Who are they and what do they do?

Although efforts have been undertaken to contextualise our knowledge of Conservative women generally, to date Scottish Conservative women are an especially neglected topic.[3] Possible reasons for that are not hard to find. The comparative rarity of Scottish Conservative women – the party is not that large, after all – may account for this to an extent. Furthermore, it is still mainly women, and feminists at that, who research topics to do with women, and as Julia Bush observed in her formidable study on anti-suffragettes in Britain, 'the boundaries of feminist history are severely stretched by the inclusion of more conservative women'.[4] Those who have been interested in women in politics (not many) and those interested in Scottish politics (even fewer) were more interested in Communist women than members of the Scottish Conservative Party, or in female activists rather than 'ordinary' party members.[5]

In contradistinction to some of the recent work in political science which considers policy changes in relation to female participation in politics, I want to focus on the 'ordinary', average female member of the Scottish Conservative Party. The Conservative Party still has a larger female membership than any of the other parties.[6] Yet the relative absence of 'average' women from party politics and the dearth of knowledge that we have on them as members of the Scottish Conservatives together perpetuate some of the common stereotypes at large about Conservative women. One is of Conservative women incessantly making tea and buns;[7] other stereotypes of Conservative women as 'glamour girls' or the so-called 'blue-rinse brigade' also abound. The mainly insubstantial and undesirable meanings of these stereotypes remain unchallenged, which perhaps is also due to the comparative insignificance of the Scottish Conservative Party in the eyes of the Scottish voters and (evidently) scholars alike. Feminist and other researchers, in short, may consider Conservative women anathema to their research foci and disciplinary dispositions and therefore simply neglect them as a research subject.

The way I want to penetrate the silence about Scottish Conservative women is by focusing on the figures of speech in use about them. These figures of speech, whilst widely used in public, refer to women's roles and activities in the party outside the eye of the public. I want to refer to this sphere as the private sphere and to the sum of what can be found out about women participating in it as a 'private' account, i.e. one that can only be gained from the perspective of an insider to the party. This private account is offset by the public account, which is the comparatively well-covered sphere of Parliamentary politics and representative functions that political scientists focus on. I will briefly sum up what can be said about Scottish Conservative women there, and then will proceed to attend to the private account.

The public account: representation and feminisation

The publicly available account about Scottish Conservative women is quickly summarised. The proportion of female Conservative representatives at Holyrood is currently 40 per cent and thus above the 35 per cent threshold of female participation that is thought to effect organisational culture in the direction of greater inclusivity.[8] Six out of fifteen Scottish Conservative MSPs are women. Of these, Annabel Goldie MSP is widely known, as is Conservative MSP Mary Scanlon whose work in the health policy area is recognised across the political parties in Holyrood.[9] Ruth Davidson's rise to party leadership has put a young and openly lesbian Conservative woman into the political limelight.

That '40 per cent' translates into a mere six female Conservative MSPs aptly demonstrates the magic that numbers can achieve for representative purposes; nonetheless, as regards representation one can hardly speak of an absence of Conservative women in Scotland. On the contrary, like the other political parties in Scotland, Conservative women have also taken leading positions in the devolved Parliament. In fact, the proportion of female members of the Scottish Parliament (34 per cent) and of the National Assembly for Wales (28 per cent) is currently higher than in the Westminster Parliament (22 per cent).

As regards public representation, then, the Scottish Conservative Party is already much better placed than its counterparts in any other of the British nations. Why is that? When political parties are in disarray it is easier for women to establish their presence in politics.[10] This is as true in times of inner-party crisis as it is for restructuring political systems. During the 1990s, as constitutional reforms were discussed in the lead-up to the devolution settlements in Northern Ireland and Scotland, 'women in both countries mobilised to place gender within reform agendas, to promote women's political representation and to influence constitutional change'.[11] Party-related groups were set up, as was a cross-party group, the Scottish Women's Co-ordination Group (SWCG), which worked under the umbrella of the Scottish Trade Union Council (STUC).[12] Unlike in the English Conservative Party, which according to Rosie Campbell and associates has in the recent past witnessed the efforts of Conservative female activists, Scottish Conservative women have on the whole remained uninvolved in gender politics.[13] They were not part of the SWCG but have obviously reaped the benefits of a changing culture towards more female involvement in the Scottish Parliament anyway, as was evidenced by the fact that 17 per cent of sitting Conservative MSPs in the first Scottish Parliament of 1999–2003 were women.[14]

However, the overall proportion of female representatives at Holyrood has dropped since 1999. The downward trend is due to the alignment of the Scottish political status quo in terms of gender participation in politics with the staidness of the Westminster Parliament. In other words, as the erstwhile comparatively disorderly political situation stabilises, opportunities for policy innovation become fewer and women lose ground again.[15] Politics is and thus remains a masculine-coded field.

Despite the increase in visibility of Conservative women in Holyrood, then, all is not well in public perception. Besides, the Conservative Party has opposed positive discrimination so vehemently in the past – not least under the magnanimous Margaret Thatcher herself who notoriously said about female activists to her Cabinet ministers, 'if they have their way, you'll soon be having the babies'[16] – that the implication that women's various roles have little to do with substantive representation, i.e. one that demonstrates a strong concern with gender equality, is always in the offing. From there it is only a small step to the allegation that women's presence in all sectors of the political field, be it formal or informal, voluntary or Parliamentary politics, is always only symbolic.[17] Gender equality, in other words, far from being a worthy goal for the Scottish Conservative Party, is a useful image improvement tool, for feminisation, it is said, 'signals party "modernisation" to an electorate that has turned away from the party'.[18]

The meaning of feminisation is not exhausted by increasing the proportion of female members alone. Such positive change must come with a concomitant change in attitudes towards the role of women in the party as well as a shift in policy focus on concerns that are of vital substantive interest to women. The comparatively high number of highly visible Conservative MSPs can thus mean very little in terms of party modernisation – which, judging by the electoral failures of the Conservatives in Scotland in 2010 and of the Scottish Conservatives in Holyrood in 2011, is urgently required – if it is not undergirded by a simultaneous real readiness to change. In other words, the public account about women in the Scottish Conservative Party needs to be contextualised by the private account of the same. By that I do not mean to suggest that there is something like a 'dirty underbelly' to politics that one also always needs to look at. What I mean is rather that the political field is not defined by formal rules alone. Much political activity takes place informally and outwith the public eye – essentially in the privacy of party organisation.[19] What I want to do is go beyond looking at the percentage figures of women's representation in Parliament into ordinary party members' lives which take place within that inner-party private realm.

A closer look at how Conservative women present themselves to other Conservatives and how they are subsequently perceived and discussed within the Conservative field provides the necessary material for pursuing this question here. In looking at the private sphere I draw on observation data and interview material with seventeen young Conservatives and three older Conservatives, gathered between 2008 and 2010.

The private account: Conservatives about Conservative women

Young Conservatives through and with whom I entered the Conservative field are not, it should be pointed out straight away, 'ordinary' party members. Aged between eighteen and thirty, my research participants were in fact two to three decades younger than the average member of the Conservative Party who, in 2008, was 51.9 years old.[20] As most of them were students they were neither in gainful employment nor homeowners, as the majority of party members are. However, as potentially 'tomorrow's leaders'[21] of the Conservative Party in Scotland, they are embedded in the Conservative field, meaning they use its language and participate in the actions and interactions that, seen in total, constitute what it means to be a member of the Scottish Conservative Party.

Their position in the party hierarchy is often experienced as depressingly low, and one of the results of that is that young

Conservatives passively participate in inner-party discourse rather than suggest new directions (as the Young Conservatives so irreverently did in the 1960s and 1970s) so as to prove their worth to their elders and subsequently rise in the party hierarchy.[22] This means that young Conservatives, like most other members of the party, are part of a field whose essential character and internal workings largely precede them and which they cannot easily change. 'Siphoning off', as it were, how young Conservatives reflect on gender thus opens a path into what could be called 'Scottish Conservative culture', culture here meaning mindsets, thoughts and attitudes as well as associated behaviours.

Conservative women were spoken about in several ways by the young Conservatives. Positive reference was made repeatedly to the hard-working 'girls' who 'run' the youth branch of the Scottish Conservative Party, Conservative Future Scotland (CFS), and who are also heavily involved in organisational matters in University Conservative Associations (UCAs) of which there are currently eight in Scotland.[23] As the way in which women's contributions are positively highlighted among young party members draws structurally as well as semantically on the 'women-as-tea-makers' and the 'Conservative glamour-girl' metaphors, I want to examine these two first. A different and, on the whole, more negative way in which women were made reference to was as members of the 'blue-rinse brigade', which is the third type of Conservative woman that I want to discuss. Less explicitly commented upon but nonetheless clearly identifiable, the 'handbag-wielding matron' is the fourth type of Conservative woman that can be encountered and that I will describe in the following paragraphs.

'Conservative women make tea and buns'

Women quickly assumed a highly prominent role in my perception of the Conservative field, not least of all thanks to the housekeeping and organisational duties that they seemed to jump at wherever they were. Among the young Conservatives, women arranged venues and speakers for dinners, conceptualised and arranged social nights out and generally took care of most other organisational matters also. Early on in my time with the young Conservatives their then-president told me that 'the best members are "the girls"' and that 'it is them who have the brains and who run the Association'. I learned quickly that this was indeed a true statement. The female members did not only clean up the meeting room before the weekly meetings so that everyone could feel comfortable in it, one of the 'girls' in the end succeeded the male president to become leader of the UCA herself. CFS has seen female leaders too in recent years and their work has also been praised highly.

It is not always easy to tell, says David Jarvis, 'whether [such praise is] born of affected political correctness or affected gallantry'.[24] From the very beginning, Conservative women were involved in politics as behind-the-scenes movers rather than front-row shakers and much party organisation depends on it staying that way.[25] The first female members of the Conservative Party came together as members of the Primrose League, which strongly defended the separation of men's and women's lives into discrete spheres. The public sphere, quite in line with Victorian social thought, was considered 'natural' male territory and the domestic sphere that of femininity. It was part of the Primrose League's members' 'imperial responsibility' to uphold these and other 'Conservative principles' as the sworn supporters of the male (and mostly aristocratic) elite.[26] Female members of the Primrose League, amongst other things, resisted the extension of the suffrage to 'irresponsible' and 'untried' male electors who had neither wealth nor standing to commend them. Speaking to small female audiences, aristocratic ladies lobbied with 'feminine gentility' against the extension of male suffrage behind the scenes in so-called 'drawing-room meetings'.[27]

Publicly, Conservative women thus became involved in politics as men's help, while their activities in local associations, i.e. outwith the public eye, continued to consist of making and drinking tea. There were strong overtones of class and privilege associated with the tea-making stereotype back then. 'Drawing-room meetings', however, lose their elegant overtone quickly in the hustle and bustle of a lively local association, and making tea was increasingly seen as the only organised activity – and a rather housewifely one at that – that Conservative women were engaged in.[28] This is where the stereotype of Conservative women as tea-makers originated. It is not an inherently negative one, nor has it been intended as disparaging of women. On the contrary, it is considered an acknowledgement of the essential ontogenetical differences between the sexes, and these differences must be heeded rather than forcefully equalised (which is how opponents to the feminist cause often misrepresent feminism; see Mrs Thatcher's quote above). Nonetheless, outside the

Conservative field the tea-making metaphor is hardly ever a positive one; it is often used by outsiders to the party in question with the aim of belittling Conservative women's involvement in politics, as Rachel Ward observed in relation to Unionist women in Northern Ireland.[29]

That it is the women who make the tea and that this is quite the way it should be is a view that is perpetuated within the party itself. An interesting incident in that regard ensued at the CFS Conference in 2008. The young Conservatives, somewhat disgruntled at the time about being put to use mainly as 'bodies' who do leafleting, but who are not allowed to participate in more serious and *much* more appealing aspects of constituency organisation such as strategy planning, attended the conference poised to meet Conservative MSPs whom they wanted to convince of their great potential and superior skill level (e.g. with computers). The general attitude just then was, here in the words of one of my research participants, 'There's a lot of old Tories, old and grey, and you know we're the younger generation, we can get a lot done.'

At some point during the conference it must have seemed that they were complaining about having to help with canvassing at all, and Nanette Milne MSP presently admonished them for that in her little speech. 'When I was a young Conservative, working in my local association meant making lots of tea and scones,' she said, pointing out that this is simply where a young Conservative's apprenticeship begins, at least for female Conservatives. In Mrs Milne's case, making tea and scones did eventually lead to her having a rather private meeting with Margaret Thatcher a few years later (at which Mrs Thatcher apparently exclaimed concernedly: 'I just don't understand why the Scots don't like me!'). Such close contact with the party leader and an overall successful political career narratively reinforced Nanette Milne's point that the tea-making, or, in the case of some of the young Conservatives she had spoken to, the leafleting stage was a necessary and ultimately useful one.

Such is the received wisdom. There is indeed a pattern in existence in local associations whereby women are in charge of providing food and drink at social events and very little else besides. This pattern is by now entrenched and a mainstay of Conservative women's engagement in their local associations, and the following statement found in a Conservative Party paper of 1957 that 'women's sections provided almost all the "social" activity required by all the other sections of the Party organisation' still applies today.[30] It is not the case that women only and exclusively provide the tea and buns and that their political activity exhausts itself therein; but if tea and buns are being provided and if a social event does take place in both cases it is a group of women who put it together. However, it is not always tea they supply: a fundraising barbecue I attended in the summer months following the CFS Conference came to pass thanks to the generous support of a constituency member who offered her castle grounds as a venue, and the elderly lady herself happily mixed Pimm's cups for the attending guests.

The Conservative 'glamour girl'

A marked difference between Conservative women as regards age and position within the party hierarchy becomes apparent in the above comments. Although the stereotypical image of Conservative women as tea-makers is a widely shared one, it is hardly ever thought to apply to young party members. If young Conservatives come close to the activities captured by the first stereotype, it is in generally assuming housekeeping duties when necessary. Talking about *young* Conservative women, it is altogether more suitable to conclude that 'where women did not provide the tea, they were often consigned to another traditional role – that of providing the "glamour"'.[31] The second type of Conservative woman that I want to focus on, therefore, is the 'glamour girl'.

Being perceived as a 'glamour girl' can be quite problematic such as when the perception of a woman's official role becomes synonymous with her feminine attire and the female representative's political presence becomes sexualised as result. This happened often with Theresa May when she was party chairman.[32] On the other hand, glamorous women in highly visible positions in the party hierarchy supposedly signal feminisation, which helps secure the female vote. Men are also attracted to join, if for different reasons. This was a familiar insight for the Young Conservatives even in the 1950s, who were rumoured to be 'the best marriage bureau in the country', a description they welcomed as it suggested social success and this aided recruitment.[33] Women in visible positions in the party hierarchy thus make the party 'look good' in two distinct ways, as well as to a broad and rather mixed audience.

Accepting me as a researcher into their midst, an important concern for young Conservatives was to dispel the image that

Conservatives did not support the idea of increasing the number of women in politics. They *do* support the idea generally and try to act in line with it. One of my female research participants felt that this was one of the reasons why she and two other female members had been encouraged so much to become involved. 'They kind of trumpet the fact that myself [and the other two] are the three girls that are the most active in the society,' she said, and 'when somebody says to the president "you're all rich and you're all men" he would actually just point at us "Look, we have three girls!"' Early on, such talk gave me the impression that female members were viewed as symbolic presences who reflect positively on the Conservative Party. This impression was in fact confirmed by what a former male CFS committee member said on the subject:

> Well actually the current chairman and president of CFS are both girls. I sort of pushed the election a little bit in that direction when I had the opportunity to do so because it looks better to have an organisation led by women. It looks like we're friendlier towards women. And the way I see it is that if there are more girls more guys would then join. So it's kind of more of a means to an end if you know what I mean.

'More girls' here has a purely decorative function which means that Conservative women, at least according to this male Conservative, are not appreciated as such but in terms of the value they have for the party image. This also chimes with the historical record, according to which 'the numerical predominance of women in the Young Conservatives was regularly exploited as a tactic to entice young men into the organisation'.[34] The female member quoted above was well aware of that particular function of women for the party.

In a party whose members are on average fifty-two years old, young women do, of course, stand out even if they do not wear leopard-print kitten heels (which, by the way, none of the young Conservative women I met ever did). Wearing strong primary colours and fashionable-to-middlingly-elegant clothes, young members at local events were clearly distinguishable from the majority of middle-aged and older attendees who wore shades of beige and khaki as well as assorted pastel tints; in short, 'conservative clothing' 'made of heavier fabrics, relatively subdued in colour and restrained in cut'.[35] However, within the Scottish Conservative field, the 'glamour girl' is also a rather conservative one whose wardrobe features black dresses and skirts and, for evening events, pastel-coloured frocks. As I found out at a regional conference in 2009, the more demurely dressed 'glamour girl' interestingly meets the tea-making type of Conservative woman halfway. One of the young Conservative women there had her hair tied back in a bun and wore a knee-length emerald green pencil skirt, a cream-coloured blouse tucked in and matching pearl necklace and earrings; this outfit and the young woman wearing it altogether came close to the image of the 'twinset and pearls housewife with a penchant for coffee mornings'.[36]

The 'blue-rinse brigade'

Much more persistent than either of these types is the so-called 'blue-rinse brigade'. This type of elderly woman can be found outside the Conservative Party, too, as the label first and foremost is phenotype-based, referring to homogeneous groups of elderly women with white to bluish-white hair. Yet the 'blue-rinse brigade' is said to particularly characterise the Scottish Conservative Party membership. As one young Conservative remarked:

> To be honest, the stereotypical image [of a Conservative] probably wouldn't include a lot of young people, it's probably more like the 70-year-old woman who doesn't have anything better to do other than turn up at events. The blue-rinse brigade. That's probably the closest it can get to a stereotype.

The same research participant goes on to explain that 'at conferences what you see is a sea of white in the front of the audience'. It was like this at the 2008 Scottish Conservative Party conference, I was told, where 'the room had a terrible smell of hairspray and it kind of made you want to cringe'. There is no historical precedent to the 'blue-rinse brigade' like there is to the tea-making Conservative or the 'glamour girl', which I would attribute to the fact that the age structure of the Conservative Party has not been perceived as problematic until rather recently.

The kinds of reflections quoted above smack of bitterness and possibly even ageism, i.e. the rejection of older Conservative ladies for behaviours and demeanours characteristic of their age group (such as 'fawning' over young members).[37] While some young Conservatives certainly possess ageist attitudes, it would be more correct to suggest that the majority of young Conservatives struggle with a different kind of complication. For the problem is that young party members, when they join a local association rather than a CFS branch, thus avoiding being side-channelled into the youth wing where whatever they do can be considered 'child's play',[38] meet a lot of elderly Conservative women and hardly anyone their own age. This can cause quite some grief, as a different young Conservative reveals when talking about his first year as a party member: 'I'd go campaigning, just me and the blue-rinse ladies, that sort of thing but always sitting with people that I don't really like, with which I indulge in shit-chatting [*sic*] which I don't really like.' The absence of men as well as age peers matters more in this statement than that the presence of older women is in and of itself experienced as problematic. Thus, entering the Conservative Party can feel like (as this young man continued) 'walking into a bingo hall full of old people on a sacred holiday in a bus', a bus that in this case contains more women than men and that naturally bears little relation at all to the young member's world.

Young Conservatives distance themselves from associations with the 'blue-rinse ladies' for several reasons, age being only one of them. Another vitally important reason for some young Conservatives at least is that the older generation of Conservatives in Scotland is socially conservative. In contrast to these older Conservatives, young party members, more liberally inclined as is common for their age group, prefer to – I quote – 'take a step back from judging people on social and moral matters'. They are socially liberal, as perhaps best evidenced in the following statement made by one of the young Conservatives I interviewed:

> The Conservatives got rid of Section 28 which was there for better or for worse but now it's gone and they brought in civil partnerships which is – personally [speaking] – civil partnerships are crazy. The kind of idea that you would have a different name for it and have it in the same place but make it out like something completely different, that just doesn't make sense to me. Either you have gay marriage or you don't.

Attitudes such as these are not shared by all young Conservatives, although I would guess that when a Conservative embraces such a view he or she is most likely quite young. Liberal attitudes on social matters sit somewhat uneasily with the concomitant admiration of Margaret Thatcher who, as has been documented widely, was only liberal in relation to the economy but otherwise embraced a set of Victorian social values.[39] It is these values that are attributed to the 'blue-rinse ladies', too. 'They're very Margaret Thatcher,' a male Conservative says, and he continues:

> They are very traditional in their outlook and that still has an effect on the party today . . . There is still the image of the devastation that Margaret Thatcher wreaked on Scotland. Right or wrong, um, but that's the legacy, that's the Conservative legacy and quite a lot of these people say that they're proud of that, that they're proud of that . . .

Margaret Thatcher bestowed upon posterity that other stereotype of what elderly Conservative women might be like, that of the handbag-wielding matron, which I will now discuss.

The 'handbag-wielding matron'

It is unclear and almost beside the point to wonder whether Margaret Thatcher ever really hit anyone with her handbag, as the habit of her *Spitting Image* puppet to hit her Cabinet ministers is so firmly ingrained in public memory that it has become part of how she is known as a public figure. Thanks to Annabel Goldie, 'handbagging', as the practice is properly known, has also found its way into the Scottish Conservative Party. Ms Goldie, upon being elected as party leader in 2005, declared that she 'would not hesitate to wield her "matron's handbag" in an attempt to bring the party into line'.[40] 'Handbagging' is thus a metaphor for an assertive, clear-cut, non-compromising rather than a conciliatory and cooperative political style practised by a female politician.[41] It is a highly interesting metaphor at that, for it combines the social conservative figure of the matron with an aggressively masculine style.

Unexpectedly, considering that I was researching young Conservatives, I observed forceful and aggressive – handbagging-like, in short – behaviours among some of the young Conservative women. The female president of the UCA, when I first interviewed her long before she became president, jokingly said that if she had to be the next prime minister, 'I'd definitely be a ball-buster like Margaret Thatcher', presumably meaning that she would embrace a Thatcher-like assertive style. This is also what she did upon taking over the UCA leadership. Assuming a dominant and assertive public persona, she did in fact turn out to be a 'ball-buster'. In this, she was not so unlike her male predecessor. Unlike him, however, she met with direct as well as indirect resistance from the very start. She ordered her male committee members around – at one point telling one of them to fetch her handbag for her from the adjacent room (although she did not hit him with it) – instead of delegating tasks in a less authoritative manner as her predecessor had done. Women in leading positions in CFS were rumoured to adopt a similar approach.

At the time, it seemed to me that resorting to the symbolic violence that inheres in a rather aggressive approach was an expression of two things. On the one hand, the Conservative woman who ascends to a leadership position has to switch from her formerly rather supportive role to a quite different one within a short period of time. In that switching process, supportive and conciliatory features of interacting with other members of the UCA are dropped without immediately being replaced by a different mode of interaction. Uncertainty as to one's role turns into helplessness which is expressed as aggression. The second point is one that I (and others) have made before, i.e. that most organisations employ 'the positing of an abstract, general human being, individual, or worker who apparently has no gender. On closer examination, that individual almost always has the social characteristics of men.'[42] Leadership in particular is defined by characteristics usually applied to men, such as assertiveness and rationality.[43] In the concrete case of Scottish Conservative women aspiring for leadership, this means that they believe that one has to act as much like a social male as possible without at the same time violating the Conservative perception of what a 'good woman' is like. Handbagging, quite ironically, serves both these purposes.

Discussion and conclusion

As the above has shown, there is an impressive variety among female members' roles in and their relationship with the Scottish Conservative Party. Starting with the metaphorical language used when talking about Conservative women generally, I have presented four types of Conservative women that I have encountered in the course of my fieldwork or that were described to me in interviews. The types have several common traits. As regards age, two of the four types, i.e. the 'blue-rinse brigade' and the handbag-wielding matron, almost exclusively apply to older female party members, the 'blue-rinse ladies' metaphor doing so in a particularly negative way. The image of the Conservative woman as tea-maker, in contrast, suggests an at least middle-aged woman, while the Conservative 'glamour girl' tends to be rather young. Semantically, all four types imply the espousal of traditional social values which also includes a set of patriarchal values.

The type of the tea-maker as well as that of the Conservative 'glamour girl' have quite a long history and have been discussed by scholars at length. These two types and the older female party members that are disparagingly referred to as the 'blue-rinse brigade' are, indeed, irrevocably ingrained in the organisational structure of the Scottish Conservative Party itself. Constituency organisation depends on the existence of swathes of women who will readily oversee the arrangement and execution of social events and who generally support their constituency candidates for Westminster and Holyrood in countless hours of envelope stuffing and preparing food and drinks, as well as with donations.

The observable variety of roles for and subsequently types of women in the voluntary sector of the Scottish Conservative Party contradicts assumptions documented previously that all Right-leaning women must be tea-makers. Yet it is the case that women take on supportive roles that have little to do with formal politics. Only in times of political upheaval will Conservative women take on leading roles in larger numbers, but as situations stabilise they will 'revert to type'. This is largely because the Conservative field in the process of stabilisation will re-establish the status quo ante as regards gender-based power inequalities. Considering the difficulties, then, that are involved in changing the organisational culture of the party in view of greater female participation at all levels 'tell[s] us why women are typically less likely than men to be members of political parties and why so many women prefer informal and often less effective ad hoc political activity'.[44] In other words, women self-select against more formal involvement in politics because of the many institutional and ideological obstacles they face. This way, less struggle and strife are called for, tasks can be accomplished successfully without much difficulty and a higher degree of self-efficacy ensues which overall produces feelings of contentment as well as a more positive self-concept.[45]

The important point in this argument is that women, hampered by the organisational culture of politics generally, choose non-Parliamentary and informal politics over involvement in formal politics. To my knowledge, this argument has not been tested with Scottish Conservative women specifically yet there is a strong case to be made for its partial application in the Scottish Conservative field. In contrast with England, where women tend to engage in politics as members of party-affiliated groups or movements, Scottish female activists mainly become involved in community-based and local politics.[46] For the majority of Conservative women, this then means that they become involved in local school boards, town and regional councils as well as in their local Conservative Association in the roles I have specified above rather than as Parliamentary candidates.

There is thus a wide discrepancy between the way Conservative women are presented in public and the roles they take on in the privacy of inner-party circles. That more women are elected into representative positions and the fact that the past leader of the Scottish Conservatives as well as the current one are women signals a certain readiness to modernise in the direction of the feminisation thesis. However, in light of the attitudes that prevail among grassroots Conservatives on the question of women in politics, a caveat needs to be provided here. The presence of women in highly visible positions is itself considered desirable *regardless* of a concomitant transformation of party culture in the direction of greater inclusivity. This still does not preclude the possibility of Conservative women largely functioning as a 'means to an end', the end here being the urgent improvement of the party's standing with the Scottish electorate, as one of my research participants suggested.

For the time being it seems modernisation has arrived in the Scottish Conservative Party mainly in the form of changed interaction with and changed representation to the public but not as regards the practices constituting Scottish Conservatism. In that, the Scottish party may well be quite different from the English Conservative Party, which champions a number of female activists.[47] The traditionalism of the Scottish Conservative Party, in contrast, is obvious, not least of all in Annabel Goldie's promise of 2007 to make the wielding of a matron's handbag an integral part of the party-political process. As one commentator said, 'the party as it is today is the same as it was [50 years ago], and has not moved on a bit',[48] and modernisation in the form of feminist stances embraced by and therefore expressed in the practice of being grass-roots members is not part of what it means to be a member of the Scottish Conservative Party today.

It may take longer for the Scottish Conservatives to change substantively in how they relate to women. Younger members, more progressive in outlook than their elders, could play a pivotal role in the necessary modernisation of the party. A degree of participation of women at all levels of the political process that reflects the high proportion of women in the party membership should thus be one of their main goals.

Notes

1. I want to thank David A. Gilland, Leuphana University Lüneburg, and Thomas Spiegler, Theological University Friedensau (both in Germany), for commenting on an earlier draft of this chapter.

2. David Seawright, 'The Scottish Conservative and Unionist Party: "the lesser spotted Tory"?', in Gerry Hassan and Chris Warhurst (eds), *Tomorrow's Scotland* (London, 2002).

3. On Conservative women generally see, for instance, Mitzi Auchterlonie, *Conservative Suffragists* (London, 2007); Beatrix Campbell, *The Iron Ladies. Why Do Women Vote Tory?* (London, 1987); David Jarvis, '"Behind every great party": Women and Conservatism in twentieth century Britain', in Amanda Vickery (ed.), *Women, Privilege, and Power: British Politics, 1750 to the Present* (Stanford, CA, 2001).

4. Julia Bush, *Women Against the Vote: Female Anti-Suffragism in Britain* (Oxford, 2007), p. 12.

5. Neil C. Rafeek, *Communist Women in Scotland: Red Clydeside from the Russian Revolution to the end of the Soviet Union* (London, 2008). On female activists see especially Esther Breitenbach, Alice Brown and Fiona Myers, 'Understanding women in Scotland', *Feminist Review* 58 (spring 1998), pp. 44–65; Alice Brown, Tahyna Barnett Donaghy, Fiona Mackay and Elizabeth Meehan, 'Women and constitutional change in Scotland and Northern Ireland', *Parliamentary Affairs* 55:1 (2002), pp. 71–84.

6. A figure of 39.5 per cent compared to New Labour's 31 per cent and the Liberal Democrats' 29 per cent according to Paul Whiteley, 'Where have all the members gone? The dynamics of

party membership in Britain', *Parliamentary Affairs* 62:2 (2009), pp. 242–57.

7. This is the most widely used metaphor about Conservative women. I first became acquainted with this stereotype when I studied the cultural history of New Zealand in the 1950s. It is also prevalent in Northern Ireland, as discussed in Rachel J. Ward, '"It's not just tea and buns": Women and pro-Union politics in Northern Ireland', *British Journal of Politics and International Relations* 6:4 (2004), pp. 494–506.

8. Ruth Fox, '"Boom and Bust" in women's representation: Lessons to be learnt from a decade of devolution', *Parliamentary Affairs* 64:1 (2011), pp. 193–203; Sandra Grey, 'Does size matter? Critical mass theory and New Zealand's women MPs', *Parliamentary Affairs* 55:1 (2002), pp. 19–29.

9. Fox, 'Boom and Bust', p. 198.

10. Joni Lovenduski, *Feminizing Politics* (Cambridge, 2005), p. 58.

11. Brown et al., 'Women and constitutional change in Scotland and NI', p. 71.

12. Alexandra Dobrowolsky, 'Crossing boundaries: Exploring and mapping women's constitutional interventions in England, Scotland and Northern Ireland', *Social Politics* 9:2 (2002), pp. 293–340.

13. Rosie Campbell, Sarah Childs and Joni Lovenduski, 'Women's equality guarantees and the Conservative Party', *The Political Quarterly* 77:1 (2006), pp. 18–27.

14. Brown et al., 'Women and constitutional change in Scotland and NI'.

15. Lovenduski, *Feminizing Politics*, p. 58.

16. Quoted in Sylvia Bashevkin, *Women on the Defensive: Living through Conservative Times* (Chicago IL, 1998), p. 25.

17. Like a sports playing field, a 'field' in the way I use the term is a social space that is governed and defined by a specific set of rules that apply in a unique manner in this field only. One has left the 'field' when the rules no longer apply. As rules only matter to insiders, speaking of the structure of fields is best done from an insider's perspective. The 'Conservative field' is the sphere of social, political and cultural cogitations that comprise Conservatism in the abstract. On fields, see also Pierre Bourdieu, *The Logic of Practice* (Cambridge, 1990).

18. Sarah Childs, *Women and British Party Politics; Descriptive,*

Substantive and Symbolic Representation (London, 2008), p. 49.

19. This insight is hardly new, yet it is one that is not being discussed by political scientists. My guess is that the formal/informal divide is a convention that has become a truism, and truisms are usually difficult for those to whom they apply to reflect upon.

20. Whiteley, 'Where have all the members gone?', p. 246. Whiteley based his data on an Internet survey conducted in 2008 that was carried out across the whole of Britain.

21. Michael Bruter and Sarah Harrison, 'Tomorrow's leaders? Understanding the involvement of young party members in six European democracies', *Comparative Political Studies* 42:10 (2009), pp. 1,259–91.

22. The Young Conservatives were the predecessors of today's Conservative youth branch, Conservative Future and, north of the border, Conservative Future Scotland. For a detailed discussion of the activities of Young Conservatives as well as those of the Federation of Conservative Students that later necessitated the disbanding of both, see Keith Dixon, 'The free economy and the white state: Conservative student radicalism in St Andrews in the sixties and early seventies', *Scottish Affairs* 71 (spring 2010), pp. 16–29, and Richard N. Kelly, *Conservative Party Conferences: The Hidden System* (Manchester, 1989).

23. The University of Strathclyde, University of Glasgow, University of Edinburgh, University of St Andrews, University of Stirling, University of Dundee, University of Aberdeen and Robert Gordon University.

24. Jarvis, 'Behind every great party', p. 291.

25. Bush, *Women Against the Vote*.

26. Auchterlonie, *Conservative Suffragists*, pp. 85–95. Conservative suffragists were proposing to extend suffrage to 'responsible electors', i.e. women of wealth and standing in the community.

27. Bush, *Women Against the Vote*, p. 15.

28. Sarah Childs (2008, p. 33), for instance, wonders if 'Tory ladies' today are 'making tea or making policy'.

29. Ward, 'It's not just tea and buns'.

30. Jarvis, 'Behind every great party', p. 304.

31. Ibid. p. 304.

32. See, for instance, the prologue in Childs, *Women and British Party Politics*. On a personal note, I do not quite see why the

position title would not change to 'chairwoman' when it is held by a female politician.

33. Zig Layton-Henry, 'The Young Conservatives, 1945–70', *Journal of Contemporary History* 8:2 (1973), pp. 143–56.

34. Jarvis, 'Behind every great party', p. 304.

35. Alison Lurie, *The Language of Clothes* (London, 1992), p. 155.

36. Kelly, *Conservative Party Conferences: The Hidden System*, p. 122.

37. As one young Conservative remembers: 'When I was in CFS I quite often got confronted by old women who basically ran local associations, who didn't understand why there was a separate youth part and why the young members didn't come and get involved with them; and what I always wanted to say but never did say to their faces was "it's because of people like you that this isn't happening". It's because when young people turn up at an event and there's always a lot more women than men and they always come running over and touching you and going like "oh, it's so good to see young people like you, we never see enough young people". It puts people off and that's why the young members want to be segregated. And it's always like this. When you have a big event, like a conference, you always see the young people there and there's never that many and for most members it's almost strange having young people at these events.'

38. As suggested by Hava Rachel Gordon, 'Allies within and without. How adolescent activists conceptualize ageism and navigate adult power in youth social movements', *Journal of Contemporary Ethnography* 36:6 (2007), pp. 631–68. On p. 636, Gordon cogently points out that '*youth* movements, that is, movements organized by and for adolescents, stand as testaments to the way "politics" is not meant for them, whether electoral or social-movement oriented' (original emphasis).

39. On the relationship between Thatcherite social thought and Victorianism, see, for instance, Gertrude Himmelfarb, *The De-Moralisation of Society. From Victorian Values to Modern Values* (New York, 1995), Chapter 1.

40. According to the BBC on 8 November 2005, 'the term hand-bagging was coined to describe the verbal attacks or criticism dispensed by Margaret Thatcher in her political heyday' ('Goldie "ready to wield handbag"' at BBC Online, http://news.bbc.co.uk/2/hi/uk_news/scotland/4416194.stm).

41. On Margaret Thatcher's political style in particular, see Stephen

Benedict Dyson, 'Cognitive style and foreign policy: Margaret Thatcher's black-and-white thinking', *International Political Science Review* 30:1 (2009), pp. 33–48.

42. Joan Acker, 'From sex roles to gender institutions', *Contemporary Sociology* 21:5 (1992), pp. 565–9.

43. Joan Acker, 'Gender and organisations', in Janet Saltzman Chafetz (ed.), *Handbook of the Sociology of Gender* (New York, 1999).

44. Lovenduski, *Feminizing Politics*, p. 58.

45. The root cause of self-exclusion lies in the existence of the obstacles themselves, however, the nature of which is often summarised as 'demand-side problems', meaning that voters do not want women in representative positions. This is not quite correct, as Lovenduski (2005) and Childs (2008) discuss at length.

46. Dobrowolsky, 'Crossing boundaries'.

47. For example, Childs, *Women and British Party Politics*; Campbell, Childs and Lovenduski, 'Women's equality guarantees and the Conservative Party'. Both make reference to Conservative feminist activists.

48. Gordon Snowden, 'Reversal of fortune for Scottish Tories?', *Scotsman*, 9 June 2010.

CHAPTER 12

Conservative Unionism: Prisoned in Marble

James Mitchell and Alan Convery

Introduction

There is a distinct possibility that there would not be a Scottish Parliament today without the Conservative Party. Scottish voters went to the polls in the devolution referendum in September 1997 with the experience of eighteen years of Tory rule fresh in their minds. While polls had suggested broad support for a Scottish Parliament over the decades, this support was always shallow, as became evident in the first devolution referendum in 1979. The government of Scotland by a party with declining support in the eighteen years between the two referendums explains the different results. The emphatic vote for a Scottish Parliament in September 1997 was as much a rejection of Conservative rule as a vote for a Scottish Parliament. National identity may have been the basis of the case for a parliament but it was opposition to the Conservatives that mobilised the base.

Yet, the Conservatives, more than any other party, contributed to the development of the distinct Scottish politics that provided the base which was mobilised by supporters of a Scottish Parliament. The Scottish Office was established by the Conservatives in the late nineteenth century and its responsibilities grew under successive Conservative governments in the twentieth century. The party in Scotland was separate from the party in the rest of Britain for much of the twentieth century, contributing significantly to a distinct party system north of the border. Paradoxically, from the perspective of the present, what made the Tory Party in Scotland distinct was that it called itself the Scottish *Unionist* Party. Superficially from the vantage point of today, this Unionism is often taken to equate with a deep hostility to a distinct Scottish dimension to politics when in reality it emphasised a distinct Scottish brand of Toryism.

In considering Scottish Unionism, as manifested in the Conservative Party, we need to take account of its ideological core – its support for Union – but also how this relates to other facets of the party's ideology. At one level, Unionism is a straightforward ideology in its commitment to Union but, as we will explore, there are a number of unions and Unionism appears to have shifted emphasis in its commitment to these unions. In addition, the Conservatives are not simply a party of the Union but have other ideological positions. The party's views on state intervention appear to have influenced its views on the Scottish Question in a manner that might appear unexpected, as will be discussed below.

A key tension within any Conservative tradition lies in how and whether it should respond to challenges to the existing order. Sir Ian Gilmour, the Conservative politician, distinguished between Peelite and Disraelian attitudes to change. The Peelite response to pressure for change is to resist and defeat it. From this perspective, concessions are seen as defeats and the role of Conservatism is to be a force which defends the status quo and conserves the existing order even if others introduce changes which have to be accepted after implementation. The alternative, Disraelian view anticipates change and seeks to ensure that it is brought about without disrupting the existing order and so that the Conservative Party is credited with the change. As Gilmour expressed it, 'Where Peel usually accepted the inevitable, Disraeli tried to forestall it.'[1] The classic example of the Disraelian approach to change was when the Conservatives embraced the extension of the franchise in the 1860s. In an article published after his death, *The Times* famously reflected that Disraeli saw the 'Conservative working man as the sculptor perceives the angel prisoned in a block of marble.'[2] The present Scottish Conservative Party's inability to see such potential latent support is bound up with an approach to the Union that has become in recent years increasingly inflexible.

Conceptual confusion in the study of Scottish Unionism

As Alfred Cobban remarked in his study of Nationalism, names are more permanent than things in the history of ideas.[3] Unionism's meaning has been as malleable as any other form of Nationalism. Indeed, understanding Unionism as a form of Nationalism is itself an important conceptual first step. Unionism is usually proposed as Nationalism's opposite in Scotland's adversarial political culture. But Unionism and Nationalism are part of the same conceptual family rather than ideological opposites. While Scottish Nationalism and British Unionism may be politically opposed, they are competing nationalisms, although they can be complementary in their less fundamentalist forms. Nationalism has been described as thin-centred with a restricted core of ideas.[4] Its core idea was best articulated in Gellner's terms as the 'principle which holds that the political and national unit should be congruent'[5] but, according to the thin-centred critique, Nationalism as an ideology has little to offer beyond that core. These two nationalisms are mutually incompatible in their fundamentalist core. A purist Nationalist, whether Scottish Nationalist or UK Unionist, would view the territorial integrity of the national political unit as sacrosanct whether that integrity was challenged from outside or within. The nation is then both 'one and indivisible' and its boundaries are impervious. But in its more pragmatic forms, it is possible to imagine national and political congruence which allows for complementary national and political units.

While it may be true for comparative purposes to view Nationalism as thin-centred in the sense that there is little ideologically in common between different nationalisms, Nationalism and Unionism in the Scottish context have each developed distinctly thicker ideological bases. Each specific Nationalism, however, will be grounded in its own socio-economic as well as geographic context thus broadening out its ideological base. Nationalism in Scotland has tended to be associated with liberal-leftist politics and though there will be Scottish Nationalists with other positions on the socio-economic ideological spectrum, a consensus exists that is remarkably coherent and consistent.[6] In morphological terms, ideas adjacent to Scottish Nationalism's core include support for state intervention and welfare amounting to a social democratic set of values.

Unionism in its broadest sense has been much more diffuse, split in its ideological associations as well as organisationally between different parties. The Labour Party has exhibited both Unionist and Nationalist tendencies during its history.[7] At present, Labour's Unionism is in the ascendant, in part in reaction to SNP electoral success, to the extent that Unionism sometimes appears to have become Scottish Labour's core. However, it retains a strong social democratic set of values. For the purposes of this chapter and book, the focus is on Unionism on the Centre Right. A Centre-Right party that is not Nationalist is theoretically possible, supporting a border-less, free-market world, though it is easier to imagine a Centre-Right party that places some emphasis on the importance of territorial politics. Indeed, it is more common to find Centre-Right parties having a strong Nationalist core than an internationalist outlook.

If we consider the central Gellnerian core of Scottish Nationalism and Unionism, then we find one obvious difference but some notable similarities. The obvious difference is that the national unit of Unionism is already congruent with the state while the national unit of Scottish Nationalism aspires to statehood. However, in other respects the differences are less marked. Each displays reasonably open attitudes towards membership of the national unit and each is more inclusive, though Scottish Nationalism appears relatively more open and civic. This has been evident in debates on immigration, asylum seekers and also attitudes towards the European Union, at least as far as the Conservative Party as a whole is concerned. The extent to which the Scottish Conservatives have articulated a distinct line on these matters appears to have followed the line of the party in Britain as a whole. This may not appear surprising given that Scottish Tories see themselves as part of the larger party rather than a separate party either organisation-ally or, especially, ideologically and British Conservatism has long had a strain of antipathy towards 'outsiders'. Nonetheless, it is at least conceivable that a distinctly Scottish form of Unionism might have emerged around issues such as immigration and the EU. A number of Scottish Tories have urged either reform of the Common Fisheries Policy or withdrawal from the policy but this has rarely been a prominent part of Tory campaigns. But beyond this, it is difficult to discern any distinctly Scottish dimension to attitudes to Europe, immigration or asylum seekers amongst Scottish Tories. The Conservative Mayor of London, Boris Johnson, has articulated a highly distinct position on immigration, arguing for a more inclusive policy reflecting the needs of the City of London. A distinct attitude towards immigration, reflecting different socio-economic conditions in Scotland, is at least imaginable but has been absent. For the most part, Scottish Tories have simply followed the lead of the party south of the border leaving Boris Johnson to carve out a more distinct London position than the Scottish Tories have offered on Scotland.

Which Union?

Over the course of the twentieth century, Scottish Unionism's meaning was transformed. Its ideological, social and territorial components at the start of the twentieth century were each derivative. Scottish Unionism derived from Irish Unionism. This is at least partly explained by its social dimension. The notion of Nationalism as an 'imagined community'[8] is important here. As Anderson made clear, there is a sense of belonging amongst members of this community even though they never meet but it is limited in as much as it has boundaries, even if the boundaries may be elastic. But crucially, it is a 'deep, horizontal' *community*.[9] The Scottish Conservatives' decision to change the name of their party in 1912 to the Scottish Unionist Party was the ultimate act of communion with Ulster Unionists. For much of the twentieth century, the Scottish Tories' core support among Protestants with family ties across the Irish Sea contributed to the continuing relevance of this very real imagined community.

Ideologically, this Unionism was primarily a commitment to the Crown. The unions of most relevance were the 1603 Union of Crowns and the 1800 Union with Ireland rather than the 1707 Union of Parliaments. It was the perceived threat to these unions that gave rise to Unionism in Ireland. In 1927 Lord Balfour explained that he preferred the term Unionist because 'so much of my life was spent in attempting to preserve in its full sense the union with Ireland' and because a 'very large fraction of the future felicity of the world depends upon on the union of classes within the Empire'.[10] Unionism was malleable and as the Irish dimension receded, it was being replaced by a focus on another union. The Empire had never been far from Unionist concerns but became less significant to Unionism as it receded and the Anglo-Scottish Union came under threat. But as the Empire declined, the core itself came under threat and the 1707 Treaty became the union of consequence.

The establishment of a Northern Ireland Parliament did not resolve the Irish Question but marked divergence in attitudes as to *how* Unionism could be protected. With very few exceptions, Scottish Unionists saw a Scottish Parliament as inimical to the Union while Ulster Unionists saw a Northern Ireland Parliament as essential to Unionism. This reflected the differing threats posed in these components of the state but it also showed that attitudes to a local parliament were pragmatic and need not be fundamental to Unionism. Each position was supported as a *means* to a greater Unionist end. Moreover, the nature of devolution – the term preferred to 'Home Rule' by Unionists given Home Rule's association with Irish Nationalism – in Northern Ireland was less different to 'administrative devolution', as supported and developed by Scottish Unionists.

Over the course of the twentieth century, Unionism's focus changed. The close, often familial links with Northern Ireland did not disappear but the sense of identity of Scottish Protestants with their Northern Irish co-religionists decreased with the decline of religion in Scotland. Religion had been an important indicator of voting intentions since mass enfranchisement. Protestants tended to vote Unionist while Catholics voted Labour. This was the inverse of what was found in other parts of Europe, where Catholics were associated with the Right and Protestants as often on the Left. Religion was only part of the explanation. Scotland's Catholic community had come predominantly from Ireland, where Catholicism was strongly associated with Irish Nationalism. In Scotland's Manichean politics, Catholic Irish Nationalists were seen as an alien force by many Scots Presbyterian Unionists. The Labour Party might be better understood as the immigrants' party than as the Catholic party. It would take a number of generations from the first wave of Irish immigration fleeing the Irish famine before their descendants felt at home in Scotland. The host nation was all too often unwelcoming. Scottish Unionist politicians played a role that has become common in many liberal democracies amongst parties of the Right. For the most part they sought to take advantage of latent anti-Catholic/immigrant sentiment without fomenting this sentiment so that it went out of their control. There was no effort, for example, to remove state subsidies for separate Catholic education in Scotland but the Unionist Party engaged in what would now be called 'dog whistle politics'. Prominent Unionist politicians openly associated with the Orange Order and Catholic Scottish

Unionist Party Parliamentary candidates were rare even in the 1960s.

Religion had competed with class as the most important cleavage in Scottish electoral politics but was in decline by the 1960s. Scottish society and its economy had been under change over the century. Massive urban upheavals involving the uprooting of many communities in poorer areas and the building of vast new municipal housing estates on the peripheries of cities were mirrored in a smaller way across many of Scotland's towns. New towns were developed. These developments disrupted old traditional communities and contributed to the process of secularisation. New industries opened opportunities in which religion played little or at least less part in employment. Religion was still important especially in education but separate state-funded Catholic education offered many members of a poorer Irish immigrant community opportunities for class mobility. A process of modernisation was under way that was in danger of leaving the Scottish Tories behind. In England, the party had faced up to similar changes. It did so, sometimes enthusiastically and sometimes hesitantly, from Disraeli's embrace of the newly enfranchised working classes through reforms to party organisation under Lord Woolton and acceptance of the welfare state after 1945. It underwent further changes in the 1960s under Ted Heath, its first grammar school-educated leader. But in Scotland change came late and reluctantly within the party. In 1965, the Scottish Unionist Party was renamed the Scottish Conservative and Unionist Party and its old organisational structure with Eastern and Western Divisions replaced by a more streamlined central party organisation. Heath was convinced that the party in Scotland needed to modernise and that the old name 'Scottish Unionist Party' made no sense in the modern media age when projections of himself and the Conservative Party were compromised by the existence of the Scottish party's distinct name. Simultaneously and in contradiction to this, he was amongst the first London-based politicians to recognise that a distinct Scottish dimension existed.

But if religion was receding as a cleavage, a latent centre-periphery cleavage was emerging from the shadows. In the first Nuffield election study in 1945 one of the authors had been keen to refer to the SNP's performance while the other dismissed its relevance.[11] The 1970 Nuffield election study included an appendix on Scotland, provoked by the rise of the SNP and importance of the centre-periphery electoral cleavage.[12] But the cleavage was not new. It had merely been dormant. The key difference was the form that it was taking. Scottish Nationalism was manifested in campaigns for a Scottish Office in the late nineteenth century and that Office's development in the twentieth century, and indeed the existence of the Scottish Unionist Party as a distinct party within the Conservative tradition. Its aims were to reform the Union, giving institutional form to Scotland's voice within it, rather than bringing it to an end. Its late-twentieth-century form would be more challenging. The Conservatives had removed much that had made them distinct in Scotland three years before when the party was officially restyled the Scottish Conservative and Unionist Party. One interpretation suggests that the party suffered as a consequence by losing its Scottish distinctiveness and throwing away a plank in its appeal to its core Protestant supporters.[13] A half-hearted commitment to an Assembly which was never implemented did little to restore the party's image. The Scottish dimension was moving up the agenda just as the Unionist element to the Tory Party's name in Scotland, a mark of the party's distinctiveness, was being diluted. If the 'deep, horizontal' community with Northern Ireland was becoming attenuated, that with England was becoming more important. It was not so much that union with England was unimportant before this but that it had simply been taken for granted. It gained significance when it appeared under threat.

By the end of the century, the 'Unionist' in the Scottish Conservative and Unionist Party name was emphatically a reference to the 1707 Union. Heath's approach was initially firmly within the Disraelian tradition, anticipating change, when he proposed the establishment of a Scottish Assembly in his speech to the Scottish party conference in 1968. He established a committee under his predecessor Sir Alec Douglas-Home which reported three months before the 1970 general election. The SNP's breakthrough in the late 1960s forced Labour and Conservatives to heighten the Scottish dimension of politics and to rethink their policy on Home Rule. The Conservatives were the first to change course. Heath made no attempt to implement the policy when he became Prime Minister after the 1970 general election. Pressure for change, as measured by support for the SNP, had receded. Conceding change in the form of a Scottish Assembly, even one as weak as that proposed by Home's Constitutional Committee, was thought unnecessary. But this was a serious misreading of Scottish political behaviour. The SNP secured a breakthrough in the two elections in 1974, winning more votes than the Tories in the October election, even at a time when severe economic and industrial relations dominated the UK political agenda. But having failed to act when they had the opportunity in government, the Conservatives lacked credibility on the issue in the 1974 elections. Heath's flirtation with devolution in Opposition looks like an aberration given the party's deep-rooted stance on the issue. It is possible that devolution could have been presented as the latest development in the evolution of Conservative willingness to accommodate Scottish distinctiveness rather than as a break with the past. But the opportunity was lost.

Mrs Thatcher and the Scottish Question

It has often been noted that Margaret Thatcher initially supported the establishment of a Scottish Assembly. However, accepting inherited policy stances at the outset of leadership is no guide to a new leader's future attitudes. What became clear within a short period of time was that Margaret Thatcher was more Peelite than Disraelian with respect to devolution. The 1979 referendum result was interpreted by senior Conservatives as evidence that pressure for change in Scotland was weak. As had happened at the 1970 election, heightened expectations had proved mistaken. The narrow majority for devolution was well below expectations and the Conservatives made gains in Scotland at the subsequent general election. The Peelite approach of resisting pressure appeared to have worked. Devolution was removed from the political agenda.

It is impossible to know whether devolution would have returned to the political agenda had the Conservatives pursued a different approach in government after 1979. It is unclear at which point Mrs Thatcher concluded, as she wrote in her memoirs, that 'The pride of the Scottish Office – whose very structure added a layer of bureaucracy, standing in the way of reforms which were paying such dividends in England – was that public expenditure per head in Scotland was far higher than in England.'[14] In her mind, the very institutions that Tories had in previous decades developed and which contributed to the sense of a Scottish political community had become part of the problem in tackling Britain's decline. It was not just Mrs Thatcher who associated distinct Scottish institutions with welfare and intervention. Many Scots came to do so too. The 'Iron Lady' was a term initially intended to mock the new Tory leader but she embraced it. Strong leadership became part of Mrs Thatcher's brand. Strong leadership in pursuit of popular policies might enhance the standing of a politician but strong leadership in pursuit of unpopular policies had the opposite effect in Scotland. Even popular policies were undermined by association with the Conservatives. Following the 2005 election, Tory peer Michael Ashcroft identified a problem then afflicting the Conservative Party across Britain: the 'Conservative label was undermining its ability to sell its policies' and many voters 'had such a negative view of the Conservative Party's brand that they would oppose a policy they actually agreed with rather than support a Tory proposal'.[15] This happened in Scotland two decades before. Council house sales, for example, proved very popular but the Conservatives got little credit. Municipal tenants might have been Scottish angels in marble awaiting Thatcherite liberation but while the Conservatives may have liberated them from municipal socialism, it has been the SNP that has been the beneficiary electorally.

Jim Bulpitt argued that Margaret Thatcher's government was best understood in terms of 'statecraft', the 'art of winning elections and achieving some necessary degree of governing competence in office'.[16] Statecraft has a number of dimensions: party management; a winning electoral strategy; political argument hegemony; and governing competence. The Conservatives had been better able than their opponents since the late nineteenth century to take account of the constraints under which government occurred. However, Mrs Thatcher's statecraft failed in Scotland; as she herself admitted, the 'balance sheet of Thatcherism in Scotland is a lopsided one: economically positive but politically negative'.[17] The Scottish Tories became dependent on the party in England for electoral success. George Younger, her Scottish Secretary from 1979 to 1986, did little to lead a Thatcherite revolution in Scotland or gain credit for protecting Scotland from Thatcherism. In Wales, Peter Walker was given the challenging task of heading the Welsh Office after the 1987 election while representing a constituency in England. He gained respect for a well-orchestrated image as protector of Wales. Younger simply managed the Scottish Conservatives' decline, showing little initiative other than the introduction of the poll tax, what has become a textbook classic of public policy failure. The (future) 4th Viscount Younger of Leckie was precisely the kind of Tory that Margaret Thatcher battled with in England.

Michael Forsyth was more Mrs Thatcher's ideological soulmate but he showed little understanding of the Scottish dimension. He was in constant battle for control of the party in Scotland with the Scottish Secretary Malcolm Rifkind; Forsyth was his junior minister while simultaneously chairman of the party in Scotland. His approach chimed with his mentor's views of the Scottish Office recorded in her memoirs. Five years after her departure from office, Forsyth became Scottish Secretary under John Major and appeared more willing to embrace a distinct Scottish dimension. But the loud boos that greeted Forsyth when he wore a kilt at the Scottish premiere of the film *Braveheart* signalled contempt for a politician who failed to appreciate that the Scottish Question required more than symbolic gestures. He compounded this the following year with his 'Stone of Destiny' gimmick.

Losing all their seats in 1997 prompted some Conservative soul-searching and organisational change. Having campaigned unsuccessfully for a 'no' vote in the 1997 devolution referendum, they entered the Scottish Parliament in 1999 with a respectable tally of eighteen MSPs. Once more, an opportunity presented itself but instead the image projected by the Scottish Tories was all too often of a party in search of a better yesterday than one that embraced devolution.

Conservative Unionism today

The central problem is that the Scottish Conservatives' present conception of Unionism acts as a barrier to thinking about the type of devolution they want Scotland to have. Officially, the party accepts the Scottish Parliament and supports further powers proposed in the Scotland Bill. It played a full part in the Calman Commission. However, this official stance masks deep divisions within the party about devolution. Members who believe that the Scottish Parliament should not exist clash with those who believe that the only coherent Conservative position is to support full fiscal autonomy or federalism. Between these two positions there are debates about whether to support the Scotland Bill. It can be viewed either as a line in the sand or as a natural stepping-stone to further devolution of powers in the future.

The 2011 leadership election neatly captured these disagreements within the party. At one end of the spectrum Murdo Fraser supported the Scotland Bill and would not rule out further devolution;

at the other, Margaret Mitchell argued for a referendum on the Scotland Bill in which she would campaign for a 'no' vote. Both Jackson Carlaw and Ruth Davidson saw the Scotland Bill as the final word on devolution of powers for the foreseeable future. However, even the leadership contest did not permit the Conservatives to have an open debate about what might be the optimal balance between fiscal responsibility and defending the Union. Fundamental disagreements about Unionism hamper the party's policy thinking in many other areas. Conservatives would surely design the present Scottish Parliament differently. Its lack of fiscal responsibility precludes serious debate about the size and role of the state. From a Conservative perspective, the current arrangements dull incentives to improve economic performance or public-sector productivity. Debates focus instead on valence issues about how best to slice up the cake, rather than on the more natural Conservative territory of the proper balance between taxation and expenditure. This point is readily conceded by former Conservative Scottish Secretary Ian Lang who argues that devolution has created 'a supplicant and dependent Parliament – a sure recipe for the politics of grievance and the fostering of a dependency culture'.[18]

Nevertheless, the Scottish Conservatives' fear of independence and their interpretation of Unionism mean that they are forced to defend the status quo (or a modified status quo through the Scotland Bill) which is both politically and ideologically awkward. Three out of the four leadership candidates in 2011 seemed to interpret further powers for the Scottish Parliament as concessions to the SNP. In many ways this leaves them with the worst of both worlds: a Parliament without fiscal responsibility; and an Opposition that is able to paint their stance as 'anti-Scottish'. They are reduced to passionately defending a status quo which they themselves only half-heartedly support and which in the medium term may not exist, leaving the Conservatives stranded once more on the losing side of the Scottish Question.

Tangling themselves in these intellectual knots has serious consequences for the Scottish Conservatives. It means that debates about devolution tend to descend into name-calling from entrenched positions, rather than the serious reflection on this issue called for by the Sanderson Commission.[19] Thus 'full fiscal autonomy' has become a term of abuse. Ironically, the problem is that in defending the Scottish Parliament as it stands, the Conservatives' position is at its core a paternalistic one: Scotland needs to be saved by the discipline of the UK Treasury from its own left-wing self. Given too much power over taxes it might be tempted to raise them; given too much policy control it might flirt with independence. If a more positive Centre-Right case had a hearing, then many Conservatives might conclude that the only way to free Scotland from the grip of Centre-Left policies is if it is allowed to raise the taxes that it spends.

In this sense Unionism for the Scottish Conservatives in 2012 blinds their Centre-Right instincts in all other areas. It leads to a narrowing of debate within the party and potentially drives Centre-Right voters elsewhere. For Michael Russell (currently the SNP government's Education Secretary) and Dennis MacLeod, 'The Tories' problem is that their Unionist ideology is overcoming their free market common sense'.[20] The Scottish Conservatives fail to discern potential supporters. Such an outlook on Unionism makes it difficult for them to engage in open debates about Scotland's future in the United Kingdom.

Conclusion

In the first half of the twentieth century, Scottish Tories proved adept at 'playing the Scottish card', but as the party declined they failed to build or renew a coalition of support and became dependent for electoral success on the party in England. Apart from the brief flirtation with devolution under Heath, the Tories have consistently responded to events rather than set the agenda on the Scottish Question. While formally accepting the Scottish Parliament, the party still suffers electorally from its strident opposition to devolution. On becoming Prime Minister, David Cameron inherited an unprecedented economic and fiscal crisis and could be excused from taking no new initiative regarding the government of Scotland. However, the consequence for the Conservatives is that the return of an SNP government with an overall majority has meant that the Tories are once more having to respond to events rather than set the agenda. Mr Cameron had little choice but to accept that a referendum on Scotland's constitutional future will be held but in arguing for a straight choice between independence and the status quo he pursues the same hardline approach that proved fruitless in the past. Leaving aside the gamble inherent in such a referendum, this ignores the possibility that Scots will find means of expressing support for more powers, whether in a referendum or in support for the SNP and possibly other parties, even if they reject independence, and the Conservatives will once more find themselves on the losing side, enhancing their image as a party out of step with Scotland. But the more fundamental issue is the absence of Disraelian leadership. At the heart of Tory opposition to devolution and further powers is an inability to see potential support in Scotland. It is not difficult to conceive of a form of devolution that would create a different set of incentives. However, devolution as currently constituted encourages a type of politics and policies that is unlikely ever to suit the Conservatives. Instead of adapting Unionism for a new era, as they have done so many times before, the Conservatives in Scotland have imprisoned potential support in a block of marble of their own creation.

Notes

1. Ian Gilmour, *Inside Right – A Study of Conservatism* (London, 1977), p. 127.
2. *The Times*, 18 April 1883.
3. Alfred Cobban, *The Nation State and National Self-Determination* (London, 1969), p. 23.
4. Michael Freeden, 'Is nationalism a distinct ideology?', *Political Studies* 46 (September 1998), pp. 748–65.
5. Ernest Gellner, *Nations and Nationalism* (Oxford, 1983), p. 1.
6. See James Mitchell, Lynn Bennie and Rob Johns, *The SNP: Transition to Power* (Oxford, 2011).
7. Michael Keating and David Bleiman, *Labour and Scottish Nationalism* (London, 1979).
8. Benedict Anderson, *Imagined Communities* (London, 1983).
9. Ibid. p. 7.
10. Lord Balfour's speech at the fiftieth anniversary of the Scottish Conservative Club in Edinburgh, reported in the *Glasgow Herald*, 22 October 1927.
11. Obituary of Alison Wright (nee Readman), *The Times*, 18 December 2003. Readman was a Tory and McCallum was a Liberal.
12. James G. Kellas, 'Scottish Nationalism', in David Butler and Michael Pinto-Duschinsky (eds), *The British General Election of 1970* (London, 1971).
13. David Seawright, *An Important Matter of Principle: The Decline of the Scottish Conservative and Unionist Party* (Aldershot, 1999).

14. Margaret Thatcher, *The Downing Street Years* (London, 1993), p. 627.

15. Michael Ashcroft, *Smell the Coffee: A Wake-Up Call for the Conservative Party* (London, 2005), p. 52.

16. Jim Bulpitt, 'The discipline of the New Democracy: Mrs. Thatcher's domestic statecraft', *Political Studies* 34 (1985), p. 21.

17. Margaret Thatcher, *The Downing Street Years*, p. 623.

18. Ian Lang, *Blue Remembered Years* (London, 2002), p. 192.

19. Scottish Conservative Party, *Report of the Scottish Conservatives Commission*, (Edinburgh, 2011), p. 27.

20. Dennis MacLeod and Michael Russell, *Grasping the Thistle* (Glendaruel, 2006), p. 130.

Index